# THE FATHERS OF THE CHURCH

MEDIAEVAL CONTINUATION

VOLUME 24

# THE FATHERS OF THE CHURCH

## MEDIAEVAL CONTINUATION

# *HONORIUS AUGUSTODUNENSIS*

## *THE KEY TO NATURAL PHILOSOPHY*

*Translated by*

BARBARA NEWMAN

THE CATHOLIC UNIVERSITY OF AMERICA PRESS
Washington, D.C.

Printed in the United States of America
The paper used in this publication meets the minimum requirements of the American National Standards for Information Science--Permanence of Paper for Printed Library Materials, ANSI Z39.48 - 1984.
∞
ISBN 978-0-8132-4013-8
Library of Congress Cataloging-in-Publication Data
To be supplied by the Library of Congress

Frontispiece: The Four Divisions of Nature
Paris, BnF ms. lat. 6734, fol. 3v

## CONTENTS

In Memoriam

Sr. Nonna Verna Harrison

(1953–2022)

# ACKNOWLEDGMENTS

It gives me great pleasure to acknowledge the debts I have incurred in preparing this translation. I would like to thank Willemien Otten, a leading scholar of Eriugena, for encouraging me to undertake the project and vetting my initial proposal. At a later stage, Jeffrey Hamburger graciously shared the manuscript of his forthcoming book, *The Areopagite through the Ages: Diagramming the Pseudo-Dionysius c. 600–c. 1600*. Hamburger will publish the diagrams that accompany the *Clavis physicae* in the manuscripts, helping to clarify its sometimes-baffling logical structure. He has allowed me to cite some of his findings, and my own diagrams are indebted to his discoveries.

Chapters dealing with the history of science, especially astronomy, are among the most difficult in the volume. This is the case because Eriugena, and Honorius after him, were following Latin writers who did not fully understand the calculations of the Greek mathematicians and astronomers they cite. I thank my colleague Nick Winters, a historian of ancient science, for patiently explaining Eratosthenes's ingenious experiment to estimate the circumference of the earth through measurements made with sundials (chap. 202), and many related calculations.

With my husband, Richard Kieckhefer, I have puzzled through some of Honorius's more difficult passages as we shared our wonderment at his startling doctrines. Finally, I want to thank Carole Burnett, my editor at the Catholic University of America Press. Far more than an editor, she is an expert Latinist who checked my translation line by line against the original and suggested countless small improvements. The translation has benefited immeasurably from her help and that of all my colleagues.

# ABBREVIATIONS AND SIGLA

## *Abbreviations*

| | |
|---|---|
| CCCM | *Corpus christianorum: continuatio mediaevalis* (Turnhout: Brepols, 1966– ) |
| CCSL | *Corpus christianorum: series latina* (Turnhout: Brepols, 1953– ) |
| CSEL | *Corpus scriptorum ecclesiasticorum latinorum* (Vienna: C. Gerold, 1866–1974) |
| LXX | Septuagint (Greek Old Testament) |
| MGH | *Monumenta Germaniae historica* |
| PG | *Patrologiae cursus completus: series graeca,* 162 vols. (Paris: J.-P. Migne, 1857–66) |
| PL | *Patrologiae cursus completus: series latina,* 221 vols. (Paris: J.-P. Migne, 1861–64) |

## *Sigla*

| | |
|---|---|
| ( ) | Parentheses indicate material appearing in the Latin text. |
| [ ] | Square brackets indicate material supplied by the translator. |

# SELECT BIBLIOGRAPHY

## *Primary Sources*

### Periphyseon *and* Clavis physicae

Eriugena, Johannes Scottus. *Periphyseon* (*De divisione naturae*). Edited by Édouard Jeauneau, 5 vols. CCCM 161–65. Brepols, 1996–2003.

———. Translated by I. P. Sheldon-Williams. Revised by John J. O'Meara. Bellarmin and Dumbarton Oaks, 1987.

Honorius Augustodunensis. *Clavis physicae.* Edited by Paolo Lucentini. Temi e Testi 21. Edizioni di Storia e Letteratura, 1974.

———. *La "Clavis Physicae" (316–529) di Honorius Augustodunensis: Studio e edizione.* Edited by Pasquale Arfé. Liguori, 2012.

### *Other Works by Honorius: Editions and Translations*

Honorius Augustodunensis. *De anima et de Deo, quaedam ex Augustino excerpta, sub dialogo exarata.* Edited by Marie-Odile Garrigues. *Recherches augustiniennes* 12 (1977): 212–78.

———. *De esu volatilium.* Edited by Marie-Odile Garrigues. *Studia Monastica* 28 (1986): 75–130.

———. *De luminaribus Ecclesiae.* PL 172: 197–234.

———. *De neocosmo.* Edited by R. D. Crouse. "Honorius Augustodunensis: 'De Neocosmo.' A Critical Edition of the Text with Introduction and Notes." Ph.D. dissertation, Harvard University, 1970.

———. *Elucidarium.* Edited by Yves Lefèvre. *L'Elucidarium et les lucidaires: Contribution, par l'histoire d'un texte, à l'histoire des croyances religieuses en France au Moyen Âge.* Boccard, 1954.

———. *Elucidarium.* Translated by Clifford T. G. Sorensen. "The *Elucidarium* of Honorius Augustodunensis: Translation and Selected Annotations." M.A. thesis, Brigham Young University, 1979.

———. *Exposition of Selected Psalms.* Edited by David Welch. Translated by Ann W. Astell, Joseph Wawrykow, and the "Catena Scholarium." Medieval Institute, 2023.

———. *Imago mundi.* Edited by Valerie I. J. Flint. *Archives d'histoire doctrinale et littéraire du Moyen Âge* 49 (1982): 7–153.

———. *Imago mundi.* Translated by Nicholas Ryan Foster. "The *Imago mundi* of Honorius Augustodunensis." M.A. thesis, Portland State University, 2008.

———. *Inevitabile.* Edited and translated by Walter A. Hannam. "The *Inevitabile* of Honorius Augustodunensis: A Study in the Textures of Early Twelfth-Century Augustinianisms." Ph.D. dissertation, Boston College, 2013.

———. *Interrogatio de descensu Christi, Interrogatio de ascensu et consessu Christi,* and *Interrogatio 'Cum Johannes.'* Edited by J. A. Endres. In *Honorius Augustodunensis: Beitrag zur Geschichte des geistigen Lebens im 12. Jahrhundert.* Kösel'chen Buchhandlung, 1906.

———. *Jewel of the Soul* (*Gemma animae*). Edited and translated by Zachary Thomas and Gerhard Eger. Dumbarton Oaks Medieval Library. Harvard University Press, 2023.

———. *Offendiculum, De apostatis,* and *Summa gloria.* Edited by J. Dieterich. MGH *Libelli de lite* III: 38–80. Hannover: Hahn, 1897.

———. *Opera omnia.* Edited by J.-P. Migne. Patrologia Latina 172. Paris: Migne, 1855.

———. *Quod monachis liceat predicare.* Edited by J. A. Endres. In *Honorius Augustodunensis: Beitrag zur Geschichte des geistigen Lebens im 12. Jahrhundert,* 147–50. Kösel'chen Buchhandlung, 1906.

———. *The Seal of Blessed Mary* (*Sigillum beatae Mariae*). Translated by Amelia Carr. Peregrina, 1991.

*Other Primary Sources*

Anonymous. "Daz send gar hoch fragen und materien." Edited by Auguste Jundt. In *Histoire du panthéisme populaire au Moyen Âge et au seizième siècle.* Paris, 1875; reprinted by Minerva, 1964.

Anselm, St. *Basic Writings.* Translated by Thomas Williams. Hackett, 2007.

Berengar of Tours. *De sacra coena adversus Lanfrancum.* Edited by W. H. Beekenkamp. Nijhoff, 1941.

Bernard Silvestris. *Cosmographia.* Edited by Peter Dronke. Brill, 1978.

———. *The* Cosmographia *of Bernardus Silvestris.* Translated by Winthrop Wetherbee. Columbia University Press, 1973.

Gilbert of Poitiers. *Disputatio altera adversus Petrum Abaelardum.* PL 180: 283–328.

———. *In librum [Boetii] de duabus naturis et una persona Christi commentaria.* PL 64: 1353–1412.

Hildegard of Bingen. *Liber divinorum operum.* Edited by Albert Derolez and Peter Dronke. CCCM 92. Brepols, 1996.

Nicholas of Cusa. *Apologia doctae ignorantiae.* Edited by Raymond Klibansky. *Opera omnia* II. Felix Meiner, 2007.

Ratramnus of Corbie. *De corpore et sanguine Domini.* PL 121: 125–70.

## *Secondary Sources*

Arfé, Pasquale. "*Triplex modus theoriae de reditu:* The Doctrine of Universal Return in Eriugena." *Archives d'histoire doctrinale et littéraire du Moyen Âge* 78 (2011): 7–45.

Barstad, Joel I. "Eriugena as Translator and Interpreter of the Greek Fathers." In *A Companion to John Scottus Eriugena,* edited by Adrian Guiu. Brill, 2020.

Beccarisi, Alessandra. "Un nuovo frammento della 'Clavis Physicae' di Onorio e la diffusione dell'Eriugenismo nella Germania medievale." *Giornale critico della filosofia italiana* 21 (2001): 171–78.

Beierwaltes, Werner, ed. *Eriugena Redivivus: Zur Wirkungsgeschichte seines Denkens im Mittelalter und im Übergang zur Neuzeit.* Winter, 1987.

Bett, Henry. *Johannes Scotus Erigena: A Study in Mediaeval Philosophy.* Cambridge University Press, 1925.

Carabine, Deirdre. *John Scottus Eriugena.* Great Medieval Thinkers. Oxford University Press, 2000.

Crouse, Robert D. "Honorius Augustodunensis: Disciple of Anselm?" *Analecta Anselmiana* 4 (1972): 131–39.

———. "*Intentio Moysi:* Bede, Augustine, Eriugena and Plato in the *Hexaemeron* of Honorius Augustodunensis." *Dionysius* 2 (1978): 137–57.

d'Alverny, Marie-Thérèse. "Le cosmos symbolique du XIIe siècle." *Archives d'histoire doctrinale et littéraire du Moyen Âge* 20 (1953): 31–81.

Endres, J. A. *Honorius Augustodunensis: Beitrag zur Geschichte des geistigen Lebens im 12. Jahrhundert.* Kösel'chen Buchhandlung, 1906.

Flint, Valerie I. J. "Honorius Augustodunensis of Regensburg." In *Historical and Religious Writers of the Latin West, 5–6,* edited by Constant Mews and Valerie I. J. Flint. Variorum, 1995.

———. *Ideas in the Medieval West: Texts and Their Contexts.* Variorum, 1988.

Fulton, Rachel. *From Judgment to Passion: Devotion to Christ and the Virgin Mary, 800–1200.* Columbia University Press, 2002.

Garrigues, Marie-Odile. "Quelques recherches sur l'oeuvre d'Honorius Augustodunensis." *Revue d'histoire ecclésiastique* 70 (1975): 388–425.

———. "Qui était Honorius Augustodunensis?" *Angelicum* 50 (1973): 20–49.

Gersh, Stephen. "Honorius Augustodunensis and Eriugena: Remarks on the Method and Content of the *Clavis physicae.*" In *Eriugena Redivivus: Zur Wirkungsgeschichte seines Denkens im Mittelalter und im Übergang zur Neuzeit,* edited by Werner Beierwaltes. Winter, 1987.

Graff, Eric. "A Primitive Text of *Periphyseon V* Rediscovered: The Witness of Honorius Augustodunensis in *Clavis physicae.*" *Recherches de théologie et philosophie médiévales* 69 (2002): 271–95.

Guiu, Adrian, ed. *A Companion to John Scottus Eriugena.* Brill, 2020.

Hamburger, Jeffrey F. *The Areopagite through the Ages: Diagramming the Pseudo-Dionysius c. 600–c. 1600.* Pontifical Institute of Mediaeval Studies. Forthcoming, 2026.

Harringon, Michael. "Eriugena and the Neoplatonic Tradition." In *A Companion to John Scottus Eriugena,* edited by Adrian Guiu. Brill, 2020.

Jeauneau, Édouard. "Guillaume de Malmesbury, premier éditeur anglais du 'Periphyseon.'" In *"Sapientiae Doctrina": Mélanges de théologie et de littérature médiévales offerts à Dom Hildebrand Bascour O.S.B.*, edited by Roland Hissette, Guibert Michiels, and Dirk Van Den Auweele. Recherches de théologie ancienne et médiévale, 1980.

———. "Le renouveau érigénien du XIIe siècle." In *Eriugena Redivivus: Zur Wirkungsgeschichte seines Denkens im Mittelalter und im Übergang zur Neuzeit,* edited by Werner Beierwaltes. Winter, 1987.

Kijewska, Agnieszka. "Eriugena's Influence on the 12th Century." In *A Companion to John Scottus Eriugena,* edited by Adrian Guiu. Brill, 2020.

King, Evan. *Supersapientia: Berthold of Moosburg and the Divine Science of the Platonists.* Brill, 2021.

Lahey, Stephen. "Eriugena's Condemnation and His Idealism." In *A Companion to John Scottus Eriugena,* edited by Adrian Guiu. Brill, 2020.

Lucentini, Paolo. "La *Clavis physicae* di Honorius Augustodunensis e la tradizione eriugeniana nel secolo XII." In *Jean Scot Érigène et l'histoire de la philosophie,* edited by René Roques. Centre national de la recherche scientifique, 1977.

———. *Platonismo medievale: Contributi per la storia dell'Eriugenismo.* La Nuova Italia, 1979.

McGinn, Bernard. "The *Periphyseon* as Hexaemeral Commentary." In *A Companion to John Scottus Eriugena,* edited by Adrian Guiu. Brill, 2020.

Meier, Christel. "Scientia Divinorum Operum: Zu Hildegards von Bingen visionär-künstlerischer Rezeption Eriugenas." In *Eriugena Redivivus: Zur Wirkungsgeschichte seines Denkens im Mittelalter und im Übergang zur Neuzeit,* edited by Werner Beierwaltes. Winter, 1987.

Moran, Dermot. *The Philosophy of John Scottus Eriugena: A Study of Idealism in the Middle Ages.* Cambridge University Press, 1989.

Otten, Willemien. "Suspended between Cosmology and Anthropology: *Natura*'s Bond in Eriugena's *Periphyseon.*" In *A Companion to John Scottus Eriugena,* edited by Adrian Guiu. Brill, 2020.

Sanford, Eva Matthews. "Honorius, *Presbyter* and *Scholasticus.*" *Speculum* 23 (1948): 397–425.

Schmidt, Gleb. "From Manual to Best-Seller: The History of Honorius Augustodunensis's *Elucidarium.*" In *Books of Knowledge in Late Medieval Europe: Circulation and Reception of Popular Texts,* edited by Pavlína Cermanová and Václav Žůrek. Brepols, 2021.

Sturlese, Loris. "Zwischen Anselm und Johannes Scotus Eriugena: Der seltsame Fall des Honorius, des Mönchs von Regensburg." In *Historia Philosophiae Medii Aevi: Studien zur Geschichte der Philosophie des Mittelalters. Festschrift für Kurt Flasch zu seinem 60. Geburtstag,* edited by Burkhard Mojsisch and Olaf Pluta. 2 vols., vol. II. Grüner, 1991.

Yingst, Daniel. "*Quae omnia concorditer consonant:* Eriugena's Universe in the Thought of Honorius Augustodunensis." In *Eriugena and Creation,* edited by Willemien Otten and Michael I. Allen. Brepols, 2014.

———. "Towers in the Mud: Honorius Augustodunensis through the Lens of Pedagogy." Ph.D. dissertation, University of Chicago, 2017.

THE SEVEN DEGREES

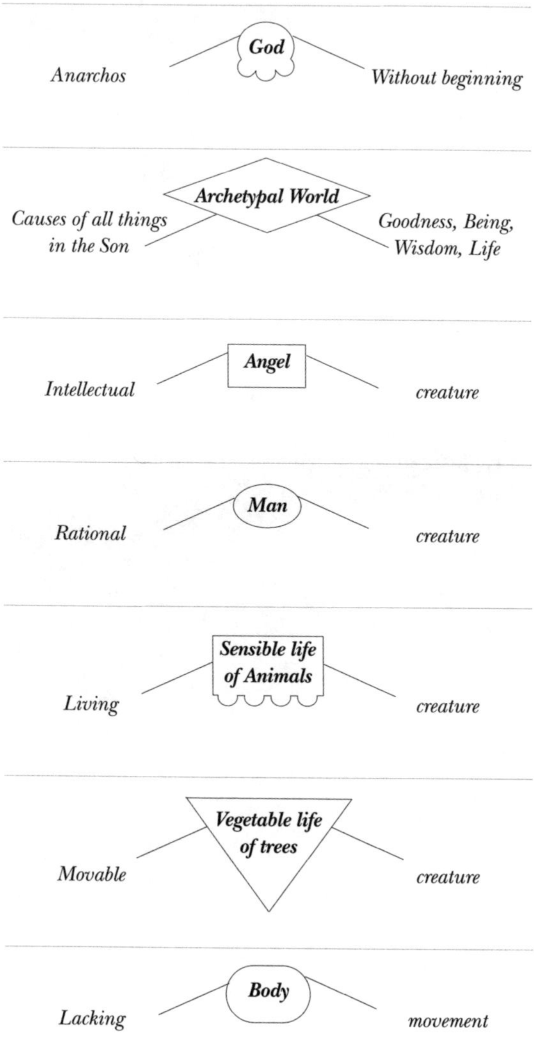


Figure 1. The Great Chain of Being
Paris, BNF ms. Lat 6734, fol. v
Vienna, ÖNB, Cod. ser. nov. 3605, 12v

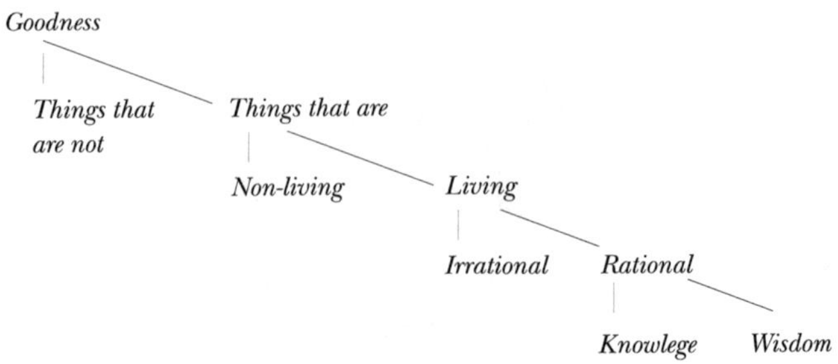


Figure 2. A "Porphyrian tree" diagram of chap. 120

# INTRODUCTION

# INTRODUCTION

Honorius Augustodunensis ("of Regensburg") is the most unjustly neglected writer of the twelfth-century renaissance. Although his works survive in more than five hundred manuscripts and his influence is widely acknowledged, not many of his prolific writings have been critically edited, much less translated.[1] To date, the only ones published in English are a liturgical commentary, *Jewel of the Soul* (*Gemma animae*); a Marian commentary on the Song of Songs, *The Seal of Blessed Mary* (*Sigillum beatae Mariae*); and a small selection from his massive exposition of the Psalms.[2] A few more can be found in unpublished theses and dissertations.[3] Even though the writer is often mentioned in surveys of the period or of a particular field, detailed studies are few. Most to date have focused on establishing his canon, chronology, and the little that can be known of his biography—

1. Most but not all of his works, along with a few spurious ones, can be found in *Opera omnia,* ed. J.-P. Migne, Patrologia Latina 172 (Paris: Migne, 1855). The *Clavis physicae* (*Key to Natural Philosophy*) is not included.

2. Honorius Augustodunensis, *Jewel of the Soul,* ed. and trans. Zachary Thomas and Gerhard Eger, Dumbarton Oaks Medieval Library (Harvard University Press, 2023); *The Seal of Blessed Mary,* trans. Amelia Carr (Peregrina, 1991); *Exposition of Selected Psalms,* ed. David Welch, trans. Ann W. Astell, Joseph Wawrykow, and the "Catena Scholarium" (Medieval Institute, 2023).

3. Robert D. Crouse, ed., "Honorius Augustodunensis: 'De Neocosmo.' A Critical Edition of the Text with Introduction and Notes," Ph.D. dissertation, Harvard University, 1970; Clifford T. G. Sorensen, trans., "The *Elucidarium* of Honorius Augustodunensis: Translation and Selected Annotations," M.A. thesis, Brigham Young University, 1979; Nicholas Ryan Foster, trans., "The *Imago mundi* of Honorius Augustodunensis," M.A. thesis, Portland State University, 2008; Walter A. Hannam, ed. and trans., "The *Inevitabile* of Honorius Augustodunensis: A Study in the Textures of Early Twelfth-Century Augustinianisms," Ph.D. dissertation, Boston College, 2013.

of which virtually all details are contested.[4] The early mistake of linking Honorius with Autun, based on his mysterious loconymic, still persists despite being refuted more than a century ago.[5]

### *The career and writings of Honorius*

Born perhaps in the 1070s, Honorius likely hailed from what is now southern Germany or Austria. As a young man he went to study with St. Anselm at Canterbury and seems also to have spent some time in Worcester.[6] The English manuscripts of his early works suggest that his baptismal name was Henricus (or Heinricus), and he may have been a regular canon before becoming a Benedictine under the influence of Anselm. While still a student he wrote his extraordinarily popular *Elucidarium* (ca. 1100), a catechism covering the whole of Christian doctrine, which survives in almost four hundred manuscripts and was translated into most European vernaculars.[7] *The Seal of*

4. The most influential accounts are those of Valerie I. J. Flint, *Ideas in the Medieval West: Texts and Their Contexts* (Variorum, 1988), which collects ten of her earlier essays on Honorius, and eadem, "Honorius Augustodunensis of Regensburg," in *Historical and Religious Writers of the Latin West, 5–6,* by Constant Mews and Valerie I. J. Flint (Variorum, 1995), 89–183. See also Eva Matthews Sanford, "Honorius, *Presbyter* and *Scholasticus,*" *Speculum* 23 (1948): 397–425; Marie-Odile Garrigues, "Qui était Honorius Augustodunensis?" *Angelicum* 50 (1973): 20–49; and eadem, "Quelques recherches sur l'oeuvre d'Honorius Augustodunensis," *Revue d'histoire ecclésiastique* 70 (1975): 388–425.

5. J. A. Endres, *Honorius Augustodunensis: Beitrag zur Geschichte des geistigen Lebens im 12. Jahrhundert* (Kösel'chen Buchhandlung, 1906).

6. My account largely follows Flint, though not her later suggestion that he was born, like Anselm, in the Italian region of Aosta. Others have proposed an English or Irish origin—a hypothesis now largely dismissed. Robert D. Crouse expresses skepticism about a master-student relationship between Anselm and Honorius, though I believe the balance of evidence favors it. See Crouse, "Honorius Augustodunensis: Disciple of Anselm?" *Analecta Anselmiana* 4 (1972): 131–39.

7. Honorius Augustodunensis, *Elucidarium,* ed. Yves Lefèvre: *L'Elucidarium et les lucidaires: Contribution, par l'histoire d'un texte, à l'histoire des croyances religieuses en France au moyen âge* (Boccard, 1954); Dagmar Gottschall, *Das 'Elucidarium' des Honorius Augustodunensis: Untersuchungen zu seiner Überlieferungs- und Rezeptionsgeschichte im deutschsprachigen Raum mit Ausgabe der niederdeutschen Übersetzung* (Niemeyer, 1992); Ernstpeter Ruhe, ed., *Elucidarium und Lucidaires: Zur Rezeption des Werks von Honorius Augustodunensis in der Romania und in England*

*Blessed Mary*, another early work, was the first to allegorize the entire Song of Songs with reference to the Virgin.[8] It too had an outsized influence. A third work with English connections, the sermon collection *Speculum Ecclesiae* (*Mirror of the Church*), is dedicated to the brothers of Canterbury and may have been written shortly after Honorius left that community. Further works probably written in England include the *Imago mundi* (*Image of the World*), a popular encyclopedia of geography and world history,[9] and two polemics that echo Anselm's relentless efforts to ban clerical marriage. The *Offendiculum* (*Stumbling Block*) attacks concubinous and simoniac priests, while *De apostatis* (*On Apostates*) argues that professed monks who leave the cloister are damned unless they repent.[10]

Around 1103, perhaps at the time of Anselm's second exile, Honorius returned to Germany, where he may have traveled for some time before ending up in the Bavarian city of Regensburg. At some point after his return to the Continent, he changed his name from Henricus to Honorius and adopted the mystifying epithet "Augustodunensis." His reasons for doing so are unclear; the one he states is a fear of "destructive envy."[11] But perhaps he wished to disguise his identity because of involvement in some controversy. In fact, Gilbert of Poitiers charged that the sower of a certain "heresy," hidden somewhere in Germany, would have been officially censured if he had dared to publish under his

(Reichert, 1993). For the figure of 400 MSS see Gleb Schmidt, "From Manual to Best-Seller: The History of Honorius Augustodunensis's *Elucidarium*," in *Books of Knowledge in Late Medieval Europe: Circulation and Reception of Popular Texts*, ed. Pavlína Cermanová and Václav Žůrek (Brepols, 2021), 140.

8. Honorius, *The Seal of Blessed Mary*, trans. Carr; Rachel Fulton, *From Judgment to Passion: Devotion to Christ and the Virgin Mary, 800–1200* (Columbia University Press, 2002), 244–88.

9. Honorius Augustodunensis, *Imago mundi*, ed. Valerie I. J. Flint, *Archives d'histoire doctrinale et littéraire du Moyen Âge* 49 (1982): 7–153; trans. Foster, "The *Imago mundi* of Honorius Augustodunensis."

10. Honorius Augustodunensis, *Offendiculum*, ed. J. Dieterich, MGH *Libelli de lite* III (Hannover: Hahn, 1897), 38–57; *De apostatis*, in ibid., 57–63.

11. "Nomen autem meum ideo volui silentio contegi, ne invidia tabescens suis juberet utile opus contemnendo neglegi." Prologue to *Elucidarium*, ed. Lefèvre, 359.

own name.[12] For most of his monastic career, Honorius probably belonged to the abbey of St. Jakob (Schottenkloster) in Regensburg, which had been founded by Irish monks and still housed many insular Benedictines.[13] At some point he began to live as a hermit—not a rare vocation for scholars at that time and place. We know this from the many manuscripts that refer to him as *inclusus* or *solitarius,* though there is nothing to suggest that he devoted himself exclusively to contemplation and abandoned the cares of the world. A bequest of manuscripts to the abbey of Lambach, including a great many works by Honorius, suggests that he had retired to that community by the time of his death around 1140.

During an active career that spanned forty years or more, Honorius ceaselessly wrote and taught across an astonishing range of fields. Aside from the texts already mentioned, his works include the *Inevitabile,* a dialogue on free will; the *Sacramentarium,* a liturgical commentary and companion piece to *Gemma animae; De Neocosmo* (*On the New World*), an exegetical work on the six days of creation; the *Eucharistion,* defending an orthodox view of the sacrament against the heresy of Berengar of Tours; the *Scala caeli* (*Ladder of Heaven*) on types of visionary experience; and two huge biblical commentaries, an *Expositio totius Psalterii* (*Explanation of the Whole Psalter*) and a second Song commentary, *In Cantica canticorum.*[14] A third commentary on the Gospels is lost. Shorter works include *De vita claustrali* (*On Monastic Life*), a glowing eulogy; *De exsilio et patria animae* (*On the Exile and Homeland of the Soul*), an allegory of the lib-

12. The heresy in question was a belief in human deification (*theosis*) after the resurrection, one of many Greek theological ideas Honorius adopted and continued to teach in the *Clavis physicae.* Gilbert of Poitiers, *In librum [Boetii] de duabus naturis et una persona Christi commentaria* (PL 64: 1397c); Endres, *Honorius,* 124–26; Sanford, "Honorius, *Presbyter,*" 399.

13. For its iconographic connection with Honorius's commentary on the Song of Songs, see J. A. Endres, *Das St. Jakobsportal in Regensburg und Honorius Augustodunensis: Beitrag zur Ikonographie und Literaturgeschichte des 12. Jahrhunderts* (Kösel'chen Buchhandlung, 1903).

14. E. Ann Matter, *The Voice of My Beloved: The Song of Songs in Western Medieval Christianity* (University of Pennsylvania Press, 1990), 58–76, includes three illustrations from this work.

eral and mechanical arts;[15] and two sets of *quaestiones* dealing with angels and mortals, written to refute the popular belief that God created human beings to replace the fallen angels.[16] Other writings are polemical. The *Summa gloria* (*Supreme Glory*) takes an extreme view in the investiture controversy, arguing for the superiority of all priests and bishops over kings and emperors,[17] while the brief tract *Quod monachis liceat predicare* (*That Monks Should be Allowed to Preach*) argues passionately against regular canons that monks could not only preach, but also celebrate Mass for the laity and absolve penitents.[18] An Augustinian dialogue *De anima et de Deo* (*On the Soul and on God*) rounds out the monk's teaching profile.[19]

Fairly late in his career (ca. 1130–33), Honorius penned a catalogue of ecclesiastical writers, *De luminaribus Ecclesiae* (*On Luminaries of the Church*), listing their dates and works. The last authors mentioned are Anselm of Canterbury, the German Benedictine Rupert of Deutz (d. 1129/30), and Honorius himself, with a canon listing twenty-two of his works. Those not mentioned in this list are either minor or must have been composed later. In this source the writer identifies himself as "Honorius, Augustodunensis Ecclesiae presbyter et scholasticus" ("priest and schoolmaster of the church of *Augustodunensis*," presumably

15. R. D. Crouse, "Honorius Augustodunensis: The Arts as *Via ad Patriam*," in *Congrès International de Philosophie Médiévale: Arts Libéraux et Philosophie au Moyen Âge* (Vrin, 1969), 531–39; Paul Michel, "'Ignorantia exsilium hominis': Zu einem enzyklopädischen Traktat des Honorius Augustodunensis," in *Strenarum Lanx: Beiträge zur Philologie und Geschichte des Mittelalters und der frühen Neuzeit,* ed. Martin H. Graf and Christian Moser (Achius, 2003), 117–43; José Miguel de Toro Vial, "'Exsilium hominum ignorantia est': Honorius Augustodunensis and Knowledge in the Twelfth Century," *Imago temporis* 13 (2019): 115–33.

16. Honorius, *Liber duodecim quaestionum* and *Libellus octo quaestionum de angelis et homine* (PL 172: 1177–92); Vojtěch Novotný, *Cur Homo: A History of the Thesis Concerning Man as a Replacement for Fallen Angels,* trans. Tim Morgan and Pavlína Morgan (Karolinum, 2014).

17. Honorius, *Summa gloria,* ed. J. Dieterich, MGH *Libelli de lite* III (Hahn, 1897), 63–80.

18. This work is edited in Endres, *Honorius Augustodunensis,* 147–50.

19. Honorius Augustodunensis, *De anima et de Deo, quaedam ex Augustino excerpta, sub dialogo exarata,* ed. Marie-Odile Garrigues, *Recherches augustiniennes* 12 (1977): 212–78.

Regensburg), and half-modestly states that he "published little works that are not to be despised." He ends the list with *De luminaribus* itself, dates his life with the comment *sub quinto Henrico floruit* ("flourished under Emperor Henry V," reg. 1099–1125), and closes with the remark, "Who will write after him, posterity will see."[20] Meager as it is, this self-description gives us virtually all the information we have about the author's life, beyond what can be deduced from the works themselves and the provenance of their manuscripts. The vast majority of these come from southern Germany and Austria, with England as runner-up.

Honorius is best known as a popularizer, a role in which he enjoyed spectacular success. He combined insatiable curiosity about the world, wide reading, and zeal for the Gregorian reform and its theology (especially Anselm's) with a passionate loyalty to the old monastic order, shared with his German colleagues Rupert of Deutz and Idung of Prüfening. Although he is sometimes dismissed as a mere compiler, some of his works (such as *The Seal of Blessed Mary*) show considerable originality. But what most distinguishes Honorius is his dedication to making clerical learning accessible to the laity. In R. D. Crouse's words, his "combination of the luminous metaphysics of Christian Neoplatonism with an intense practical engagement in the edification of the '*oves Christi*'" sets him apart from all his contemporaries.[21] A full century before Fourth Lateran, he wrote such works as the *Elucidarium*, the *Speculum Ecclesiae*, and the *Imago mundi* as preacher's aids, using a fairly simple Latin that did not require advanced training in grammar, rhetoric, or theology to understand. He had a born teacher's gift for simplification, taking difficult materials and making them accessible to the broadest possible audience. As an encyclopedist his goal was not to ask more probing questions, but to disseminate reliable answers as widely as he could.[22] Many of his works are composed in dialogue form "because this method of teaching has seemed to the highest philosophers—Socrates, Plato, and Cicero, as well

20. Honorius, *De luminaribus Ecclesiae* 4.17 (PL 172: 232–34).

21. R. D. Crouse, "*Intentio Moysi:* Bede, Augustine, Eriugena and Plato in the *Hexaemeron* of Honorius Augustodunensis," *Dionysius* 2 (1978): 156.

22. Daniel Yingst, "Towers in the Mud: Honorius Augustodunensis through the Lens of Pedagogy" (Ph.D. dissertation, University of Chicago, 2017).

as our own Augustine and Boethius—to be the most powerful way to introduce new ideas."[23]

### *The* Clavis physicae, *its manuscripts, and its sources*

That said, however, *The Key to Natural Philosophy* (*Clavis physicae*) stands apart. Written ca. 1125–1130,[24] it is an adaptation and abridgment of the *Periphyseon* (also called *De divisione naturae*) by the Irish monk and philosopher, John Scottus Eriugena (ca. 810–877).[25] But even a simplified digest of an abstruse Neoplatonic dialogue is still an abstruse Neoplatonic dialogue. This time, Honorius was not writing to help priests teach their parishioners or fellow monks justify their vocation. The *Clavis* is a work of advanced philosophy, which Eva Matthews Sanford suggests he composed "more as a labor of love than in the hope that it would be widely read."[26]

Honorius must have encountered Eriugena no later than his studies in England, for the Carolingian writer's influence can be traced throughout his works, beginning with the *Elucidarium*.[27] Like much about his career, his discipleship to Eriugena is

23. *The Key to Natural Philosophy,* prologue.

24. This is the dating given by its editor, Paolo Lucentini, in *Platonismo medievale: Contributi per la storia dell' Eriugenismo* (La Nuova Italia, 1979), 71. But like everything else about Honorius, it is contested. Pasquale Arfé prefers a date in the 1110s: *La "Clavis physicae" (316–529) di Honorius Augustodunensis: Studio e edizione* (Liguori, 2012), 9. In *De luminaribus,* where Honorius lists his works in what seems to be chronological order, the *Clavis* is the nineteenth of the twenty-two mentioned (PL 172: 234a).

25. Johannes Scottus Eriugena, *Periphyseon* (*De divisione naturae*), ed. Édouard Jeauneau, 5 vols., CCCM 161–165 (Brepols, 1996–2003). For introductions to the philosopher's thought see Dermot Moran, *The Philosophy of John Scottus Eriugena: A Study of Idealism in the Middle Ages* (Cambridge University Press, 1989), and Deirdre Carabine, *John Scottus Eriugena,* Great Medieval Thinkers (Oxford University Press, 2000).

26. Sanford, "Honorius, *Presbyter,*" 417.

27. For Eriugena's influence on works before the *Clavis physicae* see Daniel Yingst, "*Quae omnia concorditer consonant:* Eriugena's Universe in the Thought of Honorius Augustodunensis," in *Eriugena and Creation: Proceedings of the International Conference on Eriugenian Studies,* ed. Willemien Otten and Michael I. Allen (Brepols, 2014), 427–61.

something of a mystery. We might ask if the Irishman was among the *auctores* Anselm taught his more promising students—but no evidence supports such a claim, and none of the master's other students shared Honorius's enthusiasm for this author.[28] A more likely possibility is that he had encountered Eriugena's works even before his English sojourn. If he originally hailed from Regensburg, he could have found manuscripts brought there by the Irish monks who founded the Schottenkloster in the eleventh century. Textual research indicates that for Book V of the *Periphyseon,* Honorius used a version of Eriugena's work older than any that survives elsewhere, possibly based on the author's unrevised early draft.[29]

Curiously, he seems not even to have known when the philosopher lived. In *De luminaribus Ecclesiae,* Honorius inserts Eriugena into a list of authors copied from Isidore of Seville, describing him as "Joannes Scotus or *Chrysostomus,* exceptionally learned in the Scriptures, [who] wrote the book *Περì φύσεων* or *On the Nature of All Things* in an elegant style."[30] This entry falls between Paschasinus, an obscure fifth-century bishop of Sicily, and Theodulus, author of an *Eclogue* now dated to the tenth century. Could Honorius really have confused Eriugena with St. John Chrysostom (347–407), the famed preacher and archbishop of Constantinople?[31] Did he find the epithet *Chrysostomus* ("golden-tongued") appropriate because he admired the Carolingian's "elegant style"? Or did he deliberately mystify Eriugena's identity (just as he concealed his own) because he knew the theologian was suspected of heresy?[32] But Honorius was not

28. On these contrasting influences see Loris Sturlese, "Zwischen Anselm und Johannes Scotus Eriugena: Der seltsame Fall des Honorius, des Mönchs von Regensburg," in *Historia Philosophiae Medii Aevi: Studien zur Geschichte der Philosophie des Mittelalters,* ed. Burkhard Mojsisch and Olaf Pluta, 2 vols. (Grüner, 1991), II: 927–51.

29. Eric Graff, "A Primitive Text of *Periphyseon V* Rediscovered: The Witness of Honorius Augustodunensis in *Clavis Physicae,*" *Recherches de théologie et philosophie médiévales* 69 (2002): 271–95.

30. Honorius, *De luminaribus Ecclesiae* 3.12 (PL 172: 222c).

31. This seems unlikely because, in his list of Greek sources, he names "Iohannes Crisostomus" as a distinct author. *Key to Natural Philosophy,* chap. 3.

32. This is suggested by Crouse, "*Intentio Moysi,*" 150–51.

the only twelfth-century writer to use the name "Crisostomus" for Eriugena; confusion about his identity may have been widespread. Whatever the case, several of the nine surviving manuscripts identify the *Clavis* as a work excerpted "*ex perifision magistri Crisotomii*" (*sic*). None of them mention Eriugena or John the Irishman by name.

Paolo Lucentini describes the manuscripts in his excellent critical edition.[33] Five of these date from the twelfth century, although two are fragments of the same divided codex. The most famous (Paris, BnF ms. lat. 6734, or P) dates from the mid-twelfth century, not long after the work's origin; it is the only representative of the branch of the stemma closest to the original. Made perhaps in the Mosan region (diocese of Liège), P includes the *Clavis physicae* and brief excerpts from Jerome's commentaries on Ephesians and Galatians. It was read well into the fifteenth century, for its margins contain annotations by Berthold of Moosburg, a *magister* in the Dominican convent of Regensburg as of 1327,[34] as well as "isolated notes from diverse hands," possibly including glosses by Nicholas of Cusa.[35] The second, Austrian branch of Lucentini's stemma includes the other eight surviving manuscripts, as well as three hypothetical lost exemplars.

A remarkable illustration in P (frontispiece, fol. 3v), perhaps based on a sketch by the author himself, epitomizes the work's Neoplatonic cosmology even as it illustrates the four Aristotelian causes of the world.[36] In the upper register we see a beardless Christ as *Bonitas*—the Platonic "Form of the Good"—in the role of Creator, the efficient cause of the universe. This crowned, masculine figure is surrounded by seven other divine Ideas, which constitute the world's formal causes: Justicia, Virtus, Ratio, Veritas, Essentia, Vita, and Sapientia. Painted in the guise

33. Honorius Augustodunensis, *Clavis physicae,* ed. Paolo Lucentini (Edizioni di Storia e Letteratura, 1974), vii–xxvi.

34. Evan King, *Supersapientia: Berthold of Moosburg and the Divine Science of the Platonists* (Brill, 2021), 29–30, 34.

35. Lucentini, introduction to *Clavis physicae,* ix–xv.

36. First published and expounded in detail by Marie-Thérèse d'Alverny, "Le cosmos symbolique du XIIe siècle," *Archives d'histoire doctrinale et littéraire du Moyen Âge* 20 (1954): 31–81.

of veiled feminine Virtues, these figures are variously identified in the text as primordial causes, virtues, and theophanies. The second register depicts masculine Time and feminine Place flanking an image of primal matter (*materia informis*), the material cause of the universe. Portrayed as a monstrous, many-eyed tetramorph, this is the same entity that Bernard Silvestris named Silva (*hyle*), making her the unlikely "heroine" of his *Cosmographia.* In that Neoplatonic epic, contemporary with the *Clavis,* Silva's longing to receive form and beauty motivates Nature and Noys (the divine Mind) to fashion the cosmos, bringing order out of chaos.[37] In the third register, which recalls illustrations from the Genesis tradition, we see the four elements with their inhabitants: angels and stars in the empyrean (the heaven of fire), birds in the air, fish in the water, and humans and beasts on the earth. These are summed up under the heading of "Natura creata, non creans": Nature is created by God, but not in itself creative. Finally, Christ appears again in the bottom register, now bearded and labeled *Finis.* As the final cause of the world, he holds a pair of draperies as if to pull down the curtain on the whole theatrical scene. This is Christ as Omega, whom the text calls "neither created nor creative" because in the *reditus,* or return, the cosmological process has come to a definitive end.

While only the Paris manuscript is illuminated, both it and several manuscripts from the Austrian branch of Lucentini's stemma are glossed with logical diagrams.[38] Called "Porphyrian trees," these diagrams are rooted in the discipline of dialectic. As Jeffrey Hamburger shows, they help the reader visualize the dynamic process of division that defines the cosmological cycle of *exitus* and *reditus,* which is at the same time a logical process of analysis and synthesis (chap. 302). Accordingly, the diagrams can be read either from the top down or the bottom up—from "the most general genus" to "the most specific species" and back

37. Bernard Silvestris, *Cosmographia,* ed. Peter Dronke (Brill, 1978); trans. Winthrop Wetherbee, *The* Cosmographia *of Bernardus Silvestris* (Columbia University Press, 1973).

38. Reproduced in Jeffrey F. Hamburger, *The Areopagite through the Ages: Diagramming the Pseudo-Dionysius c. 600 – c. 1600* (Pontifical Institute of Mediaeval Studies, forthcoming, 2026). I thank Prof. Hamburger for sharing a draft of his manuscript.

again. The creative process leads to division, difference, and individuality, while the return reabsorbs all creatures into the primal unity and simplicity of the Divine. The importance of this process is indicated by the Latin title often given to the *Periphyseon, De divisione naturae* (*On the Division of Nature*). Fig. 1 is an anglicized version of a diagram that appears in two manuscripts, illustrating the Great Chain of Being as it descends through seven degrees, from God down to inanimate bodies. The first descent from the divine simplicity is the archetypal world, the realm of primordial causes. From this we descend to angels (intellectual creatures), human beings (rational creatures), animals (living creatures), trees and plants (creatures with movement),[39] and finally lifeless bodies such as stones, which lack the power of movement. Studying this diagram at the beginning of the text would orient the reader to the more intricate divisions that follow. Fig. 2 is my own Porphyrian tree diagram of chapter 120, which shows how broader categories (genera) can be bifurcated into narrower ones (species). In this case, from the divine Goodness proceed both "things that are not" and "things that are," the latter being divided into non-living and living, and so forth. Students might be encouraged to construct their own diagrams of this type as a mode of what we now call visual learning.

Another type of diagram, the "square of opposition," serves to illustrate adjacent and opposing properties of the four elements: hot, cold, dry, and moist, which combine in different pairs to produce earth, air, fire, and water. Such a diagram underlies the famous image of the *Anima mundi* (Paris, BnF ms. lat. 6734, fol. 1v), in which the feminine World Soul is surrounded by a rectangle composed of arms and hands, linking medallions of the four elements and demonstrating the distinctive properties of each.[40] These diagrammatic glosses show that the *Clavis* was conceived not as a work of wild metaphysical speculation,

39. The diagram reverses two of its headings. Normally animals would be called moving creatures (which are higher on the chain of being), and plants merely living creatures.

40. Reproduced in d'Alverny, "Le cosmos symbolique," and Hamburger, *The Areopagite through the Ages*. The entire manuscript can be accessed online at gallica.bnf.fr.

but as a strictly logical unfolding of natural processes. Indeed, Honorius claims that the art of dialectic, "which divides genera into species and resolves species into genera, was not devised by human invention, but created in the nature of things" (chap. 231). Although the logical diagrams cannot be traced back to manuscripts of the *Periphyseon,* their presence in both branches of the *Clavis* stemma suggests that Honorius himself devised them, perhaps by adapting earlier models that he used for teaching. This would be wholly in line with what we know of his pedagogical habits.

A wide-ranging philosophical work, the *Clavis physicae* begins with an account of the five metaphysical divisions of nature, the incomprehensible divine essence, and the ten categories of Aristotle, which apply to all created natures but not to God. Abridging and simplifying Eriugena's text, Honorius goes on to discuss the elements and their properties; human and angelic nature; the participation of all creatures in the Divine; the mystery of God's will; heavenly bodies; the six days of creation; the nature of the soul; the human being as microcosm; Adam in paradise; the origins of evil; the future resurrection; and many other theological and scientific themes. The work is non-linear and defies easy summary. Its most salient feature is its uncompromising idealism: "any soul is superior to every body" (chap. 225), and "knowledge of things is better than the things themselves" (chap. 255). "Indeed, only God is above the intellect, and there is nothing below the body" (chap. 289). Accordingly, "our true and highest being" lies in the intellect "rendered specific by contemplation of the truth" (chap. 259).

Although Honorius faithfully follows his source, he also sharply abridges it. By Lucentini's calculations, he retains only 36 percent of Eriugena's first book, 27 percent of Book Two, 52 percent of Book Three, and 38 percent of Book Four,[41] so that the so-called Part I of the *Clavis* is roughly half the length of *Periphyseon,* Books I–IV. Even less of Book Five is abridged—the portion dealing with the *reditus* or ultimate return of all beings

41. Lucentini, *Platonismo Medievale,* 72–73; idem, "La *Clavis physicae* di Honorius Augustodunensis e la tradizione eriugeniana nel secolo XII," in *Jean Scot Érigène et l'histoire de la philosophie,* ed. René Roques (Paris: Centre national de la recherche scientifique, 1977), 405–14.

to God, completing the Neoplatonic model of exemplarity, emanation, and return.[42] Honorius did adapt and abridge the first part of Book V, following the same method he had used for the rest, but soon stopped for reasons unknown. He may have found the material too difficult to summarize, or perhaps he just ran out of time and energy. It is also possible that he had an incomplete manuscript and had to search for a fuller one. So, considered as a work by Honorius himself, the *Clavis physicae* is unfinished. What is called Part II (not included in Lucentini's edition or in this volume) begins with chapter 316 and simply transcribes the rest of *Periphyseon* V in its entirety.[43] It introduces only minor changes, such as the omission of cross-references, abridgment of a few patristic citations, and spelling variants such as *sensilis* for *sensibilis.*[44] In manuscript P, this material follows Part I without a break on the same folio (fol. 143r) in the same hand; the marginal chapter titles continue in the same format until the end of the text. Since "Part II" is found in manuscripts from both branches of the stemma, the decision to proceed in this fashion must have been made by Honorius himself, but he could well have instructed a disciple or scribe to complete his manuscript with a simple transcription.

In a study of Honorius's techniques as an adapter, Stephen Gersh showed that he was true to Eriugena in both vocabulary and doctrine, but simplified the philosopher's complex arguments by eliminating digressions, unifying terminology (though not consistently), and cutting many of his Greek etymologies.[45]

42. Pasquale Arfé, "*Triplex modus theoriae de reditu:* The Doctrine of Universal Return in Eriugena," *Archives d'histoire doctrinale et littéraire du Moyen Âge* 78 (2011): 7–45.

43. There is now an edition by Pasquale Arfé, *La "Clavis physicae" (316–529) di Honorius Augustodunensis.*

44. Arfé, *La "Clavis physicae,"* 49. Graff suggests that these changes may be due not to Honorius's editorial activity but to his use of an earlier, unrevised manuscript of the *Periphyseon.* In other words, the differences may derive not from *abbreviatio* by Honorius, but from later *amplificatio* by Eriugena himself. "A Primitive Text," 282–84.

45. Stephen Gersh, "Honorius Augustodunensis and Eriugena: Remarks on the Method and Content of the *Clavis physicae,*" in *Eriugena Redivivus: Zur Wirkungsgeschichte seines Denkens im Mittelalter und im Übergang zur Neuzeit,* ed. Werner Beierwaltes (Winter, 1987), 162–73.

He also abbreviated Eriugena's long patristic citations. The resulting text is much more concise, though still difficult, and occasionally the omission of a clause or a surrounding context alters the meaning of a sentence. These slight shifts in nuance were almost certainly not intended. The brief, marginal chapter titles found in P, which break the work into small chunks for easier reading, may go back to Honorius himself. While omitting much of Eriugena's discussion of the primordial causes in Book II, the monk expands sections on the topics of greatest interest to him: anthropology, angelic nature, the redemptive role of Christ, the relationship between angels and humans, and the spiritual body.

In a short prologue that Honorius added to Eriugena's text, he cites what he takes to be its major patristic sources (chap. 3). On the Greek side, these are "the supreme theologians Dionysius the Areopagite, Gregory of Nazianzus, Gregory of Nyssa and his brother Basil, John Chrysostom, and the monk Maximus, an outstanding philosopher and bishop." On the Latin side Honorius names "the supreme Catholic doctors Hilary of Poitiers, Ambrose of Milan, Aurelius Augustine, and Jerome." Although Eriugena often cites his sources by name, the *Periphyseon* did not come with footnotes, so the adapter's bibliography is only approximate.[46]

Eriugena did rely heavily on Dionysius, a fifth-century Syrian monk, whose complete works he had translated.[47] He also translated and highly valued Gregory of Nyssa's treatise *De hominis opificio* (*On the Making of Man*), known to him as *De imagine* (*On the Image*). Basil of Caesarea's *Hexaemeron* figures largely in what Honorius, following Eriugena, presents rather tendentiously as a literal, rather than allegorical, account of the six days of creation. Gregory of Nazianzus was commonly styled "Gregory the

46. On Eriugena's direct use of these sources see Michael Harrington, "Eriugena and the Neoplatonic Tradition," in *A Companion to John Scottus Eriugena,* ed. Adrian Guiu (Brill, 2020), 64–92, and Joel I. Barstad, "Eriugena as Translator and Interpreter of the Greek Fathers," in ibid., 267–95.

47. This author is often referred to as Pseudo-Dionysius because he was neither the Athenian convert of St. Paul (Acts 17.34), his pseudonym, nor the martyr St. Denis, the patron saint of Paris. I have dispensed with this epithet.

Theologian" by later Byzantines, leading to some confusion with his more Neoplatonic contemporary, Gregory of Nyssa. Eriugena fell prey to this misunderstanding and used the honorific for Gregory of Nyssa. In fact, he knew the Nazianzene's writings only indirectly through the glosses of a later theologian, Maximus the Confessor (d. 662). Maximus's much-cited *Ambigua* also supplied him with an important commentary on the works of Dionysius. Despite Honorius's reference to John Chrysostom, that writer represented a different school of theology that was less congenial to Eriugena, so he is quoted in neither the *Periphyseon* nor the *Clavis*. Unnamed by Honorius in his prologue, but cited occasionally in the text, is a single dialogue of Plato, the *Timaeus,* which Eriugena knew from a partial Latin translation and widely read commentary by Chalcidius. A final Greek source is the *Ancoratus* (*The Well-Anchored Man*) by Epiphanius of Salamis, cited by Eriugena mainly when he disagreed with it.

Although Honorius mentions Hilary and Jerome, neither appears in his text unless we count the Vulgate Bible, which was of course translated by Jerome. Ambrose's *De paradiso* (*On Paradise*), the Latin commentary closest in spirit to the Greek works that underlie it, plays an important role in Eriugena's account of Paradise and the Fall. But Augustine is far and away his most important Latin source, especially his massive literal commentary on Genesis (*De Genesi ad litteram*). Beyond this commentary, Eriugena was well versed in the bishop's voluminous writings and cites a wide variety of his texts more selectively. In general, he is happy to follow Augustine in his more Platonizing moods, but when the Latin bishop disagrees with the Greeks (most notably on the resurrection body), the latter prevail. Boethius is cited occasionally, while the work's scientific chapters (which are not its strongest) draw on Pliny's *Natural History* and Martianus Capella's textbook of the liberal arts, *De nuptiis Philologiae et Mercurii* (*On the Marriage of Philology and Mercury*). At only one point did Honorius add a new reference to the *Periphyseon,* and this not surprisingly comes from his old teacher Anselm. In chapter 111, while presenting Eriugena's paradoxical idea that God "is not" (because he transcends all thought and language), Honorius recalls Anselm's refutation of the Fool who said in his heart, "there is no God."[48] Gersh remarks that "in this combination of doctrines from the two great medieval Platonists, the encyclopaedist indulges in a moment of genuine philosophical creativity."[49]

## *Influence of the* Clavis physicae

Eriugena was described a century ago as "the loneliest figure in the history of European thought," with few peers and few successors.[50] It is only in recent decades that scholars have begun to do him justice. In some ways his case runs parallel to that of Honorius: both are anomalous, biographically mysterious figures and, for that reason, baffling to historians. But as Daniel Yingst writes, "whereas Honorius is generally assumed to be too simple, too popular, and too unoriginal to warrant serious attention, Eriugena is perceived as too complex, too weird, and too original."[51] Yet he has emerged as a central figure in the history of medieval Platonism, not least because he steeped himself in the thought of the Greek Fathers. These debts make the *Periphyseon* a valuable source for the early reception of Greek theology in the West, especially because it synthesizes its eastern sources with Latin luminaries such as Augustine.

Outside of the Empire, Eriugena's influence in the twelfth century seems to have been direct, rather than mediated by the *Clavis.* As Agnieszka Kijewska has shown, after initial neglect his translation of the Dionysian corpus came to be widely read in France, where he had produced it. Both Dionysius and Eriugena were favored at Saint-Denis under Abbot Suger (reg. 1122–51) because the abbey's monks identified the Areopagite with their patron saint. Eriugena's thought was definitely known to Hugh of Saint-Victor and arguably also to such Chartrain philosophers as William of Conches, Thierry of Chartres, and Clarembald of

48. Anselm, *Proslogion,* chap. 4, in *Basic Writings,* trans. Thomas Williams (Hackett, 2007), 83. See also Ps 13.1 (Vulgate).

49. Gersh, "Honorius Augustodunensis and Eriugena," 173.

50. Henry Bett, *Johannes Scotus Erigena: A Study in Mediaeval Philosophy* (Cambridge University Press, 1925), 1.

51. Yingst, "Towers in the Mud," 86.

Arras.[52] The passionately christocentric Bernard of Clairvaux took little interest in so abstract a philosopher, but other Cistercians read him, including William of Saint-Thierry. Alan of Lille makes the unusual move of citing the Irishman favorably by name, though his metaphysics are quite different.[53] Special mention should go to William of Malmesbury (d. 1143), whom Édouard Jeauneau described as "the first English editor of the *Periphyseon.*"[54] In fact, William produced an early critical edition that still survives (Cambridge, Trinity College 0.5.20), by consulting multiple manuscripts from different families. He also invented a tale of the philosopher's life, with the surprising information that after growing bored at the court of Charles the Bald, Eriugena moved to England during the reign of Alfred the Great and settled—where else?—at Malmesbury, where he served as head of the abbey school until his frustrated students stabbed him to death with their pencils.[55]

That story is surely apocryphal—though it is not hard to imagine schoolboys growing restive under so difficult a master. Honorius, a more accommodating pedagogue, did his best to prune the philosopher's tangled prose so as to make him more accessible. In German-speaking lands, at any rate, the *Clavis physicae* soon became the primary transmitter of Eriugena's thought. Around 1160 Arno of Reichersberg (brother of the more famous Gerhoh) cited the *Clavis* at length in his *Hexaemeron,* not surprisingly because so much of Honorius's work treats the six days of creation. Also in the twelfth century, an anonymous work titled *Apex physicae* (*Summit of Natural Philosophy*)

52. Agnieszka Kijewska, "Eriugena's Influence on the 12th Century," in *A Companion,* ed. Guiu, 349–86.

53. Kijewska, "Eriugena's Influence," 377–78.

54. Édouard Jeauneau, "Guillaume de Malmesbury, premier éditeur anglais du 'Periphyseon,'" in "*Sapientiae Doctrina*": *Mélanges de théologie et de littérature médiévales offerts à Dom Hildebrand Bascour O.S.B.*, ed. Roland Hissette, Guibert Michiels, and Dirk Van Den Auweele (Recherches de théologie ancienne et médiévale, 1980), 148–79. See also Moran, *The Philosophy of John Scottus Eriugena,* 65–67.

55. Kijewska, "Eriugena's Influence," 352; Édouard Jeauneau, "Le renouveau érigénien du XIIe siècle," in *Eriugena Redivivus,* ed. Beierwaltes, 32.

not only cites the *Clavis,* but makes a direct allusion in its title.[56] While Hildegard of Bingen's sources are notoriously slippery, Christel Meier argued at length that she too was familiar with Eriugena, almost certainly by way of Honorius.[57] Peter Dronke, in his ambitious edition of the abbess's *Liber divinorum operum* (*Book of Divine Works*), does not cite the *Clavis physicae* but refers directly to the *Periphyseon,* as well as more popular works by Honorius such as the *Elucidarium, Speculum Ecclesiae,* and *Imago mundi.* More cautious than Meier, he identifies all these as "materials for comparison,… analogues that may be fruitful to consider in connection with Hildegard, but without any claim of an influence."[58]

The *Clavis physicae* retained its importance in the later Middle Ages for another reason. Eriugena was posthumously condemned for heresy, but the work of Honorius remained exempt, making his epitome the primary channel by which the philosopher could reach interested readers. The Irishman had long been under suspicion. In an eleventh-century Eucharistic controversy incited by Berengar of Tours, Berengar relied heavily on a treatise by Ratramnus of Corbie (d. ca. 868), which he mistakenly ascribed to Eriugena—thus tarnishing him with a heretical taint.[59] A few decades later Gilbert of Poitiers criticized Abelard for using the term *involucrum* in identifying the Holy

56. Alessandra Beccarisi, "Un nuovo frammento della 'Clavis Physicae' di Onorio e la diffusione dell' Eriugenismo nella Germania medievale," *Giornale critico della filosofia italiana* 21 (2001): 171–78.

57. Christel Meier, "Eriugena im Nonnenkloster? Überlegungen zum Verhältnis von Prophetentum und Werkgestalt in den *figmenta prophetica* Hildegards von Bingen," *Frühmittelalterliche Studien* 19 (1985): 466–97; eadem, "Scientia Divinorum Operum: Zu Hildegards von Bingen visionär-künstlerischer Rezeption Eriugenas," in *Eriugena Redivivus,* ed. Beierwaltes, 89–141.

58. Peter Dronke, introduction to Hildegard of Bingen, *Liber divinorum operum,* ed. Albert Derolez and Peter Dronke, CCCM 92 (Brepols, 1996), xxviii.

59. Ratramnus, *De corpore et sanguine Domini* (PL 121: 125–170); Berengar of Tours, *De sacra coena adversus Lanfrancum* 1.10–11, ed. W. H. Beekenkamp (Nijhoff, 1941); Willemien Otten, "Between Augustinian Sign and Carolingian Reality: The Presence of Ambrose and Augustine in the Eucharistic Debate between Paschasius Radbertus and Ratramnus of Corbie," Nederlandsch archief voor kerkgeschiedenis 80 (2000): 137–56, at 139. Others made the same error of attribution.

Spirit with the World Soul. Gilbert traced that term to "John the Irishman ... who frequently used this unfamiliar term and was himself noted for the subtlety of his heresy."[60] Curiously, however, Eriugena does *not* use the term. Neither does Honorius—but it appears prominently in an author portrait that opens the *Clavis physicae* (P, fol. 3r). That image shows a Greek abbot Theodorus disputing with an Irish scholar identified as Iohannes (John Scottus Eriugena). Their speech scrolls interlock, and the one held by Iohannes reads "Involucrum rerum petit is fieri sibi clarum" ("He asks that the significance of things—or the covering of nature—be made plain to him").[61] If this is where Gilbert acquired the term, it suggests that the Paris manuscript of the *Clavis physicae* was already a primary vehicle for the Carolingian's reception.

A Parisian council in 1210 condemned Eriugena's writings for their supposed pantheism, which was thought to have inspired the heresy of Amaury of Bène, and in 1225, Pope Honorius III decreed that all extant copies of the *Periphyseon* should be sent to Rome for burning.[62] Although the connections with Amaury are tenuous, suspicion of the work long endured. Soon after Thomas Gale published his *editio princeps* of the *Periphyseon,* based on William of Malmesbury, in 1681, it was added in 1687 to the Index of Forbidden Books, where it remained until the Index itself was abolished in the 1960s.[63] It was through the *Clavis physicae,* then, that the Irish "heretic" continued to travel incognito, reaching philosophers interested in Greek theology and the Neoplatonic tradition. One of these was Meister Eckhart, whose Latin commentary on the Book of Wisdom alludes

60. *Disputatio altera adversus Petrum Abaelardum* 3 (PL 180: 322a). Migne ascribes this treatise to William of Saint-Thierry, but it is more likely by Gilbert of Poitiers.

61. Paris, BnF ms. lat. 6734, fol. 3r. The illustration appears only in this manuscript.

62. Paolo Lucentini, "L'eresia di Amalrico," in *Eriugena Redivivus,* ed. Beierwaltes, 174–91; Stephen Lahey, "Eriugena's Condemnation and His Idealism," in *A Companion,* ed. Guiu, 447–53; Willemien Otten, "Suspended between Cosmology and Anthropology: *Natura*'s Bond in Eriugena's *Periphyseon,*" in *A Companion,* ed. Guiu, 189–212, at 189.

63. Yingst, "Towers in the Mud," 91.

to a passage from the *Periphyseon.* But Eriugena had already been banned for a century, and the passage appears in nearly identical form in the *Clavis,* making it a more likely source.[64] The work was also known to others in Eckhart's circle. A dialogue titled "Daz send gar hoch fragen und materien" ("These are Lofty Questions and Topics") translates chapters 12–15 and 17–25 into Middle High German in abridged versions.[65] These chapters deal with the vision of God, theophanies, how God can be described as "created" in his own works, the Trinity, and the difference between affirmative and negative theology. The dialogue does not identify an author, saying only that it was translated from the Latin by a learned priest. It illustrates the highly sophisticated theology that laypeople could access in the vernacular in the fourteenth century. A Latin commentator on the German mystical poem "Granum sinapis" ("The Mustard Seed") also made use of the *Clavis.*[66]

We have already mentioned that the twelfth-century manuscript P includes glosses by Berthold of Moosburg, a great admirer of Honorius's work. Writing around 1340, he cites it extensively in his commentary on the *Elementatio theologica* (*Elements of Theology*) of Proclus, a pagan Neoplatonist, which had been translated by William of Moerbeke in 1268. Although Berthold was familiar with Eriugena's thought from several sources, none of them were correctly ascribed, so he apparently did not know the Irishman by name. By far the most important of those sources was the *Clavis physicae,* which Berthold attributed on the basis of its author portrait to Abbot Theodorus. The Proclus commentary quotes no fewer than ninety-three chapters from the text, using both Part I (Honorius's adaptation) and Part II

64. Josef Koch, "Zur Analogielehre Meister Eckharts," in *Kleine Schriften,* 2 vols. (Edizioni di Storia e Letteratura, 1973), I: 387–88; Beccarisi, "Un nuovo frammento," 176. The passage (*Periphyseon* 449C) is in *Clavis physicae,* chap. 13, which represents the virtues as a *conformatio* between divine Wisdom and the human intellect.

65. Edited by Auguste Jundt, *Histoire du panthéisme populaire au Moyen Âge et au seizième siècle* (Paris, 1875; repr. Minerva, 1964), 240–46. Jundt does not identify the manuscript, which as of 1875 was in a private collection. He dates it to the mid-15th century, but the text itself belongs to the 14th and traveled with works ascribed to Eckhart.

66. Beccarisi, "Un nuovo frammento," 175.

(the *Periphyseon* verbatim). Berthold took a particular interest in the primordial causes and the spiritual body in paradise.[67]

In the fifteenth century another fan, Nicholas of Cusa, ordered a copy of the *Clavis* to be made for him. This manuscript still survives as Cusanusstift-Bibliothek 202 (C). Cusa's exemplar also survives, though now in two fragments. As of 1515 it still belonged to the Benedictine house of SS. Ulrich and Afra in Augsburg, according to a colophon by the Catholic theologian Johann Eck (1486–1543). As late as the second half of the seventeenth century, Andreas Erasmus von Seidel (1650–1707) annotated the same manuscript, noting that Honorius was "not ignorant of the Greek language."[68] (He does indeed use and expound several Greek philosophical terms, always following Eriugena.) Two other sixteenth-century manuscripts in Vienna further attest to the work's continuing readership in the early modern era.

Even Cusanus, however, recognized the danger of heresy. In his famous *Apologia doctae ignorantiae* (*Defense of Learned Ignorance*), he wrote, "All the saints rightly warn that the intellectual light should be withdrawn from those whose mental eyes are weak. By no means should the books of St. Dionysius be shown to them, Marius Victorinus's *To Candidus the Arian,* the *Clavis physicae* of Theodorus, the *Periphyseon* of John the Irishman, *De tomis* by David of Dinant, the *Commentaries on the Propositions of Proclus* by friar John of Mossbach [Berthold of Moosburg], and other similar books."[69] Cusanus thus acknowledged a long lineage of Neoplatonic philosophers who provided "intellectual light" for venturesome minds, but could endanger "those whose mental eyes are weak."

67. King, *Supersapientia,* 31–34.

68. Lucentini, *Clavis physicae,* xviii–xxi.

69. "Unde recte admonent omnes sancti, quod illis debilibus mentis oculis lux intellectualis subtrahatur. Sunt autem illis nequaquam libri sancti Dionysii, Marii Victorini ad Candidum Arrianum, Clavis physicae Theodori, Iohannis Scotigenae Περι φύσεως, Tomi David de Dynanto, Commentaria fratris Iohannis de Mossbach in Propositiones Proculi et consimiles libri ostendendi." Nicholas of Cusa, *Opera omnia* II: *Apologia doctae ignorantiae,* ed. Raymond Klibansky (Felix Meiner, 2007), 29–30. The ascription of the *Clavis* to "Theodorus" is based on the author portrait in P discussed above.

### *Radical doctrines*

It is not without reason that orthodox churchmen charged Eriugena with heresy, in particular with pantheism. While Christian Platonism took many forms, Eriugena's is the most radical to be found in the Latin West, at least until Meister Eckhart, and Honorius faithfully reproduces even his most controversial doctrines. In this section I summarize a few of these positions, which follow the Greek fathers but often carry their thought even further. While orthodox constructions can be placed on most of these doctrines, some stand in sharp contrast with the Augustinian theology that became normative for much of medieval Europe. Eriugena and Honorius downplay contradictions between their authorities, harmonizing where possible and explicitly refusing to denounce opposing views (chaps. 178, 190, 274, 312). "Indeed, we aim to support our own opinion or that of writers who surpass the rest—but to condemn the opinion of others is very dangerous, arrogant in the extreme, or surely contentious. So let us proceed cautiously, humbly, and modestly" (chap. 281). Nevertheless, when the chips are down, they consistently side with Gregory of Nyssa, Dionysius, and Maximus over against Augustine. Ambrose of Milan, one of the few Latin fathers who read Greek, offers important support.

Here are some of the propositions that might have shocked heresy-hunters or simple believers.

(a) God "does not exist." Following the apophatic theology of Dionysius the Areopagite, the *Clavis physicae* argues that all affirmative statements about God must be understood metaphorically. Thus God is not properly truth, wisdom, goodness, and so forth, but more-than-truth, more-than-wisdom, more-than-goodness. By the same logic, he is not being or essence, but "superessential" (chap. 25). Even being is not properly predicated of God, for, in the strict sense, the divine nature is "nothing" (chap. 107). Honorius argues that while affirmative theology "clothes the divine essence" in garments of beauty, the more accurate negative theology leaves it "naked of all proper signification" (chap. 25). At the same time, God is rightly understood as the source of all being, goodness, and other positive qualities. Evil is nonexistent in a different sense. Since it was not created by God, he does not know it and it has no substance (chap. 110). It can only be understood as a privation of the good, or pure nothingness. As Bernard McGinn has pointed out, this passage in Eriugena is "the first explicit appearance in Christian thought of the distinction between *nihil* as privation and *nihil* as eminence, a distinction that was to have a significant later history in thinkers like Eckhart and Cusanus."[70]

(b) God does not know or understand himself. Being infinite, he cannot be bounded or circumscribed by any definition. He is therefore incomprehensible not only to human and angelic intellects, but even to himself. We can know only *that* God is, but not *what* he is. In an audacious extension of that commonplace, Honorius proclaims that such ignorance applies to the divine Being itself because God is "truly infinite, in all and above all" (chap. 108). "In this wonderful divine ignorance, by which God does not understand what he is because he is not any thing, there smiles a supreme, ineffable wisdom" (chap. 108). This is the foundation of *docta ignorantia,* a principle that would be further developed by one of Eriugena's most important followers, Nicholas of Cusa.

(c) Nothing truly exists but God, who is one with creation. Although in one sense God does not exist, in another sense *only* God exists, for he is the being or essence of all things (chap. 19). God brings all things into being by an act of will, but since he exists beyond time, to be, to will, and to act are one and the same (chaps. 19, 35, 157, 188). Creation is therefore eternal in its primordial causes, which subsist within God. Though invisible and incomprehensible by nature, the divine becomes manifest in and even *as* all creatures (chap. 133), in which God is said both to "become" (*fieri*) and to "be created." The world, therefore, is both eternal and created (chaps. 133, 134, 155). The most eloquent statement of this view occurs in chapter 160:

> All is one and the same nature whose simplicity is inviolable, whose unity is inseparable.... [A]ll things everywhere are God: the whole in the whole, the Creator and the created, the seer and the seen, time and place and the being, substance, and accidents of all

70. Bernard McGinn, "The *Periphyseon* as Hexaemeral Commentary," in *A Companion,* ed. Guiu, 154–88, at 175.

things—and to speak simply, all that truly is and all that is not, superessential in essences, supersubstantial in substances, Creator above every creature, created within every creature, subsisting beneath every creature, beginning to exist from itself, moving itself through itself, moved toward itself and resting in itself, infinitely multiplied in itself through genera and species, yet not forsaking the simplicity of its nature, but recalling its infinite multiplication back to itself. For in it all things are one.

It is on this and similar statements that the charge of pantheism is based. Even if all things are not God, strictly speaking (a point on which the text is inconsistent), all things are certainly *in* God, and reciprocally, God is in all things as their very being.

(d) Reason supersedes authority, even that of Scripture. In chapter 64, Honorius echoes Eriugena's famous dictum that "all authority that is not proven by true reasoning seems weak, but true reasoning supported by its own merits does not need to be strengthened by the help of any authority. For true authority is nothing but truth discovered by the power of reason." When Scripture openly contradicts the arguments of "true reason," that is only because it speaks metaphorically "for the benefit of untrained and childish minds" (chap. 64). Scripture is like a mother who nurses her babes with simple doctrine, while reason is a teacher (*magistra*) who leads advanced pupils to the truth. One such truth is that God can neither love nor be loved because loving is a form of action, and being loved, a form of passivity. But to act and be acted on are accidents, and the divine nature admits no accident.

(e) The soul creates the body. As a manifestation of his extreme idealism, Eriugena asserts that the soul creates its own body by taking "matter from the qualities of sensible things," imbuing it with vital motion, and conferring the external senses (chap. 102). So just as the soul is the image of God, the body is the image of the soul (chap. 106). With God's counsel, but not by direct divine action, "man made for himself a mortal dwelling of mud" in order to expiate his sins in it (chap. 104). Although Honorius qualifies this idea, admitting that the soul precedes the body "only in the dignity and excellence of its nature," not in time (chap. 102), many theologians would have raised an eyebrow at his unconventional claim. All the more would they have been surprised by its corollary: the soul continues to govern its body after death, even after its parts have been dispersed among the elements (chaps. 213, 273).

(f) At the general resurrection, all the blessed will be deified. Here Eriugena follows a Greek patristic teaching that would become central to Byzantine and later Orthodox theology. *Theosis,* or deification, comes about through full participation in the divine nature. Human nature will not be abolished after the end of the world. But, in a favorite simile, it will "disappear" just as air illuminated by sunlight disappears into pure light, or as melted iron appears to be wholly fire even though its substance remains (chaps. 13, 15, 47, 165, 313). For human nature, this means that in the general resurrection, the body will be absorbed into the soul, the soul into the intellect, and the intellect into God. This is pure Platonism, though the *Clavis* salvages some fidelity to the Nicene Creed by falling back on Paul's conception of the "spiritual body" (1 Corinthians 15). That body will not only be immortal and incorruptible, but it will have none of the qualities we now think of as corporeal—least of all, sex and gender.

(g) Sex was not part of the original creation, and it will disappear in the resurrection. Being created in the divine image, the original human being was pure intellect and would have reproduced like the angels (chap. 70). This is *homo* as he existed, and still exists, among the primordial causes. But the omniscient God foresaw the Fall (although, properly speaking, "foresaw" implies a temporality that is alien to the divine nature). He therefore gave human beings material bodies "in the likeness of foolish animals" (chap. 247), including the division into two sexes, so the human species would not be extinguished by death. This division is perceived as secondary, punitive, and shameful; it dishonors the dignity of the divine image (chap. 271). So in the resurrection, when human nature is restored to its original glory, sex and gender—along with all forms of corruptible materiality—will vanish entirely (chaps. 71, 99), as prefigured by the risen Christ, who was already sexless (chap. 75). At the end of time, "the whole of human nature will be poured into the intellect alone" (chap. 305).

Through the figure of the Disciple, Honorius shows a keen awareness that many readers will find his doctrines problematic. When the Master boldly argues that God can neither love nor be loved because he cannot act or be acted on, the Disciple feels compelled to accept this conclusion, despite the "many arrows of holy Scripture ... clamoring on all sides and proclaiming that this is false" (chap. 63). In chapter 79, the Disciple protests Maximus the Confessor's view that sex will disappear in the resurrection. "Who would not tremble" on hearing such things, he asks, knowing that "this teaching opposes the authority of almost all the Latin saints?" (Augustine is the primary opponent.) When the discussion turns to the thorny question of formless matter, which the Master claims is eternal yet refuses to identify with the "nothing" from which God created all things, the Disciple ties himself in philosophical knots: "Don't you see that I am rightly shaken and dashed between floods of mutually exclusive thoughts? For how can these arguments be reconciled? If all things that exist in the creative Wisdom are eternal, how were they made from nothing?" (chap. 129). Paradox always troubles him, including the idea that man is at the same time one animal among others and uniquely fashioned in God's image (chap. 234).

The Disciple is especially vexed by the Master's paradoxical argument that the world is simultaneously created and eternal. In his lengthiest intervention (chaps. 138–141), he protests that it is logically impossible for anything that had a beginning in time to be (or to become) eternal. Summarizing a range of positions on the possible eternity or sempiternity of the universe (chap. 139), the Disciple finally declares that the Master's doctrine, supported by the authority of Dionysius, "is still unheard-of and unknown, not only to me but to many, in fact almost everyone." He refers to the pantheistic view that "God is everything and everything is God" (chap. 141). If the Master cannot present a better argument for his position, it will be "thought monstrous even by those who are held to be wise," and in addition he will "be accused of great heresy" (chap. 141)—as Eriugena in fact was. The Master relents and admits that he was "once deceived by the false reasoning of human opinions, far removed from the truth," and indeed he "fabricated the most foul, abominable monstrosities in human thinking" (chap. 141). Yet he goes on to support a position that differs almost imperceptibly from the one he has just repudiated. By voicing such objections, the Disciple not only compels the Master to clarify his arguments, but acknowledges the highly speculative, controversial character of the text.

Given those four hundred extant manuscripts of the *Elucidarium,* Honorius won his reputation primarily as a catechist, a purveyor of that "simple teaching" that reason perceives as suitable for "childish minds" (chap. 64). But after enjoying unparalleled success as a popularizer, at some point he turned from milk to solid food, as it were, and wrote the *Clavis physicae* for the philosophical few. We will never know why. The work had a limited readership but a long shelf life (as I dare to hope for this translation). If it had circulated more widely, might its author have been remembered less as a shepherd of the simple than as the Pied Piper of Pantheism?

### *About this translation*

Like any philosophical text, the *Clavis physicae* poses certain technical difficulties. These are compounded because Honorius, like his source, indiscriminately mingles Greek and Latin philosophical terms. In chapters 23–27 alone, for example, *substantia* is used to denote (1) the three persons of the Trinity (Greek *hypostases*); (2) the unique divine essence (Greek *ousia*); and (3) the first of Aristotle's ten categories. Words such as *essentia, substantia,* and *(o)usia* are sometimes used synonymously, while at other times they have distinct meanings. The same applies to the ubiquitous *genus* and *species,* which are relative rather than absolute terms.[71] So it is impossible to translate the same term the same way every time it appears. Since many of my readers will be historians of philosophy, I have included footnotes to supply the Latin terminology when it is of technical interest and to explain difficulties of usage.

71. For instance, "cat" would be a species of the genus "animal," but a genus containing the species "Persian" and "Siamese." *Forma* is sometimes used as a synonym for *species.*

Even the keyword *physica* is a problem. Derived from the Greek *physis* ("nature"), it is a wide-ranging term that rarely means "physics" or "science" in the English sense. Honorius uses it as both noun and adjective. In adjectival form it is best translated as "natural," and the noun sometimes means simply "nature." In chapter 4, Honorius defines it as *natura omnium rerum,* the nature of all things, which could be specified more precisely as "the Creator and creation." That indeed is the work's principal subject. But in the title, *physica* designates a discipline, which is defined in chapter 123 as "the natural knowledge of natures that are accessible to the senses and the intellect." I have decided that "natural philosophy" is the nearest equivalent, although the comprehensive discipline in question also embraces theology, metaphysics, cosmology, and biblical exegesis.

The word *homo* is problematic too. Following Eriugena and several of the Greek fathers, as we have seen, Honorius opposes Augustine and argues that sex and gender formed no part of the original human creation, which took place in the primordial causes. The gender division was added only in the secondary, material creation because God providentially foresaw the need for sexual reproduction after the Fall. So *homo* is a gender-neutral term, most often referring to this exemplary, sexless human person. For that reason I often translate it as "the human being." But that expression is cumbersome, and the term occurs constantly, so I usually fall back on "man" in the older, gender-neutral sense. "Person" is not an acceptable substitute because it has its own philosophical meaning, and switching to the plural would falsify the text's profound valuation of unity and simplicity. I apologize for this old-fashioned usage but see no way to avoid it.

Conversely, I have used both masculine and feminine pronouns for God. *Deus* is of course masculine. But when Honorius speaks of the divine essence (*essentia*) or nature (*natura*), those feminine nouns require feminine pronouns, so I have followed suit. The same is true of personified Wisdom (*sapientia*), the feminine alter ego of Christ. When Honorius represents the divine nature as universal cause, his Latin term is *creatrix,* which I have reproduced in English. Philosophically, the alternating pronouns should remind readers that gender is one of the innumerable accidents that do not apply to the Divine.

I have checked several portions of this work against the meticulous translation of Eriugena by I. P. Sheldon-Williams.[72] Unlike Sheldon-Williams, however, I do not try to replicate the tortuous grammar and syntax of the Latin text. Rather, I emulate Honorius's pedagogical instincts and aim to make my English version as accessible as so difficult a work can possibly be. To that end, I break up its long periodic sentences, frequently replace the passive voice with the active, and supply nouns as needed to clarify ambiguous pronoun references. I have also divided the longer chapters into paragraphs for the reader's convenience. Biblical citations are translated directly from the Latin. Honorius's text usually quotes the Vulgate, but not always, and the exegetical meanings he assigns to particular verses often range far from any English Bible. The numbering of psalm verses follows the Vulgate. All footnotes identifying Eriugena's (and indirectly Honorius's) sources are adapted from Lucentini's edition, though I have supplied a few additional biblical references. Explanatory notes are my own.

For all patristic sources I cite the relevant section or chapter of the original text. Where possible I also supply references from the Patrologia Graeca (PG) or Patrologia Latina (PL) because those nineteenth-century volumes are now so easy to search electronically. Readers who want to consult more recent editions can locate the passages from the internal references. Finally, although the *Clavis physicae* is divided only into chapters, I have also divided it according to Books I–V of the *Periphyseon*, for the benefit of readers who wish to compare Honorius's compendium with his source.

Finally, I dedicate this volume to the memory of Sr. Nonna Verna Harrison (1953–2022), a great scholar and translator of the Cappadocian Fathers.

72. Eriugena, *Periphyseon* (*The Division of Nature*), trans. I. P. Sheldon-Williams, rev. John J. O'Meara (Bellarmin and Dumbarton Oaks, 1987).

# THE KEY TO NATURAL PHILOSOPHY

# PROLOGUE AND OPENING DIALOGUE

## 1. *Prologue*

In my mind's eye I see that many people—not only the uneducated, but even those who shine with lofty wisdom—stray far from the path of reason in natural philosophy. I myself have examined this field, illumined by divine grace, with sharp-eyed reason, so with God's guidance I am ready to recall everyone who wishes to follow me to the way of truth. In this work, some things will seem incongruous to those who are less skilled in reasoning, yet to those who consider the truth, they will be established with the support of the highest authority and truthful argument. I have composed the book as a dialogue because this method of teaching has seemed to the highest philosophers—Socrates, Plato, and Cicero, as well as our own Augustine and Boethius—to be the most powerful way to introduce new ideas. Because many abstruse points of natural philosophy are disclosed in this little book, let its title be *The Key to Natural Philosophy,* if you like. I offer it to the judgment of the wise, despising the malicious bite of the envious. First of all, then, we must invoke the eternal Wisdom of God, which surpasses all thought,[1] to open our understanding so that we may say what is worthy of it.

## 2. *Here begins* The Key to Natural Philosophy

D[isciple]: A while ago I posed certain questions, but you said you were too busy with other things and had no time to solve them. Now that I see you have abundant leisure, I demand a solution.

1. Phil 4.7.

M[aster]: What you ask is fair. But let us agree, if you like, to commend nothing to writing except what can be proven by sacred authority and clear reasoning.

D: I fully embrace this convention, for this structure of disputation will remain unshaken if it is supported on all sides with the bulwarks of sacred authority and proven argument. First, though, I think you should name those whose authority you judge we should follow, lest the defenses of this elaborate fort be destroyed by the engine of some heresy.

### 3. *Authors in three languages*

M: We should approve the authority of persons whose faith and life are above suspicion, in all three languages used to inscribe the title of the Lord's triumph.[2] In that way no one will be left with any doubt of their authority. From the Hebrew language, then, let the Lord himself, author of both laws, provide authority, along with the prophets and apostles. From the Greek, the supreme theologians Dionysius the Areopagite, Gregory of Nazianzus, Gregory of Nyssa and his brother Basil, John Chrysostom, and the monk Maximus, an outstanding philosopher and bishop, shall lend authority.[3] From the Latin, the supreme Catholic doctors Hilary of Poitiers, Ambrose of Milan, Aurelius Augustine, and Jerome will show their authority.[4]

D: No faithful Christian may resist the authority of any of these, for the Catholic Church everywhere is firmly upheld by their teaching.

2. Lk 23.38. The title "King of the Jews" was inscribed on the Cross in Hebrew, Greek, and Latin.

3. All these authors are cited frequently except for John Chrysostom.

4. Of the Latin fathers, Augustine is cited most often across an astonishing range of his works. Ambrose figures largely in the chapters on paradise, but Hilary and Jerome do not appear—unless we count the Latin Bible (Vulgate) translated by Jerome. Boethius is another important Latin authority. Conspicuously missing from this list is John Scottus Eriugena himself, from whose *Periphyseon* the *Clavis* is adapted.

# BOOK I

## 4. *On the twofold division of nature*

M: THE CARDINAL point of your proposition, if I am not mistaken, was natural philosophy.

D: That's right.

M: Natural philosophy, then—the nature of all things—is divided into things that are and things that are not. This division has four species on account of four differences. The first is that which creates and is not created, namely God. The second is created but also creates, namely the primordial causes. The third is created and does not create, namely the generation of temporal things in space and time. The fourth neither creates nor is created, namely God as the end of all things. The third of these is opposed to the first; the fourth is opposed to the second.

## 5. *On the five modes*

D: I approve these species as they differ among themselves, but I want to know if this division can have further modes.

M: The twofold division of nature has five modes.[1] The first is perceived in Creator and creature; the second in the orders and differences of created natures; the third in the fullness of the visible world and its preceding causes; the fourth in those things that truly exist and those that do not; the fifth in the good and the wicked.

1. These modes represent different ways of dividing or thinking about nature; they are not all mutually compatible.

### 6. *The first mode*

D: I ask you to explain these modes more fully, one at a time.

M: So be it. Every nature, then, that is perceived by either the senses or the intellect is truly and rationally said to exist, such as this visible world perceived by the bodily senses and the angelic nature perceived by the intellect alone. But those things which, because of their exalted nature, escape not only the senses, but intellect and reason as well, rightly seem not to exist. This is rightly understood concerning God alone and all the essences and reasons of all things. For God alone is truly the essence of all things, as Dionysius the Areopagite says.[2] And Gregory of Nazianzus proves that no substance or essence of any creature, whether visible or invisible, can be comprehended by intellect or reason.[3] For just as no intellect can comprehend God in himself, beyond all creation, so too he is known to be incomprehensible in the mysteries of creation. But whatever is perceived by the bodily senses or examined by the intellect in any creature is nothing but an accident pertaining to its incomprehensible essence. For either by quality or quantity, form or matter, or some other accident, we know that it exists, but not what it is. This is the first mode of division of those things that are said to be and not to be.

### 7. *The second mode*

The second mode begins with the intellectual power closest to God and descends to the outermost limit of the visible creation. That is, it extends from the most exalted angel down to the meanest body. By a marvelous mode of understanding, every single order with the one below it, down to the very last, can be said to be and not to be. It is said to be insofar as it is known by those above it or by itself, and not to be insofar as it is not comprehended by those below it. For our intellect fails to grasp what transcends our senses, as if it were thought not to exist.

2. Dionysius, *De caelesti hierarchia* 4.1 (PG 3: 177d).

3. Maximus, *Ambigua* 13 (PG 91: 1225d–1228a). Eriugena knew Gregory of Nazianzus indirectly through the great 7th-century commentary by Maximus the Confessor, *Ambigua* (*On Difficulties in the Church Fathers*).

## 8. *The third mode*

The third mode is that whatever of those [primordial] causes is known through generation in matter and form, in times and places, is by a human convention said to exist. But what is still contained in the womb of nature and does not yet appear in form or matter, in place or time or other accidents, is by the same convention said not to exist. In the first man God made all human beings in his image,[4] but he did not produce them all at once in this visible world. Rather, he brought the nature he had created all at once into visible being in certain times and places in a sequence known to him. Those who have already appeared visibly in the world are said to exist; those who are still hidden, but will be born in the future, are said not to exist. We should hold the same view concerning the seeds of animals, trees, and plants.

## 9. *The fourth mode*

The fourth mode is posited, not improbably, by philosophers who affirm that nothing truly exists except things that are comprehended by the intellect alone. But things that vary according to places and times, such as bodies that can be born and decay, do not truly exist.[5]

## 10. *The fifth mode*

The fifth mode exists in human nature alone. For anyone who by sinning abandons the dignity of the divine image, in which he properly subsists, rightly loses his being and is therefore said not to exist. But one who is restored by Christ's grace to his prior state of being in the image of God is said to exist. This is the meaning of the Apostle's saying: "He calls the things that are not, just as those that are."[6] That is, God calls those who were lost in the first man, and fell into a kind of non-existence, back into being through faith in his Son, just like those who have already been reborn in Christ.

4. Gn 1.27.
5. Plato, *Timaeus* 27d–28a.
6. Rom 4.17.

This can also be understood another way. God calls things that are judged not to exist out of the secret womb of nature to make them appear visibly in form and matter—like a tree, hidden in a seed, that comes forth in a growing form.

### 11. *That God is incomprehensible to the angels*

D: These modes have been carefully distinguished, but something in them troubles me.

M: What is that?

D: If the divine essence, as well as the reasons of things that exist in it essentially, cannot be comprehended by any creature, how can St. Augustine say that the angelic nature (which was formed before all creation in dignity, not in time),[7] contemplated the causes of things that would be created, which exist eternally in God and *are* God, first in God and then in themselves, and finally knew the proper species and differences of the creatures themselves?[8]

M: Do not let this trouble you; perhaps you will see whether it is true without debate. The Apostle attests that God himself is above all that can be said or thought. Thus the causes of all things in him—which are nothing else than himself—are known to no created nature. "For who has known the mind of the Lord?"[9] No one. The Apostle says again, "The peace of Christ surpasses all understanding."[10] Peace and the mind of God are one. If the cause of all things is remote from all creatures, certainly the reasons of all things, which exist eternally and unchangeably in God, are utterly remote from all beings whose reasons they are. Yet Dionysius proves that within the angelic intellects are the *theophanies* of these reasons—that is, divine appearances that can be grasped by an intellectual nature—rather than the reasons themselves, or the principal exemplars.[11] It is by these theophanies, Augustine says, that the angels contemplated the reasons of things first in God, then in themselves,

7. Augustine, *De Genesi ad litteram* 1.17 (CSEL 28.1, 24).
8. Augustine, *De Genesi ad litteram* 4.24 (CSEL 28.1, 123–24).
9. Rom 11.34; 1 Cor 2.16.
10. Phil 4.7.
11. Dionysius, *De caelesti hierarchia* 4.3 (PG 3: 180c).

then in creatures.[12] For it is not only the divine essence that is called "God," but also the mode by which he is revealed to intellectual and rational creatures according to their capacity. This too is often called "God" in holy Scripture, as in the verses "I saw the Lord sitting"[13] and "God spoke with Moses face to face."[14]

D: What then shall we say about the future happiness promised to the saints, which we think is nothing other than the pure, immediate contemplation of the divine essence itself? As the evangelist John says, "we know that we are children of God, and it has not yet appeared what we shall be. But when he appears, we shall be like him, for we shall see him as he is."[15] The Apostle Paul also says, "Now we see through a mirror in a mystery, but then face to face."[16] Again, I believe Augustine says in his book *On the City of God* that the divine essence will be seen: "Through the bodies we will have, we will see whatever we wish to see in every body, wherever we turn our bodily eyes; and we shall contemplate God himself in absolute clarity."[17] If the sublimity of the divine essence to be contemplated surpasses the purest angelic nature, how will human nature be able to contemplate it? For no other happiness is promised to us than equality with the angelic nature.

### 12. *How the angels and saints can see God*

M: According to the supreme theologians Dionysius, Gregory, and Maximus, the divine essence in itself is not comprehensible to any sense, any reason, or any human or angelic intellect. Therefore, no angel or human being will see God in himself, for this is impossible to any creature. Scripture proclaims, "No one has ever seen God,"[18] and Ambrose affirms, "No one ever will or ever could see him."[19] "He alone has immortality and

12. Augustine, *De Genesi ad litteram* 4.24 (CSEL 28.1, 123–24).
13. 1Kgs 22.19; 2 Chr 18.18; Is 6.1.
14. Ex 33.11.
15. 1 Jn 3.2.
16. 1 Cor 13.12.
17. Augustine, *De civitate Dei* 22.29 (CCSL 48, 861).
18. Jn 1.18; 1 Jn 4.12.
19. Ambrose, *Expositio evangelii secundum Lucam* 1.24–27 (CCSL 14, 18–20).

dwells in unapproachable light."[20] But we will contemplate God through certain theophanies that he will create within us. This is the way the angels always see God;[21] the righteous, rapt into ecstasy like Paul, see him this way in this life; and in the future life, all the elect will see him thus. In that life, the one and only form that all things desire—the Word of God[22]—will fashion a divine appearance for everyone according to the loftiness of their holiness and wisdom. This form says of itself in the Gospel, "In my Father's house there are many dwellings."[23] The Father's house is that form which—abiding as one and the same, in itself unchanging—will nevertheless be seen as manifold[24] by those to whom it grants a dwelling. For each will possess in himself as much knowledge of the only-begotten Word of God as grace bestows on him. As many as the number of the elect will be the number of dwellings. As many as there are holy souls, so many will possess divine theophanies.

### 13. *What the substance of the virtues is*

D: This seems plausible. But I would like you to explain briefly what a theophany is, where it is and whence it comes, and whether it is formed outside of us or within us.

M: You ask a deep question, but Maximus the Theologian resolves it. He says that when the Wisdom of God condescends to human nature by grace, and human nature ascends to Wisdom by love, a theophany occurs—that is, an appearance of the Divine.[25] Augustine also speaks to this question when he expounds the Apostle's saying, "He has become for us wisdom and justice."[26] Augustine says that the uncreated, creative Wisdom of

20. 1 Tm 6.16.

21. Mt 18.10.

22. Augustine, *De vera religione* 55.113 (CCSL 32, 259–60); *Sermo* 117 (PL 38: 662–63).

23. Jn 14.2.

24. Wis 7.22, 27.

25. Maximus, *Ambigua* 3 (PG 91: 1084c); 6.3 (PG 91: 1113bc); 27 (PG 91: 1280d); 29 (PG 91: 1288a); 56 (PG 91: 1385bc).

26. 1 Cor 1.30; the passage in Augustine has not been identified.

the Father, in whom and through whom all things were made,[27] unites our intellect to himself, and, by an ineffable condescension of his mercy, causes a kind of composite wisdom to take shape ineffably in our souls. It is formed on the one hand by Wisdom coming down to us and dwelling in us, and on the other by our intelligence being caught up to him through love and conformed to him. We should think the same way about justice and the other virtues, which come about by a marvelous, ineffable conformity between divine Wisdom and our intelligence. To the same degree that the human intellect ascends through charity, as Maximus says, divine Wisdom descends through mercy; and this is the cause and substance of all the virtues.[28] So every theophany—that is, every virtue—that begins to be formed in the righteous in this life and is perfected in the future life, is formed not outside but within them, both by God and by themselves. For as Maximus also says, whatever the intellect can grasp, it becomes.[29] Inasmuch as the mind comprehends a virtue, then, it becomes that virtue.

Consider an analogy. Air illumined by the sun seems to be nothing but light, not because it loses its own nature, but because light has so much power in it that it seems itself to be light. In the same way, human nature united to God is said to be God in every way. This is not because it ceases to be human, but because it gains participation in divinity in such a way that only God seems to exist in it.[30] Further, although the air is dark without light, sunlight as it subsists in its own nature cannot be grasped by any bodily sense. But when sunlight is mixed with air, only then does it become visible. In itself, it cannot be grasped by the senses, but when it is mixed with air, the senses can grasp it. In the same way, understand that the divine essence is incomprehensible in itself, but appears in a marvelous way when it is joined to an intellectual creature, such that this divine essence

27. Jn 1.3; Col 1.16.

28. Maximus, *Ambigua* 6.3 (PG 91: 1113d).

29. Maximus, *Ambigua* 11 (PG 91: 1220ab).

30. Maximus, *Ambigua* 3 (PG 91: 1073d–1076a and 1088d); 6.19 (PG 91: 1137bc); 6.20 (PG 91: 1140c).

can only appear at all in some intellectual creature.[31] For its ineffable majesty transcends every nature that shares in it. So, while nothing but that essence is encountered in every intelligence that partakes of it, as we have said, it can by no means appear in itself.

### 14. *How God will be all in all*

D: This seems to agree with St. Augustine's words quoted above: "Through the bodies we will have, we will see God in every body."[32]

M: Indeed, it does. He will be seen through bodies in bodies, not in himself. In the same way, the divine essence will appear through the intellect in intellects and through the reason in reasons, not in itself. For in the future life, the great majesty of divine virtue will be manifest to all who are found worthy of that vision, so that nothing will shine for them but that—whether in bodies or in intellects. For "God will be all in all"[33] because God alone will appear in all. Hence Job says, "In my flesh I shall see God,"[34] as if to say: just as nothing but death and corruption appears now in this flesh of mine, so in the future life, nothing will appear in it but God alone, who is truly life, immortality, and incorruption.

### 15. *On the glory of the saints*

D: If so great a glory is promised concerning the happiness of the body, what shall we think about the dignity of the mind?

M: Precisely what Gregory the Theologian says: The bodies of the saints will be transformed into reason, reason into intellect, and intellect into God; and by this means their whole nature will be changed into God himself.[35] It is just as when iron melted

31. Maximus, *Ambigua* 6.3 (PG 91: 1113bc).

32. Augustine, *De civitate Dei* 22.29 (CCSL 48, 861). Cf. section 11 above.

33. 1 Cor 15.28.

34. Jb 19.26.

35. Gregory of Nazianzus, *Epitaphios in Caesarion,* cited in Maximus, *Ambigua* 17 (PG 91: 1249d–1252a).

in fire dissolves into liquid. To the senses, nothing of its nature seems to remain, but all is turned into the quality of fire. Reason alone knows that it still keeps its nature, although it is molten.[36] Just as all the air appears to be light and all the melted iron to be fiery, or rather fire itself, as we have said, yet the substance of each remains. In the same way a sound intellect should understand that after this world has ended, every nature, corporeal or incorporeal, will seem to be God alone—yet the integrity of nature will remain. So that God, incomprehensible in himself, may be comprehended by some means in the creation, nature itself will be changed by an ineffable miracle into God.

## 16. *The first division of nature*

D: Everything that you have proven by reason is corroborated by venerable authority. But I think we should return to the proposed division of nature.

M: The first distinction in the division of nature, then, seemed to us to be that which creates and is not created. This species is rightly predicated of God alone, who alone creates all things and is created by none. He is *anarchos,* which means "without beginning"—the principal cause of all things that are. He is the beginning, for all things are from him; he is the middle, for all things subsist through him;[37] he is the end, for all things tend toward him and seek in him rest for their movement and the stability of perfection.

## 17. *Why he is called "God"*

D: I would like to know why, in the books of the saints, the all-creating God is said to be created or to become, when reason teaches that he is created by none.

M: You are rightly troubled. First, then, if it seems right, I think we should consider from the word itself why he is called "God," and in this way perhaps we will more easily find what

36. Maximus, *Ambigua* 3 (PG 91: 1073d–1076a, 1088d); 6.20 (PG 91: 1140c).

37. Col 1.16–17.

we seek. For although the divine nature is designated by many names, such as goodness, being, and truth,[38] holy Scripture most often uses the name "God."

D: This is clear.

M: The word "God" (*theos*) comes from the verb *theōrō*, "I see," or else from *theō*, "I run."[39] For he sees all things that exist in him, while he can see nothing outside himself because nothing exists outside himself. He also runs through all things because he fills all things. For God to run through all things is the same as to see all things. As by his seeing, so by his running, all things come to be. Hence it is written, "His word runs swiftly."[40]

## 18. *On the moving and the standing of God*[41]

D: I do not clearly see where God can move himself, for he is everywhere. Without him and outside of him, nothing exists, for he himself is the place and boundary of all things.

M: God does not move outside of himself, but by himself, in himself, and toward himself. His movement is the desire of his will, by which he wills all things to come into being. By his standing we understand the changeless purpose of his will, by which he decrees that all things should remain in a stable order. Neither standing nor moving is properly spoken of him. But by a divine metaphor they are referred from creation to the Creator, for he himself is the cause of all creatures that are standing and moving. From him they begin to run into being, since he is the beginning of all. By a natural motion they are carried through him and toward him so that they may changelessly and eternally stand in him, for he is the end and the rest of all. Beyond him they desire nothing, for they find in him the beginning and end of their movement.

38. Lk 18.19; Ex 3.14; Jn 14.6.

39. Macrobius, *Saturnalia* 1.23.3; Dionysius, *De divinis nominibus* 12.2 (PG 3: 969c).

40. Ps 147.15.

41. *De motu Dei et statu.*

### 19. *Why God is said to become or to be created*

The will of God is his essence. To God, being is not one thing and willing another, but to will and to be are one and the same. God therefore brings all things into being by willing, and he "becomes" by accomplishing the movement of his will in all things. Further, he creates all things that he brings forth from nothing, that is, from non-being into being, so that they may exist. But he himself is "created" when he exists in all of these, for nothing essentially exists but him. He is the essence of all things. There is no natural good but him; everything that is called "good" is good by participation in the one supreme good. In the same way, everything that is said to exist, exists not in itself, but by participation in that nature which truly exists.

The Word of God is born in a marvelous, ineffable way in those who are refashioned in faith, hope, charity, and the other virtues, as the Apostle says: "He has become for us wisdom, justification, and sanctification from God."[42] Moreover, God, who is invisible in himself, "becomes" in all things in which he appears. Just as our intellect, which in itself is invisible and known only to God and ourselves, becomes accessible to memory when it clothes itself in phantasms (that is, the forms of objects or words, by which it can be known to listeners' senses), in the same way the divine essence, which subsists in itself and transcends every intellect, is rightly said "to become" and "to be created" in the creatures in which it is known to those who rationally seek it.

### 20. *How God may be created*

D: If the divine nature both creates and is created, why is it called only Creatrix[43] and not also created?

M: The divine nature is the creatrix[44] of the universe and is created by nothing except herself. But when she is said to create

42. 1 Cor 1.30.

43. When speaking of the divine *essentia* or *natura,* both feminine nouns, Honorius characterizes God as *creatrix.* In such passages I have used feminine pronouns, though gender is one of the innumerable accidents that do not apply to God.

44. *Conditrix.*

herself, this rightly means that she creates the natures of things. For her creation means her manifestation in anything, or her subsistence[45] in all beings that exist.

### 21. *God is not defined*

D: All of this seems probable. But I would like to hear what theology can teach about the ineffable, incomprehensible Creatrix of all things and her causative nature. What is it, or what is it like, and how can it be defined?

M: In the branch of philosophy that deals especially with the divine nature, those who behold the truth clearly understand from the things she has created that the divine nature alone essentially exists. But what that essence is, no one understands. For it transcends not only the efforts of human reasoning, as we have often said, but even the purest intellects of the celestial beings. Rightly training the gaze of the mind, theologians have discovered only that she exists, from the things that exist; that she is wise, from their divisions into essences, genera, species, differences, and numbers; and that she is alive, from the stable movement and moving stability of all things.

### 22. *Why God may be called a Trinity*

By this reasoning, too, they have most truly discovered that the cause of all things subsists in a threefold way. As we have said, it is understood to be from the essence of things that are;[46] to be wise from the wonderful order of things; and to be life from movement. So the cause and creative nature of all things exists, is wise, and is alive. For this reason, seekers of the truth have handed down that by essence we should understand the Father, by wisdom the Son, and by life the Holy Spirit.

### 23. *Trinity and Unity*

D: I perceive that these things are very true, and I see that what God is or is like cannot be defined. For anything reason

45. *Substitutio.*

46. *Essentia* can be translated as either "essence" or "being."

cannot understand at all, it cannot define at all. Yet I would like to hear why theologians predicate both unity and trinity of the cause of all things.

M: Dionysius the Areopagite solves these mysteries for us.[47] He says that the supreme and causative essence of all things cannot be signified by the meaning of any words, names, or articulate sounds. For neither the Unity nor the Trinity is the sort of entity that any human or angelic intellect can conceive or imagine, not even the purest or most serene. Yet religious men, insofar as they were illuminated by the divine Spirit, have contemplated the one, ineffable cause of all things and the one, simple and undivided, universal Beginning, and called it the Unity. Further, perceiving that Unity not in singularity, but in a marvelous multiplicity, they understood that it has three hypostases:[48] unbegotten, begotten, and proceeding. They named the relation[49] of the unbegotten to the begotten hypostasis "Father"; of the begotten to the unbegotten hypostasis "Son"; and of the proceeding to the unbegotten and begotten hypostases "Holy Spirit." These words discovered by holy theologians have been handed down to provide a rational account of the Christian religion, so that we may believe in our heart and confess with our mouth[50] that the divine goodness subsists in three hypostases (or persons) of a single essence.

D: I would like to know whether these mystical names of the Holy Trinity (Father, Son, and Holy Spirit) are predicated substantially and naturally of God, or relatively.

M: They are names not of substance but of relation.[51] By the name "God" we express the substance of all three;[52] by the three

47. Dionysius, *De divinis nominibus* 1.4–5 (PG 3: 592c–593b); 13.3 (PG 3: 980b–981b).

48. *Substantias.*

49. *Habitum.*

50. Rom 10.10.

51. Augustine, *De Trinitate* 5.5–7 (CCSL 50, 210–15); Maximus, *Ambigua* 22 (PG 91: 1265cd).

52. The word *substantia,* used above to denote the three persons (*hypostases*), is here applied to the single essence (*ousia*). In early Latin theology *substantia* was used indiscriminately to translate both Greek terms, *hypostasis* and *ousia,* leading to confusion and charges of heresy. To avoid misunderstandings, when

names, we distinguish the property of the persons—the relation of the Father to the Son, the Son to the Father, and the Holy Spirit to both. Similarly we understand the same humanity in Abraham, Isaac, and Jacob, but they are all different persons. The relation of father applies only to the son Isaac, and the relation of son applies only to the father Abraham.[53]

### 24. *On the affirmative and the negative*

D: I see now that the name of relation cannot be predicated of substance or essence, whether in divine or human nature. But I want to learn from you, clearly and briefly, whether all the categories of the one essence can be predicated of the three persons.

M: I do not know if anyone can speak clearly and briefly of this matter! For either we must be utterly silent about such a case, which surpasses all thought,[54] or else we must necessarily use many arguments in a disputation that spans the two principal parts of theology: affirmative and negative. One denies that the divine essence or substance is any of the things that exist, that is, anything that can be named or understood. But the other predicates everything that exists concerning that essence and is therefore called affirmative. It does not affirm that the essence is any of the things that exist, but rather, urges that all things that derive from it should be predicated of it.[55] The causal can be reasonably signified by the causative; therefore this type of theology says that God is truth, goodness, being, light, justice, and many other things that, as Dionysius argues, are stated of God not properly but metaphorically.[56]

---

Honorius speaks of three *substantiae*, I translate as either "hypostases" or "persons."

53. Augustine, *De Trinitate* 7.4 (CCSL 50, 255–58), 7.6 (CCSL 50, 263).

54. Phil 4.7.

55. Dionysius, *De caelesti hierarchia* 2.3 (PG 3: 140c–141a); 2.5 (PG 3: 144c–145a); *De mystica theologia* 3 (PG 3: 1032d–1033c).

56. Dionysius, *De divinis nominibus* 1.6 (PG 3: 596a–c). For these divine names see Jn 14.6; Lk 18.19; Ex 3.14; Jn 8.12; and 1 Cor 1.30.

### 25. *That nothing can properly be said of God*

D: But I thought that goodness, truth, justice, wisdom, and other things of that kind signified the very substance or essence of God—not just metaphorically, as transferred from the creature to the Creator.

M: Nothing can properly be said of God if it is open to opposition or contradiction. For example, God is said to be essence or being, but non-being is opposed to being. Therefore, he is not properly essence but superessence; not substance but supersubstance, as we say in the Lord's Prayer: "Give us today our supersubstantial bread" (that is how it reads in Greek).[57] Again, he is called "goodness," but evil is opposed to goodness, so he is not properly goodness but more-than-goodness. We should think the same way about the other names for God.

D: I agree. For if the divine substance could properly be described by any words, it would seem not to be ineffable. But return to what you called the two principal parts of theology.

M: All right. Do you not see that these two—affirmation and negation—are mutually opposed?

D: I see that nothing could be more contrary.

M: Yet when these two contraries are applied to the divine nature, they agree in every way. For example, affirmative theology says, "God is truth." The negative contradicts this: "God is not truth." When we look more carefully at this form of contradiction, we find no debate. For the proposition "God is truth" does not affirm that the divine substance is properly truth, but only that it can be called such metaphorically, by transference from the creature to the Creator. With such names it clothes the divine essence, left naked of all proper signification. The proposition "God is not truth," by clearly acknowledging the divine nature to be incomprehensible and ineffable, does not deny

57. Mt 6.11, Lk 11.3. The Greek adjective *epiousion* occurs nowhere else in the Bible or in ancient literature, making it difficult to interpret. In the Vulgate, Jerome used the coinage *supersubstantialem* in Matthew but translated the same word as *quotidianum* ("daily") in Luke. Most scholars now reject the meaning "daily" because that idea could have been expressed much more simply. In traditional Orthodox and Catholic theology, the "supersubstantial bread" of the prayer is the Eucharist.

that it exists, but asserts that it can neither be, nor properly be, called truth. In short, negative theology strips the Divine of all the significations with which affirmative theology clothes it. The one says, "God is wisdom," clothing him; the other says, "God is not wisdom," stripping him. The one says, "God can be called this," but stops short of saying that he properly *is* this. The other says, "God is not this, although he can be called this."

D: I now see more clearly, if I am not mistaken, that affirmative and negative theology concur about the Divine and in no way disagree. I also perceive how much more fittingly the negative theology speaks of God than the affirmative.[58] For when we say, "God is superessential," that seems to me nothing but a denial of essence. Anyone who says, "he is superessential," plainly denies that he is essential.

M: I highly approve your response. Now you see how the two aforementioned parts of theology, taken together, are fully comprehensive: they attain the form of affirmation in speech, but the virtue of abdication in the intellect. For example, "superessential" is at the same time an affirmation and an abdication.[59] On the surface it does not seem to be negative, but to the intellect it is a powerful negation. For the proposition "God is superessential" states not what he is, but what he is not; it says that he is not essence, but more-than-essence. Yet it does not express what that more-than-essence might be. The proposition says that God is not any of those things that exist, but possesses more being than anything that exists. But it in no way defines what that being is, for it transcends every word and every definition. The ineffable nature cannot be properly signified by any word, name, or perceptible sound; but whatever is said about it is said metaphorically.

## 26. *On the ten categories*

D: Now, if it seems right, we should consider the nature of the categories.

58. Dionysius, *De caelesti hierarchia* 2.3 (PG 3: 140c–141a); 2.5 (PG 3: 144c–145a); *De mystica theologia* 3 (PG 3: 1032d–1033c).

59. *Abdicatio,* literally "unsaying."

M: Aristotle, that keen investigator of nature, included all things after God within ten universal genera, which he called categories or predicaments.[60] There is nothing in the multitude of creatures that cannot be included in some of these genera. But, as Augustine says, when we come to investigate the divine essence, the categories are useless. For created natures they are extremely useful, but with regard to that nature that can be neither spoken nor understood, they completely fail.[61] Yet whatever is predicated of creatures can be applied without absurdity to the cause of them all—not properly, but metaphorically.

D: I perceive clearly that the categories cannot be properly predicated, in any rational way, of the ineffable nature. For if anything were properly predicated of God, it would necessarily follow that God was a genus. But God is neither genus nor species. No category, therefore, can properly signify God.

M: You perceive rightly. Let us run briefly through the ten categories and see whether any of them can be properly predicated of God. They are substance, quantity, quality, relation, position, condition, time, place, action, and passivity. By the following argument, you will see that each of these is alien to the divine essence.

## 27. *That God is not a substance*

Everything that exists is either Creator or creature; but what is a creature is not the Creator. A creature is a substance, and the nine accidents inhere in that substance.[62] God therefore is not a substance, for nothing is accidental to him. Yet he is more-than-substance because he is the Creator of all substances.

60. Aristotle, *Categories* 4.1b.25–27.

61. Augustine, *De Trinitate* 5.1 (CCSL 50, 206–7).

62. *Substantia* here means "subsistent being," but I retain the Aristotelian term. In *De animae exsilio et patria,* Honorius says that "the citadel of the city [of Dialectic, governed by Aristotle] is *substantia;* the towers surrounding it are the nine accidents" (PL 172: 1244b).

## 28. *Nor quantity*

In the same way God is not quantity. Every quantity is extended in three dimensions: length, breadth, and height. These are further extended in six directions, for length entails up and down, breadth right and left, and height forward and backward.[63] But God is not spatial; therefore, he lacks quantity. Again, quantity consists in a number of parts, either naturally joined together (as in a line or time) or naturally distinct from each other (like numbers, whether corporeal or intelligible).[64] But the divine substance is neither composed of continuous parts nor marked by divisions; therefore, it is not quantity. Rather, it is more-than-quantity because it is the beginning of all quantity in virtues and in objects.

## 29. *Nor quality*

In the same way, God is not quality, and nothing is accidental to him. He does not participate in anything—neither goodness nor justice nor wisdom nor truth, nor the other virtues that are said to be qualities. Rather, he is more-than-virtue because he is the source of them all.

## 30. *Nor relation*

Relation is not properly predicated of God. For the predicate "toward something," such as a father toward a son or a son toward a father, does not indicate the same relationship in those exalted hypostases of the divine essence as in the things created by God. For just as he surpasses every essence, wisdom, and virtue, he ineffably transcends every relationship. We cannot imagine the same kind of relationship between the Father and his Word as between Abraham and Isaac.

63. *Longitudo* and *altitudo* appear to have been switched. Cf. Plato, *Timaeus* 43b; Maximus, *Ambigua* 13 (PG 91: 1232a).

64. Aristotle, *Categories* 6.4b.20–5a.14; Boethius, *In Categorias Aristotelis* 2 (PL 64: 201b–206a); *De institutione musica* 1.6, 2.3; pseudo-Augustine, *Categoriae decem* 74–79.

### 31. *Nor position*

Position cannot be predicated of God except metaphorically. For if God truly and properly lies, sits, or stands, as pertains to this category, then he does not lack position. If he does not lack position, he is local. But God is not local, so he is contained by no position. Yet he is the cause of standing and lying because all things stand firm in him, that is, they subsist unchangeably according to their reasons. They also lie, which means that they rest in him.

### 32. *Nor condition*[65]

Condition is not properly predicated of God, for if it were proper, he would not by any means be his own, but another's. Indeed, every condition is understood to exist in some subject to which it is accidental. But it would be impious to believe this concerning God, to whom nothing is accidental. We understand that he is accidental to nothing in any way, and nothing in him is accidental. Yet it can be predicated of him [metaphorically] because he is the cause of every condition.

### 33. *Nor place*

In the same way, God is neither place nor time. Yet he is metaphorically called the place and time of all things, for he is the cause of all places and times. Everything in the world necessarily moves in time and is bounded by place, while place itself is bounded and time moves. But God is neither moved nor bounded. Therefore, he is not place but more-than-place, because he gives place to all things within himself while being set in place by nothing.

### 34. *Nor time*

God moves all times and is moved by none. All things emanate from him and return to him, for he is the cause of all; therefore, he is not time.

65. *Habitus.*

### 35. *Nor action*[66]

Action is not properly predicated of God, for action is movement. But God lacks movement, so he also lacks action. He is moved toward nothing because he contains all things within himself and encompasses all.

D: Then how is he said to be the maker of all?

M: For God, it is not one thing to make and another to be. Therefore, he did not exist before he made all things. If he had, making would be accidental to him, but he is without accidents; therefore, he did not exist before he made all things. When we hear that God made all things, we should understand that he exists in all; he subsists as the essence of all things. For God alone truly exists by himself. Whatever is truly understood in him receives being by participation in him—the only one who truly exists by himself.

### 36. *Nor passivity*[67]

In the same way, passivity is not fitting to God, for "passivity is movement proceeding from one entity to another."[68] But no one's movement touches God because all things are moved from him, through him, in him, and toward him. Therefore, neither action nor passivity is properly predicated of God.

### 37. *Motion and stability*

D: It seems clear that nothing is said of God properly, but all is metaphorical.

M: Four of these ten genera [categories] are stable, that is, substance,[69] quantity, position, and place. But six are in motion: quality, relation, condition, time, action, and passivity.

D: Where is this discussion heading?

66. *Facere.* The verb means both "to act" and "to make."

67. *Pati.* The verb means both "to suffer" and "to be passive."

68. Maximus, *Ambigua* 3 (PG 91: 1072b).

69. *Usia.* The Greek philosophical term *ousia* ("being"), widely used in Trinitarian theology, could be translated as either *essentia* or *substantia.* Honorius uses all three terms interchangeably in this section.

M: To teach you that the ten aforesaid categories can be included within two more general ones, motion and stability. These in turn are gathered under the most general of all, which is called the universe.

## 38. *"Subject" and "of a subject"*

D: This is very pleasing on account of those who think that in the nature of things, there is no genus more general than the ten categories. But I would like to know whether these three—quantity, position, and place—are accidents in a substance or substantial in themselves.

M: I see this as a worthy question. According to the opinion of dialecticians, everything that exists is "either a subject, of a subject, in a subject, or both in and of a subject."[70] Yet true reason replies that "a subject" and "of a subject" mean the same thing and there is no difference between them. For Cicero (a subject) and "a man" (of a subject) are one in nature, differing only in number and species—although species is nothing but the unity of numbers, and number is nothing but the plurality of species. Thus it does not mean one thing to be "in a subject" and another to be "in a subject and of a subject." For a discipline is one and the same, both in itself and in its species and numbers. Nor is a discipline predicated as proper to any one individual, but it is one and the same in the whole and in its parts. By this argument, it has been shown that to be "in a subject" and "of a subject" are one thing.[71]

As Gregory of Nazianzus says, substance (*usia*) is altogether incomprehensible in all things that exist by it, not only to the senses but also to the intellect. Therefore, it is understood to exist only by its circumstances, so to speak. I mean place, quantity, position, and time.[72] Substance is known to be circumscribed within these categories as within certain set limits. Thus accidents do not subsist in it, for they are extrinsic; but neither can

70. Martianus Capella, *De nuptiis Philologiae et Mercurii* 4.361.

71. Aristotle, *Categories* 5, 2a, 11–19; Martianus Capella, *De nuptiis* 4.361–62; Boethius, *Commentarii in librum Aristotelis Peri hermeneias* 1.3; pseudo-Augustine, *Categoriae decem* 31–41.

72. Maximus, *Ambigua* 13 (PG 91: 1225d–1228a).

it exist without them, for it is their center around which times revolve and places, quantities, and positions are arranged on every side. In it, too, are quality, relation, condition, action, and passivity, which are also understood in the other categories.

## 39. *On being (usia)*

D: I see that almost all the categories are so mutually intertwined that reason can scarcely distinguish them. So I beg you to explain by what property individuals can be discerned.

M: Being, or substance, is universally and properly contained in all things. It is in the most general genera; the more general genera; the genera themselves and their species; and again in the most specific species, which are called atoms—that means "indivisible." Universal being descends from the most general categories to the most specific individuals, and ascends from these back up to the most general. It subsists in all of these as in its natural parts.[73]

Quantity pertains to number, weight, and measure. Quality is contemplated in figures, colors, disciplines, virtues, and in all incorporeal things. Relation to some other is understood in things that reciprocally look to one another. Position can be demonstrated either generally in the position of the whole world or specifically in its parts. Condition is perceived in the fixed possession of virtues or vices, but not properly in bodily things, which can be taken away. Place is constituted in the boundaries of things that can be delimited by space.[74]

## 40. *What place is*

Place is nothing but the space within which anything is enclosed by fixed boundaries. There are many kinds of places, for there are as many places as there are things that can be circumscribed, both corporeal and incorporeal. For example, a body is a composite of the four elements assembled in a certain shape. All bodies, which consist of matter and form, are included in

73. Maximus, *Ambigua* 6.37 (PG 91: 1177bc).
74. Boethius, *In Ciceronis Topica* 1 (PL 64: 1051c–1054b).

this general definition. Again, a spirit is an incorporeal nature without form or matter. Every spirit in itself is formless,[75] though a rational spirit is formed in the Word of God, an irrational one in the phantasms of things. Hence we can agree that on the one hand, angels and souls are local because they are enclosed within their own boundaries. On the other hand, they are not local because they are not circumscribed by the boundaries of any corporeal place.

There are also many places to be found in the liberal disciplines. In dialectic a "place" is identified by genus, species, name, and so forth. So too in the other arts, there are places encompassed by their own boundaries.

D: I am compelled by these arguments to assert that place exists only in the mind. For if every boundary exists in a discipline and every discipline is in the mind, then every place, because it is a boundary, necessarily exists only in the mind.

M: You perceive rightly.

D: What then should we say of people who maintain that places are the dwellings of human beings and other animals? They judge that air and earth are the places of all that dwell in them, and in the same way they think water is the place of fish, ether of the planets, and the heavenly sphere of the stars.

M: True reason laughs at those who say such things. For if a body is one thing and place another, it follows that place is not a body. But earth, air, water, and heaven are bodies; therefore, they are not places. This whole world that appears to our senses revolves with ceaseless motion around its axis. I mean the earth—the center around which the other three elements (water, air, and fire) revolve with ceaseless rotation. So as they move with invisible motion, never resting, these universal bodies (I mean the four elements) combine with each other to fashion the particular bodies of individual things. When these are dissolved, they return again from the particular to the universal. As the center of all individual things, their proper and natural substance remains forever immutable; it can neither be moved nor increased nor diminished. Only accidents are in motion, not substances. Nor does their very participation in being suffer

75. Augustine, *De Genesi ad litteram* 1.5 (CSEL 28.1, 8); 1.9 (CSEL 28.1, 13).

changes. Indeed, every nature is immutable, whether substances or accidents. Only their participation is in motion.

### 41. *On the elements*

According to Plato, part of the visible universe stands in eternal stability—the earth. Part moves with eternal swiftness—the ethereal spaces. Part neither stands still nor swiftly moves—the water. And part moves swiftly but not extremely so—the air.[76] But according to Gregory of Nyssa, the earth remains forever immobile because it is heavy, and heavy objects are not easily moved. Set in the middle of the cosmos, it marks its inmost boundary and occupies its midpoint. The ethereal spaces forever revolve around the midpoint with ineffable swiftness because of their light nature, which cannot stand still, marking the outermost boundary of the visible world. The two middle elements, water and air, are balanced proportionally between heaviness and lightness. Constantly moving, they come closer to the boundary nearer to them than the one farther removed. Water moves more slowly than air because it clings to the heavy weight of the earth; air is stirred more quickly than water because it is joined to the lightness of the ether. Although the ethereal spaces are in motion, yet the stars are stable. In the same way, the earth is stable, yet all things that arise from it are in motion: being born, growing, and diminishing again until they reach dissolution.[77]

### 42. *That quantity is one thing and locality another*

The confusion of these two things is the chief if not the only cause of error for many—for practically all who think that this visible world and its universal and specific parts are places. If they keenly distinguished the genera of all things with right reason, they would conclude that body and place are by no means of the same genus. No one who rightly considers their natures will mix places with bodies in one genus. For quantity contains bodies, while place contains boundaries; and in themselves,

76. Plato, *Timaeus* 55d–56a.

77. Gregory of Nyssa, *De hominis opificio* 1 (PG 44: 128c–132a).

quantity is one category and place another. Further, bodies and boundaries differ greatly between themselves. Therefore, place is not body because locality is not quantity. For quantity is the fixed dimension of bodies and a natural extension of space (length, breadth, and height). But place is the enclosure of things within fixed boundaries. This world with its parts, therefore, is not a place but is contained in place, that is, within the fixed ambit of its boundaries.

## 43. *The ten categories are incorporeal*

D: I do not see why this world is not a place, considering that many things are placed in it.

M: Perhaps you will see. Considered in themselves, the ten categories are not accessible to the bodily senses. For substance is incorporeal, and everything that adheres to it or subsists in it (and cannot exist without it) is also incorporeal. So all the categories, understood in themselves, are incorporeal. Yet some of them, by a marvelous union among themselves, as Gregory says, fashion visible matter.[78] Others, however, appear in nothing and are always incorporeal. Substance, relation, place, time, action, and passivity are never touched by any bodily sense. But quantity, quality, position, and condition, when they come together and unite with matter, can be perceived by the bodily senses.

Note that place is listed among the incorporeal categories. (By "bodies" I refer to those formed by the union of the four elements of the world. For even though the four elements are bodies distinct in themselves, they transcend all mortal sense by their ineffable, natural subtlety and purity.) Therefore, place is one thing, and body another.

## 44. *What matter is*

D: I clearly see this. But what you have said troubles me, namely that visible matter united to a form is nothing but an assemblage of accidents.

M: Do not let this trouble you. For as the great Gregory says,

78. Gregory of Nyssa, *De hominis opificio* 24 (PG 44: 212d–213b).

matter is nothing but a composite of accidents proceeding toward a visible material.[79] For if an immutable substance were inherent in a corporeal material, it could by no means be utterly dissolved. But because it is in fact dissolved, nothing indissoluble enters into it. For genera, species, and individuals exist and remain forever because there exists in them something indivisible that can be neither dissolved nor destroyed. Further, the accidents themselves remain immutably in their nature because something indivisible inheres in all of them, in which they all naturally subsist as one.

### 45. *That bodies cannot be places*

D: I think that nothing is truer. But what shall we say about places?

M: Only bodies exist within bodies, just as we see that our own bodies are formed of this earth and surrounded by this air. In the same way, fish in the waves, planets in the ether, and stars in the firmament are bodies within bodies: the lesser in the greater, the denser in the more subtle. Light bodies are found within lighter ones, pure bodies within purer ones. True reason teaches that all these sensible things, like intelligible ones, are contained within their own places, that is, their natural boundaries.

D: I am amazed at our human custom of speaking about larger bodies as if they were places that contain smaller bodies within themselves. Where does that come from?

M: By metonymy, or *transnominatio,* we are accustomed to name things that are contained after their containers, due to the poverty of human speech. As we have seen, whatever is knowable by the bodily senses, reason, or intellect can be predicated of God, even though he is none of those things. In the same way, everything that exists in some place can be called a place, even though none of them are properly places. Thus by this figure, illuminated air is called light, the eye is called vision, and a family is called a house, as it is written, "He and his whole house believed."[80]

79. Ibid.
80. Jn 4.53.

### 46. *That place existed before all things*

D: Can you expound the nature of place itself more thoroughly?

M: As Gregory the Theologian proves, everything whatsoever—except God—is understood to be in a place, which must always be understood along with time. For place cannot be understood without time, just as time cannot be defined without a simultaneous understanding of place. These two categories are forever inseparable, and without them no created being can exist or be known. The substance of all that exists is spatial and temporal; it can by no means be known except in place and time, and under the categories of place and time. Even the universe is enclosed in a place, for place itself is the space beyond the universe and is the all-encompassing boundary in which all things are comprehended. The universe is also shown to exist in time, for everything that exists—except God—began to be; and from the moment it began, it existed in time. God himself does not possess being; rather, being is from him. He is above being itself, for he transcends all that is said and understood. Everything that occupies a position is in a place, and everything that has a beginning is in time.[81]

Place and time, therefore, as Augustine testifies, are prior to all the things that are in them.[82] The measure of all things naturally precedes their creation, for the measure of anything is called (and is) a place. In the same way, everything that began to exist began at some time. So time is prior, just as a cause precedes its effect, fire precedes a conflagration, and a voice precedes a word. Only God is infinite. All other things are not without place and time.

### 47. *That eternal life is beyond place and time*

You should know, however, that in the beatitude promised to the saints at the end of this world, all who attain the glory of *theosis,* or deification, will rise above places and times. For those

81. Maximus, *Ambigua* 6.38 (PG 91: 1180b–1181a).
82. Augustine, *De musica* 6.17.58 (PL 32: 1192).

who are constrained by place and time are finite, but eternal beatitude is infinite. Therefore, those who participate in eternal, infinite beatitude will be circumscribed by neither place nor time. All who return to the eternal reasons—which have no beginning in time and no end in dissolution and are circumscribed by no location in space—will themselves have no local or temporal boundaries. These reasons alone and nothing else will exist in the blessed. Indeed, they will become infinite and cleave for infinity to the cause of all things, which, being infinite, is circumscribed by nothing. God alone will appear in them when they transcend the bounds of their nature. It is not that nature will perish in them, but he who alone truly is, will alone appear in them. This is what it means to transcend nature: nature will disappear, just as air filled with light disappears because light alone reigns in it.[83]

Place, then, is nothing but the natural boundary and measurement of everything, just as time is nothing but the movement of things from non-being into being and the fixed dimension of mutable things—until the coming of that stable end in which all things will stand immutably.

## 48. *There are two kinds of things*

D: I think that place, boundary, limit, definition, and circumscription all mean the same thing. This is the space that encloses a finite nature: the whole is contained within it and does not extend beyond it. But I do not really see why the definition of any substance is said to be outside of it, not within itself. In other words, it can be called neither the whole nor a part.

M: Pay attention, and you will see more clearly. There are two kinds of things: visible (whatever is perceived by our bodily senses) and invisible (whatever is understood by the intellect). Place, boundary, definition, and circumscription, being incorporeal, pertain to invisible things. Point, line, surface, and solid, considered in themselves, are also incorporeal. Substance itself is incorporeal; form, which contains all the matter of bodies, is

83. Maximus, *Ambigua* 3 (PG 91: 1073d–1076a and 1088d); 6.19 (PG 91: 1137bc); 6.20 (PG 91: 1140c).

incorporeal; and even matter itself is composed of incorporeal qualities.[84]

D: I think that definitions—that is, the places of things that are circumscribed—belong to the genus of invisible things.

M: You judge rightly. But the genus of invisible things is divided into many species. For example, there is that which understands itself and is not understood, namely God; that which both understands itself and is understood, such as angels and souls; and that which is understood, but does not understand itself, such as the spirits of all [non-human] animals and the life of trees and plants. To which species do you think definition belongs?

D: To a reasoning, intelligent nature, which both understands itself and is understood. For a nature that does not understand that it exists cannot define what is equal or inferior to itself.

M: You are paying close attention.

### 49. *Definition in angels and humans*

D: So skill in definition belongs only to an angel or a [human] mind. But I would like to know whether an angel or a man can define himself. Or can a man define an angel, or an angel a man?

M: They cannot define either themselves or each other. For if a man could define himself or an angel, he would be greater than himself or the angel; that which defines is greater than that which is defined. They can be defined, therefore, only by him who created them in his own image.[85]

D: It seems to me that a rational mind can define only natures inferior to itself, whether visible or invisible.

M: Anyone who says this does not stray from the truth. So wherever there are definitions of any creatures, their places are also circumscribed. For place is definition, definition place.

D: So it is agreed.

M: But the definitions of bodies and things exist only in the

84. Gregory of Nyssa, *De hominis opificio* 24 (PG 44: 212d–213b).

85. Grammatically, the sentence implies that angels are also created in the divine image, though the idea is not scriptural.

rational soul. In it, therefore, are the places of all things that are contained in space. The soul is incorporeal, and whatever is understood by it is also incorporeal. But since place is understood within the soul, it too is incorporeal.

D: I see that this conclusion is correct. But I wish to know whether the angelic nature contains the definitions of things inferior to itself.

M: It does. According to Augustine, angels are believed to govern things below themselves and to gaze constantly at those above themselves, that is, the eternal causes of things.[86] Even the human mind, if it lives purely, can comprehend the created causes of natures below itself. But the angelic mind gazes on the eternal reasons of all things. Moved by charity, it constantly attracts human nature toward this contemplation.

D: I see that place is nothing but the action of an intelligent mind, by which it comprehends both sensible and intelligible things. But the intellect which understands itself, because it defines itself, seems to be its own place.

M: God alone is the intellect of all things, and every intellect is circumscribed by him. But no intellect after God understands itself, so none will be its own place. Rather, it will be situated within the one superior to it.

## 50. *Souls are one thing and the arts another*

D: Now I would like to know whether the nature of the defining mind is the same as the place or definition of whatever is located or defined.

M: Souls are one thing and the arts another. This is clear because many arts can exist in a single soul, or a single art in many souls, yet each person has only one soul. The soul is the subject of the arts, as it were, but the arts seem to be inseparable and natural accidents of the soul. The discipline of defining pertains to the arts and is ascribed to dialectic, for the property of that art is to divide, unite, and distinguish the natures of all things that can be understood, and to distribute their proper places to each.

86. Augustine, *De Genesi ad litteram* 4.24 (CSEL 28.1, 123–24).

As Dionysius testifies, three things are considered inseparable in every rational and intellectual nature: being, virtue, and operation.[87] These three are as one and can be neither increased nor diminished, for they are immortal and immutable.[88] The soul has being because it exists; virtue because it can understand that it exists; operation because it *does* understand that it exists. The liberal arts are ascribed to the operation of the soul. Indeed, philosophers have truly discovered that the arts are eternal and always cling immutably to the soul—not as if they were its accidents, but as its natural virtues and actions that by no means depart from it, nor can they ever depart. They do not come from elsewhere but are naturally inherent in it. So it is uncertain as to whether the arts bestow eternity on the soul because they are themselves eternal, or eternity is conferred on the arts by their subject, namely the soul. For the soul's being, virtue, and action are eternal.

## 51. *That being is incomprehensible*

D: How can being be defined in its genera, species, or indivisible parts (atoms), when we concluded above that it is incomprehensible to both the bodily senses and the intellect?

M: No one can define being in itself and say what it is. Every created being can be defined only by place and time, without which it cannot exist. By this means we can determine that it exists, but by no means define what it is. For it is spatial because it is not infinite, and temporal because it began to be what it had not been before. Further, the cause of all things, which is God, is known to exist only from the things he created. But we cannot understand what he is by any argument from creatures. Therefore, this definition alone may be predicated of God: that he is more-than-being.[89]

D: No one will oppose this argument.

87. This triad—*essentia, virtus, operatio*—is central to the work's ontology. *Virtus* and *operatio* are distinguished as potential and actual; see chap. 315 below.

88. Dionysius, *De caelesti hierarchia* 11.2 (PG 3: 284d); *De divinis nominibus* 4.23 (PG 3: 724c–725a).

89. Maximus, *Ambigua* 6.38 (PG 91: 1180b–1181a); 13 (PG 91: 1225d–1228a).

## 52. *That the air is not a place*

M: Now then, some people hold the opinion that the parts of this visible world are the natural places of the other bodies that exist within them. You can see more clearly than the sun that such people should be laughed at, or rather pitied. By this argument they should be recalled to true discernment, if they are willing, or if not, utterly forsaken if they prefer to follow their habitual view, which is most inimical to the truth.

It is not a question of the soul, for it is extremely impudent to imagine that the soul is contained in the bodily spaces of this world. But if the air is the place of the body, it follows that one-fourth of the body would be its own place. For everyone knows that all visible bodies are composed of four parts: fire, air, earth, and water. But nothing is more irrational than to think that a whole body can be located in a part of itself. The whole in fact encompasses all its parts; no part is rightly judged to encompass the whole. Again, if a body is said to exist in the air as its place, it follows that it can have no fixed place at all, for the air is constantly moving around the earth. For this reason, a body located in it would necessarily occupy innumerable places in a single moment—a view that reason can by no means grant. For place is stable and not altered by motion.

Here is an analogy. A person standing in a river cannot hold back part of it to say that he owns a certain place in the river, when it is agreed that the river flows without ceasing. In the same way, no one should say that the place of his body is the air, which moves without ceasing and is never stable for a moment.

## 53. *That the earth is not a place*

But if anyone should object that the earth is rightly called the place of bodies because it is always stable, let them know that earth is the matter of bodies, not their place. For what rational person would dare to say that the matter of bodies is also their place—especially since matter, considered in itself, is neither in motion nor stable? It is not in motion because it has not yet begun to be contained by a fixed form, for matter is moved by form. It is not stable because it does not yet possess the end of its perfection, for stability is the end of motion. How then can the matter of a body be the place of the same body that is fashioned from it, when matter in itself can be circumscribed by no fixed place, measure, or form, nor can it be defined by any argument except negation? Matter itself is none of the things that exist, because all created things are believed to be fashioned from it.

Again, if the parts of this visible world are the places of our own or others' bodies, our places cannot always exist. For when the parts of a dead animal return separately to their natural elements, the animal's place will be neither air nor water, earth nor fire. Rather, its individual parts will mingle with the individual elements in such a way that they become one with them, rather than being "in" them the way one body can be in another. What returns to the air will *be* air—not merely as if it were in some airy place, nor as a confusion of bodies. But by a marvelous natural process, everyone will have his own part in the individual elements: the whole suffused through the whole, not as a part within a part. So at the time of the resurrection, no one will receive anything that is not his own. It is like the way light from many lanterns comes together, with neither mingling of the lanterns nor separation of the light. Even though there appears to be only one light, yet every lantern possesses its own light, unmixed with the light of another. But all the lights marvelously become a whole, producing a single light. And if one lantern is removed, it takes nothing with it except its own light.[90]

Air, then, is one thing, and its place another. Here is a different argument. If a body's place is everything that surrounds it, then color will be the body's place, for every visible body is surrounded by colored light. Who is oppressed by such stupidity as to say that the quality of a body is its place? But the color of a body is an incorporeal quality. Thus color is neither a place nor an element.

D: You have said enough to persuade the wise that a body is not a place, although this may seem ridiculous to fools.

M: Nothing is more laborious than to fight against folly, for it will never admit defeat by any authority or be persuaded by any argument.

90. Dionysius, *De divinis nominibus* 2.4 (PG 3: 641a–c).

## 54. *That body is one thing and substance another*

D: Leaving these questions aside, tell me whether a body is one thing and its being another, and whether its being or substance is corporeal, visible, and palpable.[91] For almost everyone is troubled by such an error, being unaware of the natural differences among things.

M: A body is a compound of form and matter, and every compound will be dissolved. But substance is simple; it is not composed of matter and form, so it is indissoluble. No substance, therefore, is a mortal body. Yet all being is understood to be composed of essence and essential difference. Not even incorporeal essence can lack such composition. Even the divine being, which is not only simple but more-than-simple, admits essential differences, such as unbegotten, begotten, and proceeding. Yet this composite, which is recognized not in any act but by reason alone, should be reckoned simplicity.

Again, every mortal body is corruptible. But being or essence, as Dionysius testifies, is so incorruptible that not even the demons can corrupt it in any way.[92] Essence, therefore, is not a body. Again, all human beings possess one and the same essence, for all participate in one essence. Because this is common to all, it belongs properly to none. But the body is not common to all humans because everyone has his own. Essence, therefore, is not a body. The same argument holds true of other animals.

Again, every body is measured by length, height, and breadth. But substance has no measurements. So no body that is extended in space is a substance, for substance is incorporeal. Among the categories, substance is one and quantity another. Bodies pertain to quantity; so quantity, like body, is not a substance. Further, substance is divided into genera and species, just as a whole body can be separated into parts. A body is not whole in its parts, but substance is whole in each of its individual forms and species. It is no greater in all of them together, nor any less

91. This chapter uses the terms *substantia, essentia,* and *usia* synonymously. Their equivalents in the translation—substance, essence, being—all mean the same thing.

92. Dionysius, *De divinis nominibus* 4.23 (PG 3: 724c–725a).

in individuals. For the being of all humans, all animals, and all things is no less in individual species than in all genera taken together.

Further, the essential reason of all numbers is unshaken in unity; it can neither be increased nor diminished. But bodily numbers can be increased and diminished to infinity. So being, although it may be divided by reason alone into genera, species, and numbers, remains indivisible by its natural virtue and is not separated by any visible act. The body, however, is separated into different parts.

A fantastic or imaginary body is not like a real one. A fantastic body lacks substance, but a real one needs substance in order to exist. Substance, however, does not need a body in order to exist, for it subsists in itself. A body, therefore, is not a quantity of substance, just as the visible color we see around a body is not a quality of substance. But the "how" of quality (*quale*), [such as color], subsists within the "how much" of quantity (*quantum*), [namely measurements].

## 55. *What form is*

D: What we have said of these things is enough for me. Now I want you to treat matter and form. Is the form that belongs to a genus the same as the form that is united with matter to produce a body?

M: Some forms are understood to exist in a substance, others in a quality. Those that exist in a substance are the substantial species of a genus, for genus is predicated of them because it subsists in them. The genus is whole in each of its forms, just as the individual forms are one in their genus. And all these things, both genera and forms, flow from a single source of being and return to it in their natural course.

The forms attributed to quality are properly called "forms" in natural bodies and "figures" in geometrical ones. For every geometrical body is contained in its spatial dimensions and its figure alone, not in any substance. Every imagined body possesses three dimensions (length, breadth, and height), but not all geometrical bodies are circumscribed by the same figure, for triangles, quadrangles, pentagons, and circles are all different. As the number of lines increases, beginning with three, the manifold arrangement of figures and surfaces also changes. The number of dimensions and lines in a geometrical figure is reckoned as quantity, but the arrangement and position of their sides and angles, together with the relationship of their surfaces, are ascribed to quality. This is what we properly call "form" or "figure."

In natural bodies, the distinction of limbs is ascribed to quantity, but their arrangement and position to quality. Because substance is the subject of quantity and "quantum," but quantity and quantum are accidents in a substance, it is crystal clear that there are two different kinds of forms. One is the form that is observed in a substance, not as an accident but as its own being. The other is the form that derives from quality joined to quantity and produces a complete body.

D: I now see that three things inhere in all natural bodies: substance, quantity, and quality. But substance is always discerned by the intellect alone. Quantity and quality, which are joined together to compose a sensible body, appear visibly when they become manifest in particular characteristics (*quantum* and *quale*). For it is the form, derived from quality added to quantity assumed from matter, that completes a natural body.

## 56. *Matter is from the elements*

M: That is true—and the matter of bodies derives from a combination and balance of the four elements. When the form derived from any quality is added to this, a complete body is produced.

D: We seem to be asserting quite contrary things. For now we say that matter is born of a union of the four elements, and now that the cause of matter is the joining of quantity and quality to a substance.

M: This is no wonder, for it is a hidden truth that the elements of this world come from nowhere else. They are composed by a combination of the aforesaid accidents of a substance. Indeed, warmth joined to dryness produces fire; warmth joined to moisture, air; moisture joined to cold, water; and cold joined to dryness, earth.[93] And because these qualities cannot appear in themselves, they become visible through quantity. So if the elements are produced by quantity and quality, and bodies by the elements, then bodies also derive from quantity and quality. Substance can by no means appear visibly and palpably in space. But a combination of accidents that inhere in it, or are understood to surround it, can create a sensible object existing in space through generation.

### 57. *All bodies come from quantity and quality*

Indeed, quantity and quality, the "how big" and the "how" (*quantum* and *quale*), are joined together and reveal a complete body. The other accidents seem to be added onto these. For these four things are perceived in all bodies: how big it is, what kind of thing it is, when it was born or produced, and by what measure it is bounded, that is, where it is located.

We must also know these three things: what we are, what is ours, and what is around us. We ourselves are a vital, intelligible substance, which exists above the body and all its senses and visible form. What is ours, but not ourselves, is the body that clings to us. It is composed of *quantum* and *quale* and other accidents, and it is sensible, mutable, dissoluble, and corruptible. In it are the instruments or seats of the senses by which the soul, being incorporeal, visibly performs its actions. Around us are all the sensible things we use, such as the four elements of this world and the bodies composed of them. For our mortal bodies cannot survive without these: our bodies feed on the earth, drink water, breathe air, and are warmed by fire.[94] They grow and are nourished by two elements, earth and water, and live by the other two, air and fire. Two elements, earth and water, pertain to things passing through the body, while the others, air and fire, maintain the workshop of the body. Fire, residing in the heart, warms the whole body and distributes food and drink through

93. Basil, *Hexaemeron* 4.5 (PG 29: 89c); Bede, *De natura rerum* 4 (PL 90: 196a).

94. Gregory of Nyssa, *De hominis opificio* 24 (PG 44: 212d–213b).

its different parts. Air, breathed by the lungs, blows on this fire like wind from a bellows. Earth and water (that is, food from the stomach and drink from the bladder) nourish the fire like tinder lest it be quenched. When the fire is extinguished, at once the whole structure of the body dissolves, collapses, and turns rigid. This is called death.

### 58. *Incorporeal things*

D: How can quantity and quality fashion matter that is far removed from them? And how do things that are incorporeal and invisible in themselves fashion visible bodies by their combination? For Boethius, the supreme philosopher skilled in both languages, asserts that incorporeal things are "qualities, quantities, forms, great and small sizes, equalities, relationships, acts, dispositions, places, and times." These and similar things "are incorporeal by nature, flourishing by reason of an immutable substance. But by participation in a body, they are altered, and by the touch of a variable thing, they pass into changeable inconstancy. Wisdom is comprehension of the truth about things that exist and how they are allotted their immutable substance. But those things that truly and properly exist neither grow by extension nor shrink by retraction, nor are they changed by any variation. But they always preserve themselves by their own power, upheld by the support of their own nature."[95] By this we can plainly understand that quantity and quality are immutable by nature, but matter and body are mutable.

M: Let us inquire into these things by reason and confirm them by authority, for by these two the whole truth is established.[96]

D: Excellent! For these truths are sought by many but discovered by few.

95. Boethius, *De institutione arithmetica* 1.1.

96. Augustine, *Contra Academicos* 3.20.43 (CCSL 29, 60–61); *De ordine* 2.9.26 (CCSL 29, 121).

## 59. *What matter is*

M: Matter is that from which formed bodies come into being, although in itself it is formless, contemplated not by the senses but by reason. For matter without form cannot be perceived by any bodily sense, since it is incorporeal.

D: I know this from the holy fathers, who clearly deduced that only two entities can by no means be defined, namely God and matter.

M: God is infinite and formless, for he is formed by nothing while he is "the form of all things."[97] Matter similarly is formless and infinite. It is said to be formless because nothing is formed by it, but it receives diverse and innumerable forms. Formless matter, according to Augustine, is "the mutability of things that are mutable, and is capable of all forms."[98] According to Dionysius the Areopagite, unformed matter is a certain formlessness that lacks participation in appearance, form, and beauty.[99] It is by participation in all of these—appearance, form, and beauty—that this formlessness or mutability is turned into a specific material.[100] All of these can be contemplated only by the mind's eye.

D: So we agree. For whatever lacks form and appearance, without which there is no beauty, is agreed to be altogether incorporeal.

M: So do you see how something corporeal, I mean matter and the body, is created out of incorporeal things, namely that mutable formlessness that is capable of receiving forms, and form itself?

D: I clearly see that bodies are produced by the union of incorporeal things.

97. Augustine, *De vera religione* 55.113 (CCSL 32, 259–60); *Sermo* 117 (PL 38: 662–63).

98. Augustine, *Confessions* 12.6.

99. Dionysius, *De divinis nominibus* 4.28 (PG 3: 729a).

100. The text distinguishes between formless matter (*materia*) and specific materials (*materies*).

## 60. *What a shadow is*

M: You know this as well: bodies can be resolved into incorporeal things so that they are no longer bodies, but totally dissolved. But incorporeal things, by their natural combination and marvelous harmony, produce bodies without losing their own natural stability and motionless vigor. For example, a shadow is born from light and a body, yet neither light nor the body moves into the shadow. But when the shadow dissipates, it is understood to return to its causes, namely the body and the light. Indeed, true reasoning teaches that body and light are the cause of shadows. They naturally fade when they cannot appear in any place because bright light surrounds a body on all sides. Those who think a shadow perishes when it does not appear to the senses are mistaken.

A shadow is not nothing, but something, as Scripture says: "And God called the darkness night."[101] God does not name anything except what has being from him. We understand that darkness and night are nothing but the shadow of the earth, like a cone created by the surrounding rays of the sun and always opposite the orb of its light. The same reasoning applies to lesser shadows cast by any kind of light and any bodies, whether the shadows are finite or infinite and whatever their forms.

Thus corporeal things can be created from incorporeal causes and resolved back into them. The created causes themselves proceed from one and the same creatrix of all things.

## 61. *What form is*

D: And from what source are they formed?

M: The Word of the Father is "the form of all things."[102] From this every form is created, whether substantial or qualitative; and when joined to matter, it generates a body. All things that are said to be or not to be flow from the same source of all, and from it the matter of all things also derives. "But all matter con-

101. Gn 1.5.

102. Augustine, *De vera religione* 55.113 (CCSL 32, 259–60); *Sermo* 117 (PL 38: 662–63).

sists of certain qualities. If it were stripped of them, it could by no means be grasped in itself."[103]

## 62. *What a body is*

Now if a body were something other than a combination of accidents in a substance, it would subsist in itself and through itself, even if the accidents were taken away. Indeed, every subject that subsists in itself, like a substance, has no need of accidents in order to exist. But a body cannot subsist in itself at all if its accidents are taken away, for it is not supported by any substance of its own. If you were to take quantity away from a body, it would not be a body, for it is contained by the dimensions of its parts and by number. Similarly, if you remove quality from it, it will remain disfigured—nothing, as it were. So whatever cannot subsist in itself without accidents should be understood as nothing but a combination of those accidents. As Boethius proves, nothing is variable and mutable except a material body, which is made of a combination of things that truly exist.[104]

D: I see that things immutable in themselves are perceived one way by the mind in their simplicity. But they are discerned another way by the bodily senses in composite form, when they are united with some kind of matter by a combination of accidents. For this massive earthly globe is composed of four simple elements. The globe is corruptible and dissoluble as long as it exists, but the elements from which it is fashioned remain indissoluble in their simplicity. And this seems to be the case with almost all bodies.

But it remains to speak of action and passivity.

## 63. *Concerning action and passivity*[105]

M: Tell me, is not loving and being loved a question of action and passivity?

D: No one trained in the liberal arts is unaware that these verbs and others like them are active and passive.

103. Gregory of Nyssa, *De hominis opificio* 24 (PG 44: 212d).

104. Boethius, *De institutione arithmetica* 1.1.

105. *De facere et pati,* the last of the ten categories.

M: So if these verbs have active and passive meanings, they cannot be predicated of God properly, but only metaphorically. Properly speaking, God neither acts nor is acted on; therefore, God neither loves nor is loved.

D: I find this conclusion deeply troubling, for in my opinion the authority of all holy Scripture seems to contradict it. Scripture manifestly proclaims that God acts and is acted on, loves and is loved. For instance, in the Gospel he says, "He who loves me will be loved by my Father, and I will love him,"[106] and many similar verses. And St. Augustine says that "the creator Spirit can move itself without time and place, move a created spirit in time without place, and move a body in time and place."[107] So if acting and being acted on cannot properly be predicated of God, it follows that he neither moves nor is moved, for to move is to act, and to be moved is to be acted on. Further, if he neither acts nor is acted on, how can he be said to love all things and be loved by all things that were made by him? For to love is the movement of an agent, and to be loved of a patient; it is the cause and end of movement.

M: Does the divine nature admit any accident?

D: No, for otherwise it would be passible and mutable.

M: Are acting and being acted on accidents?

D: They are.

M: Therefore, the supreme cause and beginning of all things, which is God, does not admit acting and being acted on.

D: I am caught in a trap! For if I say this is false, true reason mocks me, but if I say it is true, it will necessarily follow that God neither acts nor is acted on, and therefore he neither loves nor is loved. And you see how many arrows of holy Scripture oppose this, clamoring on all sides and proclaiming that this is false. Nor, I think, can you fail to see how arduous and difficult it could be to persuade simple souls of such reasoning, especially when those who seem wise are horrified to hear what they hear.

106. Jn 14.21.

107. Augustine, *De Genesi ad litteram* 8.20 (CSEL 28.1, 259).

## 64. *Reason and authority*

M: Fear not! We must follow reason, which investigates the truth and is oppressed by no authority. Nor does it fret about how it should publicly disclose what it has truthfully discovered. In all things we must follow the authority of holy Scripture, in which the truth lies hidden beneath a veil. But we should by no means believe that it employs the proper signification of words when speaking of God. Rather, it speaks simply and metaphorically in a variety of ways, using analogies for the benefit of untrained and childish minds. Hence the Apostle says, "I gave you milk to drink, not solid food."[108] Scripture, then, clothes the King of glory in varied beauty, but reason displays him stripped of all coverings. Yet, as Dionysius the theologian testifies, no one who discusses the ineffable nature is permitted to use words other than the ones she has harmoniously sung about herself in her holy instruments—I mean the theologians.[109]

Reason proves that nothing can properly be said of God, for he is above all that is said and understood. Therefore, whatever Scripture affirms about God, reason denies. True authority does not resist right reason, nor does right reason resist true authority. Indeed, there is no doubt that both flow from a single fountain, divine Wisdom. Scripture, like a mother, nurses her faithful children in the cradle of the Church with simple teaching. Reason, like a teacher, advances those who are trained to contemplate the truth.[110] Authority predicates of God that he is life, virtue, light, splendor, and similar things.[111] Reason teaches that all these things are said of God figuratively, but he is above life, light, and all things. In the ineffable sublimity of his nature, he transcends every essence and substance, every accident and movement, action and passivity, and all that is said and understood. Therefore, God is metaphorically called love, for he is more-than-love and transcends all love. In the same way he is said to love, while he transcends every movement of love be-

108. 1 Cor 3.2.
109. Dionysius, *De divinis nominibus* 1.1–2 (PG 3: 588ac–c).
110. Jn 1.4, 14.6.
111. 1 Cor 1.18, Jn 8.12, Heb 1.3.

cause he desires nothing beyond himself, that he alone may be all in all.[112]

D: You strongly urge me to confess this, but I would like reason to be strengthened by the authority of the fathers.

M: I think you are not unaware that what is prior in nature has greater dignity than what is prior in time.

D: I know this.

M: Reason is prior in nature, but authority is prior in time.[113] Indeed, authority proceeds from true reasoning, but reason does not in any way proceed from authority. For all authority that is not proven by true reasoning seems weak, but true reasoning supported by its own merits does not need to be strengthened by the help of any authority. For true authority is nothing but truth discovered by the power of reason. Therefore, although authority asserts that God made all things, reason proves that he makes nothing. For one who makes anything moves himself to do so because he desires to act. But God is without movement; therefore, he moves himself to no act.

## 65. *What movement is*

D: And what is movement?

M: Natural movement, according to Maximus, is defined in three ways. "Movement is a natural power hastening toward its end; or movement is a passion proceeding from one toward another, whose end is impassibility; or movement is an active operation whose end is perfection in itself." God is the beginning and end of all things, and all things are moved by him, through him, and toward him. He himself is moved toward none of them.[114] Therefore, he admits no movement because he has no place to move, since he himself is the fullness, the place, the perfection, the stability, and the whole of all things. Or rather, he is more than all that is said or understood about him, however it may be said or understood. So either you will grant movement to God, without which he cannot be understood to

112. 1 Cor 15.28.

113. Augustine, *De ordine* 2.9.26 (CCSL 29, 122).

114. Maximus, *Ambigua* 3 (PG 91: 1072b, 1073c).

act, or you will at the same time take both movement and action away from him.

D: I cannot grant movement to God because he has no place to move, since all things exist in him. But I cannot take action away from him because he is the maker of all things.

M: Are movement and action at one in God?

D: I am hemmed in on all sides! For if I affirm that God made this world, reason mocks me, but if I deny it, the whole world will spit at me.

M: What seems right to you? Did God exist before he made all things?

D: It seems to me that he did.

M: Then the act of making was accidental to him. For whatever is not coeternal and coessential with him is either outside of him or accidental to him.

D: I should believe that nothing exists beyond God and outside of him. For in him are all things, and outside of him is nothing, and nothing is accidental to him. Otherwise, he would not be simple, but a composite of substance and accidents. For if anything is understood to be with him that is not himself, or if anything is accidental to him, then he is neither infinite nor simple. But he is the simplicity of all simple things, the circumference of all that exists, the likeness of what is like, the unlikeness of what is unlike, the opposition of opposites, the contradiction of contraries. He gathers and assembles all these things in a beautiful, ineffable harmony, in a single concord. For whatever seems to be opposed, contrary, and mutually discordant in the parts of the universe, when contemplated in the most general harmony of the whole, is apt and concordant.

## 66. *What time is*

M: You understand rightly. God therefore did not exist before he made all things. For if he did, making all things would be accidental to him, and thus we would understand movement and time to exist in him. But time is proper to mutable things, and movement is a fixed, rational dimension. For if he moved himself to make things that he had not already made, some time would precede his action that was not coessential with him.

D: Now I see that for God, his being and his action are one, simple, and undivided.

M: Therefore, since it is the same thing for God to be as to act, that God made all things means nothing but this: God is in all things, that is, he subsists as the being of all things. We should think the same way about God willing, loving, seeing, or doing anything else.

## 67. *What love is*

D: But I would like you to argue more plainly, so that I can clearly see what it means for God to love and be loved.

M: First receive a definition of love. Love is that connection and bond that binds the whole universe in ineffable friendship and unbreakable unity. Or love is the natural movement of all that is in motion, and the end and tranquil stability beyond which no creature's movement can proceed. Dionysius defines love as "a simple power that moves itself toward a unifying balance, from the best of all existing things to the least, then back from the least through all to the best. It cycles constantly from itself, through itself, and toward itself, and always returns in the same way within itself."[115] God is rightly called love,[116] therefore, because he is the cause of all love. He is diffused throughout the universe, gathers all things into one, and cycles back to himself in an ineffable return, bringing the amorous movements of the whole creation to an end in himself. God is said to love all things because he diffuses the gaze of the rational mind through all creatures, moving them to seek and to find him—and as far as possible, to understand him. It is he who fills all things to make them exist, and he gathers the whole universe within himself in a peaceful bond of love. He is said to be loved by everything he has made. This is not because he, the only impassible one, can be affected in any way by creatures. Rather, it is because all things desire him; his beauty draws all creatures to itself.

Just as a magnet attracts iron that is near it yet does not move in order to do so and remains unaffected by the iron, the

115. Dionysius, *De divinis nominibus* 4.17 (PG 3: 713d).

116. 1 Jn 4.16.

universal cause calls everything that draws being from it back to itself by the force of beauty alone, without ever moving. In the same way the light of the world, which itself never moves, draws the gaze of all animals and attracts them to look at it. St. Dionysius in his book *On the Celestial Hierarchy,* as well as St. Basil, affirms that the substance of light, namely fire, is everywhere and fills the whole sensible world.[117] But its natural activity is to break through in the lights of the world [the sun and moon], not only to illuminate, but also to mark times by the movement of heavenly bodies. In the same way the liberal arts, unmoving in themselves, vehemently move all minds to seek them and attract all minds to study them. This is the same way that God, the unmoved mover, moves all things from non-being into being and draws them all to himself. So God is not properly said to act or be acted on. Yet without moving, he is the cause of every movement, whether of acting or of being acted on. He is also the cause and beginning of all accidents and all substances.

D: Sharp-eyed reason proves that this is so, and firm authority supports it.

117. Dionysius, *De caelesti hierarchia* 15.2 (PG 3: 329a); Basil, *Hexaemeron* 2.7 (PG 29: 44c–45b).

# BOOK II

## 68. *On the nature that is created and creates*

M: I THINK we have disputed enough concerning the nature that creates and is not created, so let us now turn our pen to the nature that is created and also creates. For this topic, the discipline that philosophers call "analytic" is necessary. *Analetice,* then, is the return and resolution of individuals into forms, genera, and substances, into the wisdom and prudence from which every division arises and in which it ends. For every division descends from above, as it were, and from the first thing that is defined it descends to infinite numbers, that is, from the most general to the most specific. But every recollection, which is like a return, begins from the most specific and ascends to the most general. Thus all creation proceeds from the supreme God and will return to him. Just as he is the beginning, therefore, he is also the end of all things.[1]

D: The order of disputation requires that after the first form, we should move on to the second.

M: That second form of universal nature, which is created and creates, is understood to be in the primordial causes of things. These primordial causes are also called primordial exemplars, predestinations, definitions, or divine volitions.[2] According to Plato, an idea is also the species or form in which the unchangeable reasons of all things still to be made were fashioned before they came into being.[3] The Father, who is the beginning of all, pre-formed in his Word, the only-begotten Son, the reasons of everything that he willed to make, before they

1. Maximus, *Ambigua* 3 (PG 91: 1073c).

2. Dionysius, *De divinis nominibus* 5.8 (PG 3: 824c); Maximus, *Ambigua* 3 (PG 91: 1085a).

3. Augustine, *De diversis quaestionibus* 46 (PL 40: 29–31).

proceeded into genera, species, numbers, differences, and everything else that can be and is considered (or not considered) in the created world.

### 69. *A fivefold division*

D: First I would like you to tell me the division of things, to make the principal causes shine more clearly.

M: Maximus the philosopher hands down a tradition from the successors of the apostles. Here is their fivefold division of all things that exist: (1) Creator and creation; (2) intelligibles and sensibles;[4] (3) heaven and earth; (4) paradise and the world; (5) male and female. All these divisions will be reintegrated in the human being through Christ. Indeed, man contains all creation within himself; he possesses the sensible insofar as he is body, the intelligible insofar as he is soul. Therefore, human nature is the midpoint joining the two opposite extremes of creation: the highest, or intelligible essence, and the lowest, or bodily substance. No creature from the highest on down is not found in man, which is why he is called the workshop of all things. In that workshop, everything created by God converges and composes a single harmony from diverse natures, as if from high sounds and low. Thus the division of all things, "proceeding through the central link, receives its end in God through the unity of ascent, in which there is no division."[5]

D: Did human nature lose its dignity after the Fall?

M: No. For nothing in the nature of things is lower than the body or higher than the intellect. As Augustine says, no creature is interposed between God and the human mind, by which we understand him.[6] So it is agreed that after the Fall, man did not lose his dignity but still retains it. In fact, the soul's leprosy does not destroy the mind's keenness, in which the Creator's image was formed.[7]

4. Objects understood only by the intellect vis-à-vis those perceived by the senses. A key distinction.

5. Maximus, *Ambigua* 37 (PG 91: 1304d–1305c).

6. Augustine, *De vera religione* 55.113 (CCSL 32, 259).

7. Augustine, *Enarrationes in Psalmos* 42.6 (CCSL 38, 479); 48.2.11 (CCSL 38, 574); 54.3 (CCSL 39, 657).

D: I see in the human being a marvelous composite of all created substances.

### 70. *The human being before sin*

M: The division of substances, which began from God, reached its endpoint in male and female. Conversely, the reunion of the sexes begins from the human being and ascends to God, in whom all things are one. The reunion of natures, when human nature will be restored to its original state, begins from the human side through the grace of the Savior, in whom, as the Apostle says, "there is neither male nor female."[8] Maximus asserts that if the first human being had not sinned, she would not have suffered the partition of her nature into two sexes, but remained immutably in her primordial reasons, in which she was created in God's image.[9] For she would have been merely a human being in the simplicity of her nature, and would have multiplied in the same way as the holy angels multiplied in intellectual numbers. But, overwhelmed by the guilt of her fall, she suffered the division of her nature into male and female. Because she did not wish to preserve the divine method of multiplication, she was reduced by a just judgment to a beastly, corruptible multiplicity derived from male and female, and into many and various qualities, quantities, and differences within a single form.[10]

### 71. *Why human beings are diverse*

Indeed, the differences among human beings, such that everyone looks different from everyone else and people vary in height, come not from nature but from the defects and diversity of places and times, as well as the different kinds of land, water, air, food, and other similar conditions under which people are

8. Gal 3.28.

9. Although *homo* is grammatically masculine, I use feminine pronouns in this paragraph to avoid any implication that the primordial, sexless human being was "really" male.

10. Maximus, *Ambigua* 37 (PG 91: 1305cd), 27 (PG 91: 1276b), 37 (PG 91: 1309a); 38 (PG 91:1320d–1321a and 1345d–1348b).

born and raised. But the diversity of morals and thoughts began with the [sexual] division of nature after sin, for the human being does not truly subsist in the conditions under which he now appears. Rather, his real being is contained in the hidden causes of nature, according to which he was first created and to which he will return. Then he will be neither male nor female, but simply a human being. Humanity is better than gender:[11] male and female are not natural names, but "human" is the special designation of their nature.

## 72. *The glory of man*

Through Christ, man will be recalled to the pristine glory of his nature, which he abandoned by sinning, and will gather the whole sensible creation beneath himself into one so that he seems to be one with it and in it. The human mind, ascending above all creatures, will attain to God himself and contemplate him in all of them. The whole person will become a light spirit, no longer detained on earth by bodily heaviness or prevented from ascending to the heavens. When humanity becomes equal to the angels, then earth will be united to paradise and paradise to heaven. The whole human being will be encompassed by the whole God and will *be* God (except for likeness of essence) to possess the whole of God. This is the end of his movement and the firm stability to which he is carried by love. This is the endless end and limitless limit of reason, intellect, and nature.[12]

## 73. *On the angels*

D: Is there any ignorance in the angels?

M: We read that certain angels are not yet purged of all ignorance.[13] But in the highest, all created substances are united through their knowledge,[14] just as an extremely wise soul has a single, inseparable knowledge of diverse arts. In rational souls,

11. *Melior est homo quam sexus.*

12. Maximus, *Ambigua* 37 (PG 91: 1305d–1308c). A double paradox: *finis ac terminus infinitus et interminatus.*

13. Dionysius, *De caelesti hierarchia* 5 (PG 3: 196bc); 7.3 (PG 3: 209a–c).

14. Maximus, *Ambigua* 37 (PG 91: 1308ab).

too, the union of separate things comes about through knowledge. For the understanding of things is truly the same as the things themselves, as Dionysius says: "The knowledge of things that exist *is* the things that exist."[15]

## 74. *Man*

D: Return to man.

M: Among the primordial causes of the universe, man was made in God's image and composed from the whole creation, which in him is one and inseparable; he is the midpoint and union of all creatures.[16] For there is no creature that cannot be understood in man, as the Evangelist says: "Preach the Gospel to all creation."[17] The Apostle adds, "All creation is groaning."[18] If he had not sinned, there would have been no division of sexes in him, but he would have been simply human. The world would not have been separate from paradise, but in him all earthly nature would have been paradise, that is, a spiritual way of life. Heaven and earth would not have been separate in him, for he would have been all heavenly, and nothing earthly, heavy, or corporeal would have appeared. For he would have existed and multiplied, as the angels did, to the number preordained by the Creator. Sensible nature in him would not have differed from intelligible, for he would have been all intellect, clinging forever immutably to his Creator. By no means would he have departed from his primordial causes, in which he was created, and no creature formed in him would have suffered division.

## 75. *The mystery of Christ's incarnation*

But since the first human being did not remain in such felicity but fell from it through pride, and the unity of human nature was scattered in infinite partitions and variations, the divine mercy created a new man in whom the same nature that had been divided in the old man might be recalled to its former

15. Dionysius, *De ecclesiastica hierarchia* 1.3 (PG 3: 376a).
16. Maximus, *Ambigua* 37 (PG 91: 1305a–c).
17. Mk 16.15.
18. Rom 8.22.

unity. God decreed that he would be born in the world, from the world—that is, as a human being, from humans, for the sake of humans. And because all creation is found in man, not in an angel, he was born not of an angel but of man, from whom he received all creation in order to restore all things that exist in heaven and on earth.[19] Uniting the division of nature (male and female) in himself, he rose from the dead not in a bodily sex, but simply as a human being. In him there is neither male nor female,[20] even though he appeared to his disciples after the resurrection in the same male sex in which he was born of the Virgin and suffered death. This was to confirm their faith in his resurrection, for otherwise they would not have recognized him if they had not seen his familiar form. Indeed, they had not yet fully received the Holy Spirit, who taught them all things.[21]

Soon after the resurrection he united the world to paradise in himself. Returning from the dead into paradise, he conversed with his disciples in this world, showing them plainly that paradise is nothing but the glory of the resurrection, which appeared first in him and will be given to all his faithful. And he taught that our world is no different from paradise according to the reason of nature.[22] For the two are not separated by nature but only by qualities, quantities, and other variations that were added to this habitable earth because of universal sin, in order to punish human nature. Paradise is not distinguished from this habitable world by mass or dimensions, but rather by a different way of life and a difference in beatitude. For if the first man had not sinned, he could have lived happily even in this world. In the principal causes, the world and paradise have one and the same reason.

### 76. *Christ was in the world and in paradise at the same time*

Our Lord very clearly revealed this in himself after the resurrection, for at the same time he was in paradise and lingered

19. Eph 1.10; Maximus, *Ambigua* 37 (PG 91: 1308c–1309a).
20. Gal 3.28.
21. Jn 14.26.
22. Maximus, *Ambigua* 37 (PG 91: 1309b).

with the disciples on this earth. We should not believe that he arrived locally from some other place to appear to his disciples, or departed to some other place when he did not appear. After the resurrection, not only his divinity but even his humanity transcended the nature of times and places. In fact, spiritual bodies are not constrained by place or time, just as they are not affected by qualities, quantities, or the boundaries of any form, for their nature is utterly simple. We can see this especially in the argument from pure fire, which is diffused through all the bodies of the sensible world but is of such subtlety that it is not confined by any place. Yet it is known to manifest its operation in all places. In the same way, Christ appeared to the disciples at one and the same time, in one and the same place, in that form in which he had suffered, in order to nourish their faith until they were illumined by the virtue of true knowledge, which later suffused them. When the momentary apparition ended, Christ at once returned to the intellectual, invisible character of the spiritual body, which transcends all time and place. Or—this seems more credible—he never departed from the glory of the resurrection in place or time, quantity or quality (for no one doubts that spiritual bodies have none of these) when he manifested himself to his disciples after the resurrection. He revealed himself in the same form in which he had appeared and lived in the world for its salvation, for human reasoning cannot prevail where divine power alone flourishes. He who said, "Behold, I am with you always, even until the end of the world,"[23] indicates clearly enough that he is present always and everywhere—not only according to the Word, by which he fills all things and is above them all, but also according to the flesh, which he received and raised from the dead in the unity of his substance, and transformed into God. But he is not present in place or time, nor is he limited in any way.

In a marvelous and ineffable manner, he is with the Father above all celestial beings according to his humanity, which is united to the Father's Word; and as God he rules the world everywhere and appears, invisibly or visibly, to those who love him. Without forsaking heaven, he rules the world and sits at the right hand of the Father (which he himself is), governing all in the

23. Mt 28.20.

heights and ministering salvation to human nature in the depths. Do not imagine that Christ's humanity is in any place, for after the resurrection it was translated into his divinity, just as air becomes light. The divinity of Christ is not in any place, so neither is his humanity. We should understand the same way concerning time, quality, quantity, and limited form. For we piously believe that the whole humanity of Christ—body, soul, and intellect—has none of these, and we understand this most clearly after the victory of the resurrection. After the universal resurrection, he will bring his elect to the same glory to be one in him and with him.

Christ, therefore, was simultaneously in paradise and in the world, showing that the world and paradise have a single natural reason and uniting the world and paradise in himself.[24] For true reason does not contemplate and honor him in the world as if he had bodily mass, extended in space, with multiple, diverse, changeable parts. Rather, he is contemplated in his natural and primordial causes, most beautifully united in himself, into which he will return and eternally remain when the end comes. For the end of this world will consist in nothing but a return to God and the world's primordial causes, in which it naturally subsists.[25] If man had preserved the unity of nature, it would by no means have been divided into different parts. But when he abandoned it through pride, he learned how to return to it through the diverse troubles of the world. God did not thrust sinful man into this world as if to avenge an injury to himself, for he is without anger. Rather, man, who had failed to preserve the dignity of his nature through free will, might be instructed by pains to seek the Creator's grace, through which he will return to his former state. And he will never wish nor be able to fall again.

## 77. *Christ restored all things*

D: I would like you to return to the words of Maximus.

M: Christ, he says, "gave life to the earth through his assumption into heaven. With this earthly body of the same nature as ours," but changed into a spiritual substance, "he returned

24. Maximus, *Ambigua* 37 (PG 91: 1309b).
25. Maximus, *Ambigua* 3 (PG 91: 1073b).

to heaven and revealed all sensible nature to be one. Next he united sensible and intelligible beings, consequently passing through all the heavenly, divine, intellectual orders with soul and body, that is, with our complete nature. Thus he perfectly revealed the inseparable, immovable convergence of all creation in himself according to its most primordial reason."[26] "And he comprehended all creation together with us and for our sake, joining paradise and the world, heaven and earth, sensibles and intelligibles. Having body, soul, senses, and intellect, he recapitulated all things in himself."[27]

### 78. *All nature is in Christ*

D: Through these four components, it seems to me, all nature was assumed by Christ and restored in him.

M: So it is. Christ received the four parts of human nature and united the whole creation in himself; for in the human being, which he took on in its wholeness, the whole creation was fashioned. Receiving a body, he united the whole bodily creation to himself. Assuming senses, he joined all sensible being to himself. By the soul he received, he coupled the whole rational creation and all the life of nourishment and growth to himself.[28] Through the intellect he assumed, all intellectual beings inseparably cleave to him.

### 79. *A question about the resurrection*

D: The division of the human being into male and female troubles me greatly. Maximus says it proceeded not from the first human creation in God's image, but from punishment for sin. He also says this division will no longer exist after the universal resurrection, but [humankind] will return to the unity of the primordial creation of nature.[29]

26. Maximus, *Ambigua* 37 (PG 91: 1309bc).

27. Maximus, *Ambigua* 37 (PG 91: 1312a).

28. *Omnem vitam nutritivam et auctivam.* Nourishment, growth, and reason are the three functions of the soul.

29. Maximus, *Ambigua* 37 (PG 91: 1305cd, 1309a); 27 (PG 91: 1276b); 38 (PG 91: 1320d–1321a, 1345d–1348a).

On hearing such things, who would not tremble and burst out at once in these words? "So after the resurrection, the male and female sexes will no longer exist if both are utterly removed from human nature! In what form will a human being appear, if no one has the form of a man or a woman? Or how will people recognize each other if both sexes are to be eliminated? In what simple, indistinguishable union of the different forms will all people appear—spiritual and incorporeal, or visible and corporeal, bounded by place and time?" This teaching opposes the authority of almost all the Latin saints, who unanimously assert that after all people are resurrected, the integrity of both sexes will remain. So a man will rise in masculine form and a woman in feminine form, with every sign of the bodily parts by which both sexes are recognized; and this form will remain eternally, whether in glory or in punishment.

Similarly, the return of creatures to the first causes seems difficult and obscure to me. For I do not clearly see how the union of both human sexes in Christ took place when he first rose from the dead, and how it will exist in all human beings at the end of the world. For we believe that Christ rose in the same form in which he lived in the flesh, and remains and will always remain in that form. But who will deny that he was clothed in a masculine form before he suffered and rose again? We also believe that all people will be raised in the same form in which they die.

Further, I do not see how the world is united to paradise, earth to heaven, and the whole sensible creation to the intelligible, and how all of these will be united to God, such that in him all will be one and no difference will appear among them. I do not see how the return of all substances into one and the future unification will take place. Will it take place in reality, that is, by the passing of all sensible beings into intellectual ones, such that when this sensible world completes its course, all things will be spiritual and nothing corporeal or sensible will remain? Or will the natural unity of all things be apparent only to the mind's eye as it contemplates them in their reasons and primordial causes?

### 80. *All things subsist in their reasons*

Things may outwardly appear to the bodily senses as many and varied. But to someone who understands them in their reasons, where they truly subsist, they seem to be—and in fact are—one and undivided. Consider a tree that displays variety in its wood, its bark, its sap, pith, branches, leaves, flowers, and fruit; yet all of these are one in the seed. Thus there are many exterior natures—sensible and bodily—that vary according to place, time, and other accidents; and these are beloved by carnal people who are far from the truth. But just as many are the interior natures—or intelligible essences—that display in themselves their simple, undivided unity. Contemplation of this truth, therefore, is promised to the wise who desire their beauty.

### 81. *How the angels see the world*

The heavenly powers (the angels) do not see this visible world with bodily senses. Yet they are not ignorant of it, since we believe it is ruled and served through them, and they administer the divine law to human beings.[30] But they contemplate it in its eternal causes, where it is neither divided by the dimensions of space, nor distinguished by the varied movements of time, nor scattered in the multiplicity of its parts, nor subject to unlikeness through the many differences of qualities and quantities, nor swollen by the magnitude of weight, nor extended in space by differences of length, breadth, and height. Rather, they simultaneously see the world whole, simply and immutably subsisting in its reasons.

I ask you to resolve all these matters for me.

### 82. *What this means: "In the beginning God made heaven and earth"*

M: First let us see about the primordial causes, and perhaps then the things that now seem obscure to you will be clearer.

D: As you wish.

30. Augustine, *De Genesi ad litteram* 4.24 (CSEL 28.1, 123–24).

M: The divine prophet Moses says, "In the beginning God made heaven and earth,"[31] a saying that many have expounded in many ways. Some think these words imply a succinct grasp of the whole perfect creation. Under the name of "heaven," they believe, is implied the forming and fashioning of the whole intellectual and spiritual creation, while "earth" designates the founding of all that is corporeal and sensible in its most perfect definitions. Others argue that the verse designates the formless beginning of both creations, the spiritual under the name of heaven, this corporeal world under that of earth. Others affirm that these words indicate the perfection of the whole sensible creation in its two principal parts, heaven and earth.[32]

As for me, this is the interpretation that I take to be most probable and closest to the truth. Under the names of heaven and earth, these words denote the primordial causes of the whole creation, causes that God had created in the beginning. That is, the Father created them in the Son before all that was made. I take the principal causes as signified by the name of "heaven" to be those of intelligible creatures and celestial beings, while "earth" indicates the causes of the sensible creatures with which this whole bodily world is filled. In these causes all things, which were made simultaneously all at once, subsist forever. But they break through in a fixed order in their effects, that is, into genera and visible forms, appearing through generation in space and time; and they return again to their causes.

D: As it seems to me, they are called "primordial causes" because they are created in the beginning by a single, creative cause of all things, and they themselves create the things beneath them. For they create the formless matter from which this sensible world and everything in it were made.

### 83. *What it means that the earth was empty and void*

M: That is true, but let's see what follows. "The earth was empty and void" (or as another translation says, "invisible and

31. Gn 1.1.
32. Augustine, *De Genesi ad litteram* 1.1 (CSEL 28.1, 4).

without order"), "and darkness covered the face of the abyss."[33] Once again, many interpret this in a variety of ways. Some think the formless state of the earth—empty and void, or invisible and without order—signifies the visible creation, while the dark abyss denotes the formless state of the invisible essence. They assert that the visible (that is, corporeal and sensible) creation, which consists of matter and form, was formed when it was circumscribed by the fixed boundaries of its nature. The invisible (intellectual and rational) creation was formed when it was changed into the form of the Creator.[34] Others, including Basil, think the void and empty earth signifies the mass of this earthly globe when it was first created, still empty and devoid of the different kinds and forms of seeds and animals. It was invisible because it was covered by the waters on all sides, or else because man, who would be able to see it, had not yet been formed. They say that darkness covered the abyss because the air that surrounds the abyss on all sides was not yet luminous.[35]

For my part, I understand by "earth" the primal exemplar of bodily nature, which the Father had created in the Son in order to make the world. The prophet saw it as empty before it proceeded by its effect, through generation in space and time, into the genera and forms of sensible nature. It was void because it had not yet assumed any quality or quantity in bodily substances.

## 84. *What "empty" means*

"Empty and void" is sometimes used as a term of praise for corporeal things. All the space between heaven and earth is divided into two parts. The lower part, reaching from the earth to the moon, is called air. The upper part, extending from the moon to the stars, is what the Greeks call ether, which means "pure spirit." But the Latins call it "empty and void," for it is

33. Gn 1.2. The Vulgate reads *inanis et vacua;* the alternate reading *invisibilis et incomposita* follows the LXX.

34. Augustine, *De Genesi ad litteram* 1.1 (CSEL 28.1, 5). See also 1.5 (CSEL 28.1, 8–9); 1.9 (CSEL 28.1, 13); 1.15 (CSEL 28.1, 22); 2.11 (CSEL 28.1, 49); 5.5 (CSEL 28.1, 146).

35. Basil, *Hexaemeron* 2.1 (PG 29: 29a–c); 2.3 (PG 29:33c–36b); 2.4 (PG 29: 37ab); 4.2 (PG 29: 80d–81a).

agreed to be extremely pure and bright at all times. It enjoys a most serene peace in eternal silence, except for the harmonious intervals of the planets, which transcend all mortal, earthly sense in the keenness of their tones and semitones.[36] It glides with extremely subtle motion and is full of daylight beyond the little portion allowed by the shadow of the earth, which is called night. Therefore, it is said to be empty because it is free of all crude, earthly mass and burdened by no corporeal weight.

### 85. *The planets*

In fact, the spheres of the planets are very light and spiritual; they are weighed down by no earthly quality and cause no darkness. The moisture of the moon and the spots that appear in it do not come from the purity of its own nature but derive from the vapors of the earthly globe and the nearness of the moist abyss.[37] Also, the cloudiness and darkness of this heavier, lower air come not from itself, but from the nearness of water and earth. From the same source as the moisture of the moon comes the cloudiness of the air. Thunder and lightning, rain, showers, snow, ice, and the various winds are caused by no other source than earthly and watery vapors.

### 86. *What darkness and the abyss mean*

By darkness and the abyss, I understand the principal causes of intellectual being. They are called an abyss because of their incomprehensible depth and infinite self-diffusion through all things, which is perceived by no sense and understood by no intellect. They are called darkness because of the loftiness of their ineffable purity, for even this sensible sun often inflicts darkness on its beholders, who cannot bear to gaze on its exceptional brightness. Darkness covered this abyss because, before the principal causes proceeded into celestial beings, no created intellect could know what they were.

D: I would like to know if this mystical earth will remain per-

36. The music of the spheres.

37. Pliny the Elder, *Natural History* 2.9.46.

petually invisible and this intellectual abyss will be eternally dark. Or after the end of this world, will they come to the knowledge of intellectual and rational beings?

M: Just as the wisdom of God the Father, in which all things were made and truly subsist, remains incomprehensible and invisible, so too the causes of all things will remain eternally invisible and incomprehensible. But they do not cease to appear in their effects, as if brought forth into a certain light of knowledge.

D: I would like to know whether or not the principal causes of things understand themselves before they flow out into the things whose causes they are.

M: Just as wisdom knows itself, so too the things that were made in it not only know themselves but also have knowledge of the things whose beginnings they are. For we should not believe that anything foolish and ignorant of itself was created in the divine Wisdom.

### 87. *What this means: "The Spirit of God was borne over the waters"*

D: What do the next words mean? "And the Spirit of God was borne over the waters."[38]

M: This means that the Creator Spirit alone surpasses created causes in excellence of knowledge. The Spirit is the one and only preceding, supereminent cause and primordial source of all the causes it had created, which flow forth from it into infinity and return to it again. In it, nothing was created earlier or later in the course of time, but all things exist in it eternally and were made by it once and for all. Yet some things precede others in an ineffable order, and these are rightly called the most primordial beginnings of the created universe. From there some descend from others, from the highest on down—that is, from the beginning of the intellectual creation down to the lowest of all, which is the body.[39]

Another translation reads, "And the Spirit of God was warm-

38. Gn 1.2: *Spiritus Dei ferebatur super aquas.*

39. Dionysius, *De divinis nominibus* 5.5–6 (PG 3: 820b–d).

ing the waters."[40] This means that the Holy Spirit fostered the primordial causes, which God made in the beginning (that is, the Father made them in the Son), so that they might proceed into various effects—into genera, forms, and species. The Spirit nurtured them in the warmth of divine love.

D: I see that the Trinity is named in the creation of the principal causes, as I believe. If I am not mistaken, by "God" is meant the Father, by "beginning" the Son, and by "the Spirit over the waters," the Holy Spirit.[41]

### 88. *All things were created at once in the Word*

M: You are correct. We should say a few things about this first and supreme cause of all, which is the Holy Trinity.

D: There is nothing I would rather hear. For the salvation of faithful souls consists in nothing but believing what is truly preached—and understanding what is truly believed—about the one Beginning of all things.

M: Tell me then: when you hear that the Father made all things in his Word, do you understand that the Father first begot his Word and then made heaven and earth in him? Or do you think he universally begot his Word and eternally made all things in him, such that the procession of the Word from the Father through generation in no way precedes the procession of all creatures from nothing through creation in the Word? To speak more plainly, didn't the primordial causes always exist in the Word of God, in which they were made? Did the Word exist when there were as yet no causes, or are they coeternal with him, such that the Word was never without the causes created in him?

### 89. *The generation of the Word and the creation of the world are simultaneous*

D: The Father's generation of the Word does not temporally precede the Father's creation of all things in the Word.[42] For in

40. Gn 1.2: *Spiritus Dei fovebat aquas.* Basil, *Hexaemeron* 2.6 (PG 29: 44ab); Augustine, *De Genesi ad litteram* 1.18 (CSEL 28.1, 26–27).

41. Augustine, *De Genesi ad litteram* 1.6 (CSEL 28.1, 10).

42. Augustine, *In Iohannem tractatus* 21.4 (CCSL 36, 214).

God there is understood to be no accident, no temporal movement or progression in time. Therefore, the generation of the Word and the creation of all things in the Word are coeternal with him. All at once the Father both begot his Wisdom and made all things in him, as the prophet says: "In wisdom you have made all things."[43] Again, the Father says, "My heart has uttered a good word; I tell my works to the king."[44] This is as if he said: just as my Word is born from the secret depth of my being, I do my works in him, which I myself give him as he reigns. Again, the prophet says to the Father, "With you is the beginning in the day of your power."[45] This means that "the beginning" of all things (that is, your Word) is always "with you" and in you "on the day" (that is, in the intellectual and rational creature's knowledge) of your generation "of your power" (that is, your wisdom). Therefore, if the beginning is always in and with the Father, there was never a time without those things whose beginning he is. The verse continues: "In the splendor of the holy ones" (that is, in the knowledge and predestination of the elect), "I bore you from the womb" (that is, from the secret bosom of the Father's being) "before the morning star" (that is, before the world).

By the morning star[46] or the sun is understood this world, as Solomon says: "There is nothing new under the sun,"[47] that is, in the world. For there is nothing new in the course of the present life that has not appeared before in the natural order of things. Nothing is perceived and understood in time except a perpetual round of the same things. Or as Maximus says, what was before this world will be again after the world. That is, only things that are eternal existed before the world and will be after it.[48] This whole world is called "new" because it is not eternal. Therefore, it is nothing, for it will perish with all that is in it. As Augustine testifies, in the Word of God "all things unchangeably live—not only those that have been, but also those that will be. Yet in him

43. Ps 103.24.

44. Ps 44.2.

45. Ps 109.3.

46. *Lucifer.*

47. Eccl 1.10.

48. Maximus, *Ambigua* 67 (PG 91: 1412d); *Quaestiones ad Thalassium* 59 (PG 90: 613d–616a).

they neither were nor will be, but simply *are.* And all things are one, or rather, all *is* one."[49] As John the theologian says, "What was made in him was life."[50]

## 90. *So all things exist because they were foreknown*

M: You are proceeding well. The Father understands all things in the Son, but the understanding of all things is the being of all. God's knowing, therefore, is the same as his acting. God did not know all things after they were made, but before they came into being, he knew all things that were to be made; and therefore all things exist because they were foreknown.[51] The being of all things is nothing other than the knowledge of them in divine wisdom.[52] "For in him we live and move and have our being."[53]

D: The principal causes, therefore, are coeternal with God and the beginning in which they were made.

M: Not altogether coeternal. For the Creator does not by any means begin to be. He alone is true eternity, without beginning or end, since he is the beginning and end of all things. But every creature begins to be, for there was a time when it was not. In the Trinity, the Father begetting precedes the Son begotten, and the one who sends comes before the one who proceeds.[54] So in the same way, the cause of all things precedes the principal causes that are eternally established in it. What is made cannot be coeternal with the Maker, for the Maker precedes the things he makes. Even if he were to make nothing, he can still exist in himself; but what is made cannot subsist in itself without the Maker. The primordial causes, therefore, are not altogether coeternal with God, for they have a beginning of existence not from themselves, but from the Creator.

49. Augustine, *De Trinitate* 4.1 (CCSL 50, 162).

50. Jn 1.3–4.

51. Augustine, *De Genesi ad litteram* 5.18 (CSEL 28.1, 161); *De Trinitate* 6.10 (CCSL 50, 241); *De Trinitate* 15.13 (CCSL 50A, 495).

52. Dionysius, *De ecclesiastica hierarchia* 1.3 (PG 3: 376a).

53. Acts 17.28.

54. The Holy Spirit.

### 91. *What is appropriate to each Person*

D: I beg you to explain clearly what special attributes should be ascribed to the Father, the Word, and the Holy Spirit. This seems proper to the Father: "God sent his Son" into the world.[55] Proper to the Son: "Although he was in the form of God, he emptied himself, taking the form of a servant."[56] Proper to the Holy Spirit: "What is born in her is of the Holy Spirit."[57]

M: Theology attributes the creation of natures properly to God the Father as their cause: "In the beginning God made heaven and earth."[58] It asserts that the substantive reasons of all things were created in the Word: "All things were made through him."[59] And again, "He is the image of the invisible God, in whom all things were created in heaven and on earth, whether visible or invisible."[60] It applies the distribution of all causes to the Holy Spirit: "To some the word of wisdom is given by the Spirit, to others the word of knowledge," and so forth up to this verse: "All these are effected by one and the same Spirit, distributing to each as the Spirit wills."[61] In the Holy Trinity we understand the unity of a common operation, yet the property of distinct operations is not excluded. Another theologian says, "Every good gift and every perfect gift comes down from above, descending from the Father of lights,"[62] that is, the Father of all goods that exist according to nature or grace. All gifts are called "lights" because they descend from the unbegotten Light through the begotten Light. The substances of each gift, whether general, special, or individual, are distributed through the proceeding Light, in accord with the capacity of nature and the generosity of grace.

This question of the Apostle can be asked of every creature:

55. Gal 4.4.
56. Phil 2.6–7.
57. Mt 1.20. "What is born in her" is Jesus, born of Mary.
58. Gn 1.1.
59. Jn 1.3.
60. Col 1.15–16.
61. 1 Cor 12.8–11.
62. Jas 1.17.

"What do you have that you did not receive?"[63] For if a creature exists, it has being from God; if it lives, it received life from him; if it perceives, it received perception; if it enjoys reason, it received this; if it has understanding, it received intellect from God. Therefore, a creature is nothing but the gifts of the Creator, whether essential or accidental.

So do you see how Scripture assigns to the Father the making of all things? To the Word it assigns all the primordial causes of things that eternally come to exist in him—universally, essentially, and simply. To the Holy Spirit it ascribes the distribution of those primordial causes that were created in the Word by making them fruitful in their effects, that is, in genera and species, numbers and differences—whether of celestial beings with no bodies at all; or beings with very pure spiritual bodies, made from the simplicity of the universal elements clinging together; or of sensible beings in this visible world, universal or particular, separated by place and moving in time, differentiated by quality and quantity. It is agreed that the primordial causes have no bodies at all, whether visible or invisible, and they have no quality or quantity. By an invisible body we mean a simple entity understood in its own right, subsisting from the individual elements of the world.

## 92. *Angels have bodies*

Celestial beings, that is, the angelic powers, are not unfittingly thought to lie beyond this sensible world in the excellence of their intellectual nature—yet not entirely. According to the holy fathers' opinions, they are judged to possess spiritual bodies.[64] For they often appear to human senses not in foreign bodies, but in their own spiritual bodies, which cleave to them at all times.

63. 1 Cor 4.7.

64. Augustine, *De diversis quaestionibus* 47 (PL 40: 31); *Epistola* 9.3 (CSEL 34.2, 21).

## 93. *The human trinity*

D: I would like to hear a proof of what is said about a likeness of the Trinity in our nature, for it is said to be similar to God.

M: Our human nature subsists in three terms: being or essence, power or virtue, and operation.[65]

D: No one with any learning doubts this.

M: But our nature, as Scripture says, was created "in the image and likeness" of God.[66]

D: Anyone who doubts this is not human.

M: Do you think that God is body or spirit?

D: "God is spirit, and those who worship him worship in spirit."[67]

M: Therefore, the image of God was impressed on our nature in the soul, not the body.

D: This also is very true.

M: God is Trinity and unity, that is, three hypostases in one essence and one essence in three hypostases, or persons. In this triad our being expresses the image of the Father; our virtue, that of the Son; and the operation of our nature, that of the Holy Spirit. For to the Father is ascribed the being of all things; to the Son, their virtue; and to the Holy Spirit, the operation of gifts. In the being of our nature, therefore, we distinguish the property of the Father's person; in our virtue, the Son's; and in operation, the person of the Holy Spirit.

## 94. *Another trinity*

There is also another trinity in our nature, which is understood to consist of intellect, reason, and sensation. There are two kinds of sensation, inner and outer. The inner is coessential with reason and intellect. The outer seems to be a kind of messenger between body and soul. Augustine defines it this way:

65. *Essentia, virtute, operatione.* Dionysius, *De caelesti hierarchia* 11.2 (PG 3: 284d). Contrast Augustine's more famous "human trinity" of memory, understanding, and will.

66. Gn 1.26.

67. Jn 4.24.

"Sensation is a receptive capacity[68] of the body that is not in and of itself hidden from the soul."[69] Or again: "Sensation is a phantasm of sensible things received through the instruments of the body."[70] The body is like the city of the soul, whose gates are the five senses: sight, hearing, smell, taste, and touch. But although sensation has five parts, it is simple and uniform and possesses its seat in the heart as its principal place. It is said to be fivefold because of the fivefold instrument of the body, for the senses admit the likenesses of sensible things coming through the five gates of the body. From the quality and quantity of the outer world, along with other things by which the outer sense is formed, the inner sense receives these likenesses and, like a doorkeeper and messenger, announces the things that sensation introduces from without to the presiding inner sense.

D: Although two trinities made in the image of God are ascribed to our nature, yet in truth there is only one. For the being of our soul is intellect, by which we understand God above all nature. The virtue is reason, by which we distinguish the principal causes from God and from creation. But the operation is sensation, by which we sense the visible and invisible effects of those causes.

Yet I wonder why you did not include life in the substance of human nature.

### 95. *The five parts of the human being*

M: We are not speaking now of the whole of human nature, which consists of five parts (body, vital motion, sensation, reason, and intellect), but only of that part in which the Creator's image and likeness reside. This consists of intellect, reason, and inner sensation, or of being, virtue, and operation. At another point we will examine vital motion, by which the soul nurtures and gives life to the body, and the body itself, which occupies

68. *Passio.*

69. Augustine, *De quantitate animae* 25.48–49 (PL 32: 1063); 30.59 (PL 32: 1068).

70. Augustine, *De Genesi ad litteram* 3.5 (CSEL 28.1, 67); *De musica* 6.5.10 (PL 32: 1169).

the lowest place in all creation. For these lie outside what is proper to our intelligible being.

By "body" I mean this still-corruptible habitation of the carnal soul, which is justly embroiled in diverse calamities because of its disobedience and pride. I am not speaking of that celestial, spiritual body that was created in paradise with the soul, as it will be again after the resurrection. The mortal body by which we are now oppressed comes not from nature but from transgression, and when our nature is restored to its original state, we will be free of it. For what clings to our nature on account of sin cannot be coeternal with it.

### 96. *The three motions of the soul*

D: Return to the soul, then, in which we are seeking the Trinity whose image it is.

M: Maximus says that the soul has three motions: the first pertains to the mind, the second to reason, and the third to sensation. The first is simple and above the soul's own nature; it has no knowledge of the very thing around which it is moved. For it does not by any means know what God is from anything that exists, because of his excellence. God transcends all that exists, and what he is can by no means be defined. The second motion is that by which the soul defines the unknown God as the cause of all things. This motion is within the soul's nature; by it, the soul expresses all natural reasons in itself through knowledge.

The third motion is compound, and by it the soul outwardly recognizes the effects of causes. First receiving the phantasms of objects through the five outer senses and gathering them in itself, it then divides, organizes, disposes, and fashions the reasons of things within itself.[71] There are two kinds of phantasms. The first kind is born of sensible nature in the sensory organs, and it is properly called an express image in the senses. The second kind is formed from the aforesaid image, and it is this phantasm that is properly called the external sense. The former always clings to the body, the latter to the soul. Although the former exists in the senses, it does not sense itself, but the latter

71. Maximus, *Ambigua* 6.3 (PG 91: 1112d–1113a).

phantasm both senses itself and receives the former. This third motion, working through the second, first reports the reasons of visible things. Through what it perceives from this third motion by means of creatures, the first motion understands that all things proceed from God and return to him.[72]

## 97. *What intellect is*

The movement of the soul by which it constantly revolves around God and proves all things that are predicated of God (not properly, but metaphorically), is called in Greek *noys.*[73] We call it intellect, spirit, or mind,[74] and it is substantially understood to be the principal part of the soul. For human intellects are nothing but ineffable, unceasing movements around God, in whom they live and move and have their being.[75] They have their being from the reasons through which they exist; they are moved by the reasons of the virtues, through which they can exist well; they live by the reasons through which they exist forever.[76]

## 98. *What the angels are*

So too the heavenly beings, which divine Scripture calls celestial and angelic powers,[77] are substantially nothing but intelligible, eternal, and unceasing movements around the Beginning of all things—by whom, through whom, in whom, and toward whom they move and subsist.[78] So it is handed down by the holy fathers. The angels understand that they have their being from God, and through him and in him they exercise their intellect. Like the angels, then, minds also revolve forever around their beginning with an intelligible, circular movement.[79]

72. Maximus, *Ambigua* 6.3 (PG 91: 1116a).

73. Honorius's spelling for νοῦς or mind; origin of the personified character Noys in Bernard Silvestris's epic *Cosmographia.*

74. *Intellectus vel animus vel mens.*

75. Acts 17.28.

76. Maximus, *Ambigua* 3 (PG 91: 1084bc); 6.3 (PG 91: 1116b); 38 (PG 91: 1329b); 61 (PG 91: 1392a).

77. Rom 8.38; 1 Cor 15.24; Eph 1.21; 1 Pt 3.22.

78. Rom 11.36; Dionysius, *De divinis nominibus* 4.10 (PG 3: 708a).

79. Dionysius, *De divinis nominibus* 4.9 (PG 3: 705ab).

### 99. *Man is worthier than an angel*

Man is said to have been made in God's image,[80] something we do not read about the angels. Rather, angels are found to stand before God and serve him.[81] But human nature, having been made God in the Word of God,[82] is believed to sit at the right hand of God and reign. It is said that after the resurrection, all "will be like angels of God in heaven."[83] We understand that this refers not to equal dignity of nature, but equal immortality, and it also means they will have no sex or corruptible generation. When man was first created in paradise before sin, in celestial beatitude, he was equal to the angels and, so to speak, connatural with them. Of these two natures it is said, "he who made the heavens in intellect."[84] That is, he made angels and humans to be essentially and substantially intellect. But since "man did not understand when he was in honor, and compared to foolish beasts, he became like them,"[85] he withdrew far from angelic dignity and fell into the calamity of this mortal life. But after the Word became flesh,[86] that is, after God became man, "he crowned him with glory and honor" and "put all things in subjection beneath his feet."[87]

D: O how greatly human nature was humbled in the first man after sin! And how greatly it was exalted by grace in the second man, Christ! In fact, man was not only restored to the original state of his nature, from which he fell, but exalted even above all the heavenly powers.

M: Renewed human nature not only attained to angelic dignity in Christ but was also taken up to God above all creation. And what happened in the head will also happen in the members. It would be impious to deny this.

80. Gn 1.27.
81. 1 Kgs 22.19; 2 Chr 18.18; Is 6.1; Dn 7.10; Mt 4.11; Lk 1.19.
82. Maximus, *Ambigua* 3 (PG 91: 1088c).
83. Mt 22.30.
84. Ps 135.5.
85. Ps 48.13, 21.
86. Jn 1.14.
87. Ps 8.6, 8.

### 100. *How the soul may be ravished*

D: How can the intellect, which is enclosed within the limits of human nature, ascend above itself and all creation to complete its substantial motions around the unknown God, who is far removed from all created nature?[88]

M: No created substance naturally has the power to transcend the limits of its nature and attain immediately to God in himself. This comes about by grace alone, not by any power of nature. Hence the Apostle says he did not know how he was ravished into paradise: "I know a man who was ravished, but whether in the body or out of the body, I do not know."[89] It is as if he said: I know that there is no power in the body, or outside the body in the soul, by which I could be ravished into "the third heaven. God" alone "knows," for I am not unaware that I was ravished by his grace alone. Indeed, no nature can ascend by itself to the place where the Lord says, "Where I am, there will my servant be also."[90]

### 101. *What reason is*

D: Turn the gaze of your mind to the soul's second motion.

M: The soul's second motion is that by which it impresses knowledge on itself from the primordial causes. The Greeks call such knowledge "theophanies," and the Latins, "divine apparitions." Through them the soul receives a certain knowledge of God.[91] The Greeks call this motion *logos;* we call it reason or virtue. It is born from the first motion, the intellect. Just as an artisan produces his art from himself and in himself, foreknowing the things he intends to make, so the intellect produces reason from itself and in itself, foreknowing in it everything it wishes to do. This is why it is called the form of reason.

D: As for the intellect, created in God's image, I see that what it is cannot be understood by itself or anyone else.[92] But it begins to appear in reason, which is born of it.

88. Maximus, *Ambigua* 6.3 (PG 91: 1112d–1113a).
89. 2 Cor 12.2.
90. Jn 12.26.
91. Maximus, *Ambigua* 6.3 (PG 91: 1113a).
92. Gregory of Nyssa, *De hominis opificio* 11 (PG 44: 153c–156b).

M: The soul's third motion is that by which it receives the images of sensible things, which the Greeks call phantasms,[93] and distinguishes them through their proper reasons into essences, genera, forms, and species.[94] In Greek this motion is called *dianoia;* in Latin, "sense" or "operation." This sense is substantial and interior, proceeding from the intellect through reason. Everything that the intellect, in understanding the primordial causes, imprints on its work of art, which is reason, it distinguishes in their proper reasons through sense, which proceeds from it. In reason all essences are one, but in sense they are distinguished as different beings.

### 102. *The soul creates bodies*

D: In our trinity I discern the face of the supreme Trinity as in a mirror. A very clear likeness of the Father shines out in the mind, a likeness of the Son in reason, and a likeness of the Holy Spirit in sensation. But what difference is there between the operation of the creative, uncreated Trinity and the action of our created and creating trinity, which, as we read, is not God's image, but was created *in* God's image?[95] For the only true "image of the invisible God,"[96] which is not unlike him in any way, is the only-begotten Word of God. Our trinity, created from nothing, creates the senses that adhere to it and its whole mortal body—not from nothing, however, but from something. For the soul, by joining incorporeal qualities together in one and supplying a kind of subject for them from quantity, creates a body for itself. In that body it can reveal its hidden actions, which are invisible in themselves, and bring them forth as a sensible idea.

M: The supreme Trinity, creatrix of all and created by none, made everything she made out of nothing and divided it into five parts. For certain creatures only subsist essentially; others subsist and live. To some is added sensation, to some reason, and to some intellect.[97] The first motion exists in natural bodies,

93. *Fantasias.*
94. Maximus, *Ambigua* 6.3 (PG 91: 1113a).
95. Gn 1.27.
96. Col 1.15.
97. Maximus, *Ambigua* 3 (PG 91: 1080b).

the second in that life by which trees and plants live and grow. The third is perceived in irrational animals, while the fourth properly subsists in human and the fifth in angelic nature. In these five degrees, the goodness of the supreme Trinity is perceived and its operation made manifest.

But our trinity creates nothing from nothing. Its action is twofold. By the first act, it gathers the knowledge of all things into one, and, by an act of knowledge, it unites the genera in one essence, the forms in a genus, and the numerous individuals in a form. This is the principal and supreme operation of a rational nature. The second act is recognized in the creation of its body and disclosed in its governance. First the soul takes its matter from the qualities of sensible things and, with no lapse of time, adapts vital motion to it. By this means it quickens and nourishes that matter and brings it to growth in place and time. It confers the external senses, by which the body receives the phantasms of all things and distributes the nourishment that it takes in to build up the body through the hidden networks of veins and nerves. Just as the supreme Trinity moves, governs, and orders the whole creation fashioned by it, so our trinity quickens, moves, and contains the body made by it. But lest you suppose that the creation of the soul precedes that of the body in time, this is not the case. The soul precedes the body only in the dignity and excellence of its nature, but not in place or time. In the one human being who was made in God's image, the reasons of all men according to body and soul were created all at once. By no means does the essence of the soul precede that of the body in the course of time.[98]

## 103. *The spiritual body*

That first, essential body was created in paradise, but in reason alone. And the soul was created in that general, universal human being made in God's image, in whom all humans were created in body and soul all at once, though in potentiality alone. In him all sinned[99] before they came forth in their proper

98. Gregory of Nyssa, *De hominis opificio* 28–29 (PG 44: 229b–240b).
99. Rom 5.12.

substances, that is, before each one appeared as a distinct individual with a rational soul and a spiritual body. The incorruptible body would have clung eternally to the soul if man had not sinned, and all humans will be resurrected in it. This body was substantially created by God for celestial beatitude. The true substance of each person is nothing other than the reason, known beforehand, by which God defined them in the primordial causes. But I do not see how man would have lost beatitude if he had fully, perfectly tasted its reality. As I suspect, he turned first to himself rather than to God, and thus he fell.

### 104. *The corruptible body*

But we affirm that this corruptible, material body, which was taken "from the slime of the earth"[100] after sin, as a punishment for sin, was created—and is daily created—by a certain operation of the soul, in order to exercise the negligent soul in it by keeping the commandments. Scripture says that God took mud from the earth and formed a body for man; but it speaks this way because every action of a creature can rightly be referred back to him from whom every natural action begins, since he is the cause of all. Expelled from the bliss of paradise because of his guilt, man made for himself a mortal dwelling of mud. He was advised by divine providence that because, in his pride, he did not keep the spiritual body created by God, he should enter a mortal dwelling on account of his disobedience. Punished in this body, he could repent and return to the original dignity of his nature. Hence Scripture says, "They sewed leaves together and made themselves girdles";[101] that is, after the fall man wove for himself the fragile condition of his mortal body. This was done by the counsel of God, as the same Scripture says: "God made Adam and his wife tunics of skins and clothed them."[102] That is, he permitted humans to fashion mortal bodies after their transgression. For God is immortal, and whatever he makes by himself is immortal. But whatever mortal thing

100. Gn 2.7.
101. Gn 3.7.
102. Gn 3.21.

appears in this world, both frail and transitory, we either make for ourselves or God permits it to be made because of our sin.

The vital motion in seeds does not always proceed into visible forms. The cause is either some accident that is not suited to the seeds, or some opposing power that resists the natural motion.

### 105. *Where the spiritual body is now*

D: What is incorruptible cannot perish, so where now is the incorruptible body that would have clung to the soul if it had not sinned?

M: It is still hidden in the secret bosom of nature, but it will appear in the age to come, when this mortal body will be changed into it and "this corruptible body will put on incorruption."[103] Listen to the Apostle: "it is sown an animal body, it will rise a spiritual body."[104] This is said about every human body, for all will have equal glory in eternal immortality, though not in beatitude. Indeed, all nature will be restored.

### 106. *Man as the image of God*

D: I would like to know whether our trinity resembles the supreme Trinity, whose image it is, in every way, or in what way the likeness falls short.

M: We believe that man, who was most perfectly made in God's image and likeness in paradise, fell short in no way before sin, except by reason of the subject. God subsists in himself; man began to exist from God. God has no beginning; man has a beginning of existence.[105] All other things that are said of God according to essence are perceived in his image entirely according to grace. The Creator is incomprehensible, and what our intellect is can be comprehended by no one but God.[106] God is the principal exemplar by nature; the image is God by grace. Just as God created his image in which he could reveal the knowledge of himself, that image made itself an image in which it could

103. 1 Cor 15.53.
104. 1 Cor 15.44.
105. Gregory of Nyssa, *De hominis opificio* 16 (PG 44: 184b–d).
106. Gregory of Nyssa, *De hominis opificio* 11 (PG 44: 153c–156b).

manifest its motions, which in themselves are hidden. For the soul is the image of God; the body is the image of the soul.[107]

D: There seems to be a great unlikeness between the image and the principal form, that is, between the human intellect and God the Creator—not only in reason of the subject, but also in this way: the divine form knows what it is, but the image does not know how to define either what it is or the form it substantially imitates.

M: I see that you are deceived by a likeness of true reasoning.

D: Please explain.

M: Does the divine essence seem to you infinite or finite?

D: It is not only infinite, but the infinity of all infinite essences and more-than-infinity.

M: So it is altogether infinite.

D: Yes, it is not otherwise.

M: When we ask what this or that is, do we seem to you to be asking about anything but a substance that is already defined, or else one that is capable of being defined?

D: No.

M: So in general, no wise person asks what any essence is because it cannot be defined. But from the circumstances that delimit its boundaries—I mean place, time, and the other accidents—it is manifested only as an existing substance, while what it is remains unknown. What theologian, then, would presume to ask what the divine substance is when he very clearly understands that it cannot be defined (nor can anything that exists)—and it transcends everything that can be defined? God cannot in any way be defined by a creature or even by himself, for he is universally infinite.[108]

## 107. *God is infinite*

D: I find the murkiness of this reasoning inaccessible. For if God does not and cannot define himself, he is either ignorant or impotent. But if he defines what he is, then he is not altogether infinite.

107. Gregory of Nyssa, *De hominis opificio* 12 (PG 44: 164a).
108. Maximus, *Ambigua* 13 (PG 91: 1225d–1228a).

M: What we concluded above about the categories will resolve this question.

D: I would like you to recapitulate them in the form of questions.

M: Then pay close attention to this order of inquiry. What, how much, how, toward what, in what situation, in what condition, in what place or time, does he act or is he acted on? None of these questions is properly asked about God, for none of these things is understood to be in him, whether by himself or another. These categories can be properly considered only in things that are proven to fall under the domain of intellect or sensation. For if you were to ask what God is, wouldn't you be asking about a certain proper, defined substance? And if someone were to reply this or that, wouldn't he seem to define some fixed, circumscribed substance, in and around which all accidents might be contained? Thus God would be understood within the boundaries of a definite nature, rather than beyond all that is said and understood. Now every question and response is alien to God, for he is none of the things that exist. God is neither whole nor part, neither genus nor form nor species, neither number nor essence, for he transcends everything that is, and he surpasses every essence and substance. How then can the divine nature understand what it is, when it is nothing? Or how can the Infinite be defined or understood in any way, knowing itself to be above all that is finite and infinite? God therefore does not know what he is, for he is not any thing. Indeed, he is incomprehensible in every way, both to himself and to every intellect.

### 108. *That God does not know what he is*

None of the wise, on hearing that God cannot understand what he is, should think anything but this: God himself, who is not any thing, does not know at all in himself that which he is not. But he does not know himself to be anything; therefore, he does not know what he is. That is, he does not know himself to be any thing, for he knows that he is absolutely none of those things that are known in any way, concerning which we can say and understand what they are. For if he knew himself in any way, he would show that he is not altogether infinite, incomprehensible, and unnamable. "Why do you ask my name, which is wonderful?" he says.[109] Truly wonderful is that "name which is above every name" that is named, either in this world or in the world to come.[110] There is no creature, visible or invisible, that is not confined in some way by the limits of its own nature "in measure, number, and weight."[111] But God understands that he is in none of these. He knows that he is above all orders of nature in the excellence of his wisdom, and beneath all things in the depth of his power, and within all things in the unsearchable dispensation of his providence. He encompasses all, for all things are in him and outside of him is nothing. He alone is measure without measure, number without number, and weight without weight, for he is measured, numbered, and ordered by no one, not even himself. He does not understand himself to exist in any measure, any number, or any order, for he is substantially contained in none of these. He alone is truly infinite, in all and above all.[112]

D: In this wonderful divine ignorance, by which God does not understand what he is because he is not any thing, there smiles a supreme, ineffable wisdom. For God is infinite both to himself and to everything that is.

M: Where there is no thing, it is impossible to discover any "how" or "how much" or to understand any accident.

D: I am deeply troubled as to how ignorance can fall on God, from whom nothing is hidden, either in himself or in the things that have being from him.

M: His ignorance is ineffable understanding.[113] For how can he know in himself something that cannot exist in himself? It is as if someone were to say, "I do not understand that I am a stone," meaning, "I understand that I am not a stone." Another example: "I do not understand any irrational man, for I know

109. Jgs 13.18.

110. Phil 2.9; Eph 1.21.

111. Wis 11.21; Augustine, *De Genesi ad litteram* 2.6 (CSEL 28.1, 42) and 4.1 (CSEL 28.1, 94); Maximus, *Ambigua* 6.39 (PG 91: 1181ab).

112. Augustine, *De Genesi ad litteram* 4.3–4 (CSEL 28.1, 99–100).

113. Dionysius, *Epistola* 1 (PG 3: 1065ab).

that no man lacks reason." So too in the Gospel, the Lord will say to some people, "I do not know you."[114] That means, I understand that you are not among my own. Again in the Gospel he says, "But of that day and that hour no one knows, neither the angels in heaven nor the Son of man, but only the Father."[115]

### 109. *That the Son is ignorant of the Judgment*

D: Since the Judgment pertains especially to the Son, how can he be ignorant of what the Father knows when he is one with the Father?[116]

M: Bishop Epiphanius scours the obscurity off this question in his exposition. The Father, he says, knows the judgment by experience, for he has already "given all judgment to the Son" in reality,[117] and he completed the whole judgment when he gave it all to the Son. But the Son both knows and does not know the judgment. He knows it by foreknowledge, but does not know it by experience, for he has not yet carried out the judgment in reality, that is, the separation of the reprobate from the elect.[118] We read of a similar ignorance in the Apostle: "I know a man who was ravished to the third heaven, whether in the body or out of the body I do not know, God knows."[119] This means: I do not know if it was in the body because I know I was not ravished in the body, that is, by the bodily senses. I do not know if it was out of the body because I know I was not ravished by the powers of the soul. But I know very clearly that I was ravished above all creation by virtue of divine grace.

### 110. *Four kinds of ignorance*

D: I would like to know how many kinds of divine ignorance there are.

M: There are three principal ones. First, God does not know

114. Mt 7.23.
115. Mk 13.32.
116. Jn 10.30.
117. Jn 5.22.
118. Epiphanius, *Ancoratus* 21 (PG 43: 53d–57a).
119. 2 Cor 12.2.

evil, for he is substantial good. If he knew evil, there would necessarily be evil in the nature of things, for his knowledge of all things that exist is their cause.[120] It is not that God knows the things that are because they exist; rather, they exist because he knows them.[121] God therefore does not know evil because it does not exist.

The second kind is that God is said not to know things other than those whose reasons he eternally made and knows in himself. For he possesses essential knowledge of the things over which he has eternal power. The third is that God is said not to know things that do not yet manifestly appear in their effects by the experience of action. But he does possess their invisible reasons, created in himself and known to himself.

A fourth kind is added to these. God is said not to know himself within the number of things made by him, but he knows that he is above all things. Therefore, there is no unlikeness between the image and the principal form, except by reason of the subject. As the principal form is God by nature, the image is God by grace.[122]

## 111. *"There is no God"*

D: It has been shown more clearly than sunlight that we should understand the divine ignorance as nothing other than the incomprehensible, infinite divine knowledge. But since reason proves that God does not properly exist, why does the Holy Spirit rebuke as a "fool" the man in the Psalms who "said in his heart, There is no God"?[123]

M: We speak in three ways—with the mouth, with the heart, and with the mind. We speak with the mouth when we say the word "man"; with the heart when we think the word "man"; and with the mind when we understand the substance signified by the word "man."[124] So if someone were to say with his mouth

120. Dionysius, *De ecclesiastica hierarchia* 1.3 (PG 3: 376a).

121. Augustine, *De Genesi ad litteram* 5.18 (CSEL 28.1, 161); *De Trinitate* 6.10 (CCSL 50, 241) and 15.13 (CCSL 50a, 495).

122. Gregory of Nyssa, *De hominis opificio* 16 (PG 44: 184b–d).

123. Ps 13.1; 52.1.

124. Anselm, *Proslogion* 2. This citation of Honorius's teacher is the single source he adds to the *Periphyseon.*

or in his heart, "There is no God," because he cannot see him with his bodily eyes, that person would be a fool. But if someone making an argument about God were to say, "There is no God," because he knows that God is above all that is said and understood, that person would be wise.

### 112. *God is three causes and one*

D: According to the Greeks, the divine goodness is one essence in three hypostases and three hypostases[125] in one essence. According to the Romans, it is one substance in three persons and three persons in one substance. I would like to know whether we should believe that God is one essential cause in three subsistent causes and three subsistent causes in one essential cause.

M: If God is the cause of all things, it follows that the cause of all things is God. Therefore, just as we understand that the one God exists in himself in three hypostases, which subsist in themselves, so we accept the one cause existing in itself in three causes subsisting in themselves. According to Dionysius, there is a substantial cause that is unbegotten and begetting; a begotten substantial cause; and a proceeding substantial cause. These three causes are one, and one essential cause.[126] But in the cause of all things, there is a preceding cause and there are subsequent causes. Indeed, the Father precedes the Son and the Holy Spirit, for the Son is begotten by him, and the Holy Spirit proceeds from him. Therefore, the Father is the cause of causes, for he is cause of the cause that is born, and of the proceeding cause. Hence the Son says, "The Father is greater than I"[127]—according to cause, not according to nature.[128] So the cause of the Son and the Holy Spirit is the Father. But the Son is the cause of the creation of the principal causes, and the Holy Spirit is the cause of the distribution of those causes.

125. *Substantie.* See n. 133 below.
126. Dionysius, *De divinis nominibus* 2.1 (PG 3: 637b); 2.7 (PG 3: 645b).
127. Jn 14.28.
128. Maximus, *Ambigua* 21 (PG 91: 1264c).

### 113. *The Holy Spirit proceeds from the Father and the Son*

D: Now that these questions have been plausibly resolved, I would like to know whether we should say the Holy Spirit proceeds from the Father alone, as the Greeks have it,[129] or from the Father and the Son, as the Latins believe. Does the Spirit have one cause or two causes of its procession?

M: We believe and understand that the Holy Spirit proceeds from the Father through the Son, but it does not have two causes. The Father is the only cause,[130] both of the Son who is born of him and the Holy Spirit who proceeds from him. Here is an analogy. Brightness proceeds from a fire through a ray, for the whole fire subsists in the whole ray, and brightness is emitted from the fire through the ray. In the same way the Holy Spirit proceeds from the Father through the Son, for the Father—the sole and principal cause of the procession of the Holy Spirit—is wholly in the whole Son, just as the whole Son is in the whole Father; and the Holy Spirit proceeds from the Father through the Son. The whole fiery power remains in the whole ray that is born of it, and the whole ray and the whole fiery power that gives rise to it are in the whole brightness; and the whole brightness, proceeding from the fiery power through the ray, is in the whole ray and the whole power from which it proceeds. In the same way the whole begetting Father is in the whole begotten Son, and the whole begotten Son is in the whole Holy Spirit, which proceeds from the Father through the Son; and the whole Holy Spirit, proceeding from the Father through the Son, is in the Father from whom it proceeds and the Son through whom it proceeds; and the three are one through the Trinity, which is understood in unity. The Son who was made man hints at this when he says, "I am in the Father, and the Father is in me."[131] It is implied, "and the Holy Spirit is in us, and we three are one"—that is, three substantially but one essentially.

D: We can prove this, as it seems to me, through the trinity of

129. Epiphanius, *Ancoratus* 119 (PG 43: 232d).
130. Maximus, *Quaestiones ad Thalassium* 63 (PG 90: 672c).
131. Jn 14.10.

our nature. Augustine says there is a trinity in our mind: being, knowledge, love.[132] The mind begets knowledge of itself, and from it proceeds love of itself and its knowledge, and by this love, the mind and its self-knowledge are joined together. These three are one according to nature or essence, and the one is three according to the contemplation of reason. In fact, reason contemplates three things in the one, simple nature of the soul: being, knowing, and loving. For the mind exists, it knows itself, and it loves itself and its knowledge.

But I would like you to explain whether, just as we believe that the Holy Spirit proceeds from the Father through the Son, we can say that the Son is born of the Father through the Holy Spirit.

### 114. *The Son is born through the Holy Spirit*

M: The Catholic faith confesses that the Holy Spirit proceeds from the Father and the Son, or from the Father through the Son. But we do not plainly read that the Son is born of the Father through the Holy Spirit—except that the incarnate Son was undoubtedly conceived and born of the Holy Spirit. Yet if the Holy Spirit proceeds from the Father through the Son, I do not see why we should not similarly say that the Son is born of the Father through the Spirit.

### 115. *What essence and substance are*

D: I would still like to ask you whether the Son is born and the Holy Spirit proceeds from the Father's essence or from his person (*substantia*), and what difference there is between the essence and the substance of divine goodness.[133]

M: As Dionysius and Gregory teach, the *ousia* or essence is

132. Augustine, *De Trinitate* 9.4 (CCSL 50, 297); 9.5 (CCSL 50, 300); 9.12 (CCSL 50, 310).

133. Like chapter 23 above, this chapter hinges on an ambiguity in the Latin *substantia,* which was used to translate both Greek *ousia* (essence) and *hypostasis* (person), leading to great confusion in Trinitarian theology. Here I have translated it as *essence* when referring to the one divine nature and *hypostasis* when referring to the three persons.

that unique, simple nature of the divine goodness, but the substance of each individual person is their proper, individual hypostasis. For they say there is one essence in three hypostases.[134] But Augustine and the other Latins say there is one substance in three persons.[135] So according to the Greeks, there is one and the same *ousia* of the Father, Son, and Holy Spirit, but not one and the same hypostasis. For the Father has his own proper hypostasis, which is neither the Son's nor the Holy Spirit's. Similarly, the Son has his proper hypostasis which is not the Father's or the Holy Spirit's, and the Holy Spirit has his proper hypostasis which is not the Father's or the Son's. The Latin language does not teach otherwise, pronouncing that there are three persons in one substance or essence. Therefore, the Father subsists in himself, the Son subsists, and the Holy Spirit subsists; and the three hypostases subsist in one essence, for the three are one. Each person, therefore, has his own hypostasis, but all have one essence. And because the essence is their common nature, the Son is not born of it nor does the Holy Spirit proceed from it. Rather, the Son is born and the Holy Spirit proceeds from the Father's hypostasis.

But we can think about these things more deeply and truly than we can utter them in speech. We can understand them more deeply and truly than we think about them; and they are deeper and truer in reality than what we understand, for they transcend all understanding. Yet we are bidden to say and think something about them, with holy Theology as our guide and mistress, that we may have material somehow to praise and bless her.

## 116. *The causes as beginning*

D: I think enough has been said about the supreme cause of all causes, according to our modest measure. Now let us return to the primordial causes.

134. Dionysius, *De divinis nominibus* 1.4 (PG 3: 589d–592a); Maximus, *Ambigua* 19 (PG 91: 1261a); 36 (PG 91: 1301d–1304c); 63 (PG 91: 1397c, 1400d–1401a).

135. Augustine, *De Trinitate* 5.8–9 (CCSL 50, 216–17); 7.4 (CCSL 50, 255, 259).

M: The primordial causes, which they call ideas, species, or forms, are the eternal and unchangeable reasons according to which, and in which, the visible and invisible world is formed and governed.[136] The wise call them the principal exemplars which the Father made in the Son, and he distributes and multiplies them in their effects through the Holy Spirit. They are also called predestinations because everything that is—past, present, or future—was changelessly predestined in them by divine Providence once and for all. For nothing naturally arises in the visible and invisible creation except what was predefined and foreordained in them before all times and places. Philosophers also name them divine volitions, because everything that God willed to make, he made in them primordially and causally. Things that are yet to come were made in them before the ages.[137] For this reason they are said to be the beginnings of all things, because everything that is perceived or understood in the visible or invisible creation subsists by participation in them. They themselves participate in the supreme cause, the Holy Trinity. They are therefore said to exist in themselves because no creature is interposed between them and the cause of all things.[138]

The primordial causes, then, which wise theologians call the beginnings of all things, are Goodness in itself, Being in itself, Life in itself, Wisdom in itself, Truth in itself, Understanding in itself, Reason in itself, Virtue in itself, Justice in itself, Salvation in itself, Greatness in itself, Omnipotence in itself, Eternity in itself, Peace in itself, and all the virtues and reasons that the Father made once for all in the Son. According to these causes, the order of all things is woven from the highest on down, that is, from the intellectual creation, which is closest to God, down to the lowest order of all things, which contains bodies. Whatever is good, is good by participation in Goodness in itself. Whatever subsists essentially and substantially, subsists by its participation

136. Honorius supplies a long list of synonymous terms, but the ones he uses most frequently are *causae, rationes,* and *principia.* The latter means both "principles" and "beginnings" as inseparable senses.

137. Dionysius, *De divinis nominibus* 5.8 (PG 3: 824c); Maximus, *Ambigua* 3 (PG 91: 1085a).

138. Dionysius, *De divinis nominibus* 5.5–6 (PG 3: 820b–d).

in Being in itself. Whatever lives, possesses life by participation in Life in itself. Similarly, whatever has wisdom, understanding, and reason possesses them by participation in Wisdom in itself, Understanding in itself, and Reason in itself. We should speak in the same way of the others. In fact, no virtue, general or special, is found in the nature of things that does not proceed from the primordial causes by participation. But all of these exist in the supreme cause, just as all numbers subsist in the monad and all lines in the center.[139]

139. Dionysius, *De divinis nominibus* 5.6 (PG 3: 820d–821a).

# BOOK III

## 117. *On the nature that is created and does not create*

D: IT IS TIME for you to unravel, with God's guidance, whatever the eternal light has revealed in your mind concerning the third aspect of universal nature, that which is created and does not create. But before you go on to elucidate this part of nature, I would like to know why you have positioned the nature that is set apart by its excellence from the universe of all natures, as if it were the first part of the universe.

M: By no means did I set it within a division of the created universe. Rather, I judged that it should be set in the division of universal nature, which is comprehended in a single term. Indeed, the first and greatest division is that between creative and created nature. By this division the supreme, unchangeable, self-existent, substantial Good is separated from that which is good by participation in the supreme Good, and from those things that are good through it. Similarly, the nature that exists through itself, from itself, and in itself, and is truly and unchangeably being, life, wisdom, and virtue, is distinguished from that nature that merely exists by participating in it, or exists and lives, or else exists, lives, and participates in wisdom and virtue. So the Creator of the whole universe occupies the first place among the divisions, for he is the beginning of all things and is inseparable from the whole universe that he created. All things essentially exist in him, and he is the division and ingathering of the universal creation, for all things are from him, in him, and toward him.[1] In the same way the monad is the beginning

1. Rom 11.36. "Division and ingathering" (*divisio et collectio*) denotes the whole cosmic process of creation and return (*reditus*), as well as the logical process by which both are contemplated.

of numbers and the first progression. From it the plurality of all numbers begins, and in it their return and ingathering are consummated. (Indeed, all numbers universally subsist in the monad, and in all of them it is the whole, the part, and the beginning of all division. But in itself, it is neither a number nor a part of one.) The same reasoning applies to the center in a circle or sphere, a sign in a figure, and a point in a line.

### 118. *Goodness*

D: Before you go on to consider the effects of the primordial causes, it is fitting to know their order.

M: This is the first consideration concerning the supreme, true nature. It is understood to be the supreme and true Goodness, which is Goodness-through-itself, not through participation in another.[2] From the first grant and participation [in the divine nature] derives [the primordial cause], Goodness in itself. In turn, whatever things are good, are good by participation in this cause. It is called Goodness in itself because it participates directly (*per se ipsam*) in the supreme Good. But other good things do not participate directly in the supreme and substantial Good. Rather, they participate [indirectly] through that which participates in the supreme Good-through-itself.[3] We should say the same about the other primordial causes: they are principal causes because they participate directly in the one cause of all things, which is God. But all other things are what they are by participation in those causes.

The first causes in themselves are one and simple. They are not defined by any known order or separated from each other, although they endure this separation in their effects. Just as all numbers are one and simple in the monad, while the multi-

2. The ultimate source is Plato's Form of the Good: *Republic* 454c–d and 508a–e.

3. In other words, God is the Supreme Good, and the primordial cause, Goodness in itself, participates in him directly. All other good things are good by participation in this primordial cause. Confusingly, Honorius uses the phrase *per se ipsam bonitas* to denote both God and the first primordial cause. For the sake of clarity I have distinguished between "Goodness-through-itself" (God) and "Goodness in itself" (the primordial cause).

plication of numbers proceeds to infinity, so the primordial causes are one, simple, and undivided in the beginning of all, that is, in the Word of God. But in their effects, which are multiplied, they proceed to infinity, receiving their numbered, ordered plurality. Every order is one and simple, undistinguished by differences, in the supreme cause of all and in its primal participation. There the orders do not differ among themselves, for they are one and inseparable. From this oneness, the multiple order of all things descends. Thus the order of the primordial causes is established by the judgment of the contemplating mind, inasmuch as the knowledge of them is given to those who discuss the divine causes. Pious philosophers may begin from any one of them as they wish, and set the end of their contemplation in any of them. In the same way, the center of a circle is the universal beginning of lines, the point at which all are one; all lines begin from the center and end at the circumference. If anyone wished to follow a certain order in these lines, he would find as many beginnings and ends of counting and ordering as there are spaces and lines.

### 119. *Goodness is the cause of being*

D: Yet I would like to know why you began with goodness.

M: I did this on the authority of Dionysius the Areopagite, who asserts that Goodness in itself is the most general of the divine gifts and in some way precedes the others.[4] For the cause of all things is goodness, the Creatrix, which is God. For this reason she first of all created that cause which is called Goodness in itself, so that through it she might bring all things that exist out of non-existence into being.[5] Goodness therefore precedes being,[6] and goodness does not exist through being, but being through goodness. Take away goodness, and it is not properly called being.

Not only things that exist are good, but even those that do

4. Dionysius, *De divinis nominibus* 3.1 (PG 3: 680b); 4.1 (PG 3: 693b); 13.3 (PG 3: 981a).

5. Dionysius, *De caelesti hierarchia* 4.1 (PG 3: 177c).

6. *Essentia.*

not exist are called good.[7] Indeed, those that are not are better than those that are. For inasmuch as they transcend being by their excellence, they draw near to the superessential Good, namely God; and inasmuch as they participate in being, they are distanced from the superessential Good. The things that are said not to exist are those that, because of their great excellence, can be perceived by neither the senses nor the intellect. The things that are said to exist are perceived by either the senses or the intellect, and they are circumscribed by certain definite boundaries. They are also subject to accidents, dispersed in places, and varied in times, so they cannot exist once and for all.

D: I see how much more general goodness is than being. For indeed, there is one kind of good in the things that are, and another in the things that are not. By this means, beginning with the more general gifts of the divine bounty and proceeding through the more specific ones, theology establishes a certain order among the primordial causes.

### 120. *Genera and species*

M: Whoever divides rightly should begin with the most general and proceed through the rather general to arrive at the most specific. Goodness is the genus of being, so to speak, while being is held to be a species of goodness. So being is the genus of life, for all things that exist are divided into those that live and those that do not. Not every being lives or is life, and for this reason there is one species of existing things that live or are life, another of those that do not participate in life and are not life. Life is the genus of reason: everything that lives is either rational or irrational, and for this reason there is a species of rational life and another of irrational life. Again, there are two species of reason; one is wisdom and the other is knowledge.[8]

7. Dionysius, *De divinis nominibus* 5.1 (PG 3: 816b).

8. Dionysius, *De divinis nominibus* 5.1 (PG 3: 816b); 5.5 (PG 3: 820a). See Figure 2.

### 121. *What wisdom is*

Wisdom is properly said to be that virtue by which the contemplative mind, whether human or angelic, considers what is divine, eternal, and unchangeable, whether it is turned toward the first cause of all or toward the primordial causes of things, which the Father created all at once in his Word. The wise call this species of reason theology.

### 122. *What knowledge is*

Knowledge is the virtue by which the theoretical mind considers the nature of things that proceed from the primordial causes through generation and are divided into genera and species through differences and properties—whether they are subject to accidents or lack them, whether they are joined to bodies or completely free of them, whether they are distributed in place and time or united and inseparable in their simplicity, beyond places and times. This species of reason is called natural philosophy (*physica*).

### 123. *What natural philosophy is*

*Physica* is the natural knowledge of natures that are accessible to the senses and the intellect. The discipline of morals always follows it. As with the other primordial causes, some are more general and some more specific. But in the supreme cause, supreme unity and supreme equality prevail.

D: Do the effects of the causes participate equally in those causes?

M: No. Among the effects, more creatures participate in some of the causes and fewer in others. There is more participation in Goodness in itself than Being in itself, for the things that are and those that are not participate in the former, but only things that are in the latter. Living and non-living creatures participate in Being, but only those that are alive participate in Life. Rational and irrational creatures participate in Life, but only rational ones in Reason. Wisdom and Knowledge both participate in Reason. But the only participants in Wisdom are those intellects that revolve around God and the principles of nature with an eternal, ineffable motion, beyond every nature of visible and invisible things and beyond themselves.[9] For this reason we should not look for genera or species, multiplicity or scarcity, in the principles of nature themselves, but rather in their participations. That is, difference should not be sought in the causes themselves, which were uniformly, unchangeably, and equally made in the Word of God, but in their effects, which fill the visible and invisible world. In the causes there is supreme equality without diversity, but in the effects, a multiple and infinite variety of differences.

### 124. *What participation is*

D: I do not yet understand what participation is.

M: Everything that exists either participates, is participated-in, or both—or is itself participation. That which is only participated-in, but participates in nothing above itself, is the sole, supreme Beginning of all, which is rightly understood to be God. Indeed, all things participate in him: some immediately in themselves, like the primordial causes, and some by intermediaries, like the subsequent beings that subsist in the causes.

That which only participates, is naturally constituted to participate in what is above itself, but is not participated-in by anything below itself because no natural order exists below it. For example, nothing subsists by participating in bodies. (We do not number shadows among subsistent realities.)

All other things stand somewhere on the scale between God and bodies. They are said to be both participants and participated-in, for we understand that participation is found in all things. Just as there are proportions and proportionalities among numbers, so in the orders of nature there are participations, by which [beings] are joined together in the union of all things and constitute a marvelous harmony.[10] The concord of numbers is proportion, while the combination of proportions is proportionality.[11] So too, the distribution of natural orders

9. Dionysius, *De divinis nominibus* 5.1 (PG 3: 816b).

10. Ibid.

11. Boethius, *De institutione arithmetica* 2.40.

receives the name of participation, while the union of distributions is called universal love because it gathers all things into one in ineffable friendship.

Participation, therefore, is not the assumption of some part, but the distribution of divine gifts and grants[12] through the higher orders to the lower, from the highest on down. Both gifts and grants come immediately to the first order from the highest Good of all. To receive gifts is to be; to receive grants is to be well.[13] That first order distributes being and well-being to the order that follows it. Thus the distribution of being and well-being flows down from the supreme Source of all good gifts and grants through the higher orders to the lower, on a graduated scale, down to the very lowest. We should note that there are two modes of well-being. By the one, all things that exist are said to be good because they were made by the Supreme Good, and insofar as they exist, they participate in goodness. By the other, all things that naturally subsist as good are adorned by the grants of virtues. Not only does the rational and intellectual creation participate in the gifts of grace, that is, the virtues, but even some of the lowest orders of nature participate in divine grace proportionally, according to their measure. Just as all things participate in goodness, they also participate in grace—in goodness that they might exist, in grace that they might be good and beautiful.

We should think similarly about life, sensation, reason, wisdom, and the other divine gifts and grants. In the same way, they are distributed through the higher orders to the lower as far down as they go, although not all gifts descend to the lowest order. To be sure, being and well-being are distributed according to nature even to the lowest point of the created universe. But life does not extend all the way to the lowest order. Bodies are not alive in themselves and are not life, but receive life through the order above them, which is set up for the functions of nourishment and growth;[14] it flourishes in seeds. Sensation descends down to irrational animals. Reason and intellect do not extend beyond rational and intellectual beings.

12. *Dationum et donationum.*

13. Maximus, *Ambigua* 3 (PG 91: 1073c).

14. *Nutritiva et auctiva vita,* a function of the soul. See chap. 78 above.

### 125. *What "gifts" and "grants" are*

D: What is the difference between gifts (*dationes*) and grants (*donationes*)?

M: The distributions by which every nature subsists are properly called gifts, but the distributions of grace that adorn every subsistent nature are grants. Thus nature is given and grace is donated. All being is given; all virtue is properly called a grant. Hence theology says, "Every good gift and every perfect grant is from above, coming down from the Father of lights."[15]

### 126. *What virtue is*

You should also know that virtue is understood in three ways. First, there is a substantial virtue, because everything that subsists does so by means of a natural trinity: being, virtue, and operation.[16] There is also a virtue that fights the corruption of nature, such as health against sickness, or knowledge and wisdom against ignorance and folly. Third is the virtue that opposes evil, such as humility against pride or chastity against lust.

Participation, then, is nothing but the derivation of being, which passes from a higher being to the one after it and from the entity that first possesses being to the next, so that there might be distribution. It is like a whole river that flows from its beginning in a spring. However far it extends, water that first arose in the spring is forever diffused without intermission through its bed. In the same way the divine goodness, being, life, wisdom, and all that is in the Source of all things, flows first into the primordial causes and makes them exist. Then it runs through the primordial causes into their effects in an ineffable way, always flowing from the higher to the lower through the harmonious orders of the universe. Again, through the most secret pores of nature, all things return to their source by way of a deeply hidden channel.

15. Jas 1.17. Ordinary Latin does not make Honorius's distinction between gifts (*data, dationes*) and donations or grants (*dona, donationes*), corresponding to the theological distinction between nature and grace.

16. Dionysius, *De caelesti hierarchia* 11.2 (PG 3: 284d). Cf. chapters 50 and 95.

### 127. *Where virtues come from*

From that source comes all good, all being, all life, all sensation, all reason, all wisdom, every genus, every species, all plenitude, all orders, all unity, all equality, all difference, every place, every time, everything that is and everything that is not, all that is understood and all that is sensed, and all that transcends sensation and intellect.[17]

### 128. *God is all things*

D: It seems that the unchangeable movement, simple multiplication, and inexhaustible diffusion of the supreme, the threefold yet only true Goodness-through-itself—as it diffused from itself, within itself, and toward itself—is the cause of all things. Or rather, it *is* all things.

M: So it is. If, as Dionysius testifies, the understanding of all things *is* all things and she alone understands all things, then she alone *is* all things.[18] For the only gnostic virtue is that which knew all things before they all existed. Outside of herself she knew nothing, for there is nothing outside her, but only within her. She encompasses all things, and there is nothing within her, insofar as it truly exists, except herself; for she alone truly is. Other things that are said to exist are her theophanies, which also truly subsist within her.

God therefore is all that truly exists, for he makes all and becomes in all.[19] Everything that is understood and perceived is nothing but an appearance of what does not appear, a manifestation of the hidden, an affirmation of what is denied, incomprehensible comprehension, ineffable speech, inaccessible access, unintelligible intellect, incorporeal body, superessential essence, formless form, immeasurable measure, innumerable number, weight of the weightless, spiritual coarsening, invisible visibility, placeless locality, timeless temporality, definition of

17. Dionysius, *De divinis nominibus* 4.10 (PG 3: 705c–708a).

18. Dionysius, *De ecclesiastica hierarchia* 1.3 (PG 3: 376a). The antecedent is *bonitas,* so I follow Honorius in using feminine pronouns. "She" in this paragraph is identical with "he" in the next.

19. *Ipse facit omnia et fit in omnibus.* Dionysius, *Epistola* 9.3 (PG 3: 1109c).

the infinite, circumscription of the uncircumscribed—and other things that are known and perceived by the pure intellect, but cannot be captured in the net of memory, and that flee the mind's gaze.

This is like our intellect, invisible and incomprehensible in itself, which is revealed and understood by certain signs when it is embodied in sounds or letters. Yet it subsists incorporeally in itself, and even as it appears outwardly, it remains forever invisible within. From the matter of the air it makes itself vehicles, as it were, which can carry it to the senses of others. Quickly abandoning these, it freely penetrates hearts, mingles with other intellects, and becomes one with those to which it is joined. Even as it does these things, it always remains in itself. While it moves, it stands still; while it stands, it moves; and while it is united to others, it does not lose its simplicity. In the same way, the ineffable diffusion of divine goodness through all things makes all things, becomes in all things, and *is* all things.

### 129. *What "out of nothing" means*

D: Your analogy fails in this respect, I think. Our intellect both makes and receives the vehicles that convey it to the senses of others from created matter outside of itself. But the divine Goodness, outside of which there is nothing, did not take matter from any of her apparitions, but from nothing. When I hear that God created all things from nothing,[20] I do not understand what is signified by that "nothing." Is it a privation of all being, whether substance or accident? Or is it the excellence of the divine superessentiality?[21]

M: Although theologians say the divine superessentiality

20. 2 Mc 7.28. Following the biblical verse, this chapter uses the technical philosophical term *nichilum,* which is distinct from the ordinary Latin *nichil.* The first term is declined, the second is not. *Nichilum* could be rendered as "nothingness" but that would reify the concept, against the bias of the text.

21. Bernard McGinn notes here (i.e., in Eriugena) "the first explicit appearance in Christian thought of the distinction between *nihil* as privation and *nihil* as eminence, a distinction that was to have a significant later history in thinkers like Eckhart and Cusanus." "The *Periphyseon* as Hexaemeral Commentary," in *A Companion to John Scottus Eriugena,* ed. Adrian Guiu (Brill, 2019), 175.

is non-being, they do not argue that it is nothing, but rather more-than-being. We cannot understand what it is from any argument based on things that exist, so it is called non-being because true reasoning cannot reckon it in the number of things that exist. Yet it is not altogether nothing, for it is understood to be above all things that are and are not.

D: I ask you, then, what should I understand when I hear that God made all things that exist out of nothing?

M: Understand that existing things were made from those that do not exist by virtue of divine Goodness. For things that were not received being; they were made out of nothing, for they did not exist before they were made. The term "nothing" does not designate any matter, any cause of existing things, or any procession or occasion preceding the creation of things that exist. It is not something coessential and coeternal with God, nor something that subsists in itself outside of God, nor something from which God received matter (so to speak) for the fashioning of the world. Rather, it is a name for the absolute privation of all being—or to speak more truly, the absence of all being. For privation is the removal of some condition, so there could be no privation before there was a condition. But there was no condition before the things that exist received the condition of substance.

D: By "nothing," then, is implied the negation and absence of all being or substance, or rather, of all that was created in the nature of things.

M: So it is. For all the interpreters of holy Scripture agree on this: the Maker of the created universe made whatever he wished to make, not out of something, but out of absolutely nothing.

D: I feel myself constrained on all sides by the deep, dark clouds of my thoughts. Indeed, nothing remains to me but faith alone, transmitted by the authority of the holy fathers. But when I try to attain some pure understanding of the things I hold by faith alone, I am driven back by the great obscurity of the most subtle arguments, which elude me. Or rather, my mind's eye is dazzled by excessive brightness.

M: Tell me, I beg, what troubles you so much?

D: The things we have clearly established up to this point seem now to bear down on me obscurely. For we deduced that the primordial causes of all things were eternally made by the Father, once and for all, in his only-begotten Word, that is, his Wisdom. Just as the Father's Wisdom is eternal and coeternal with his Father, so too all things made in it are eternal. The only difference is that they were all made in Wisdom, which is unmade but begotten and creative, for the Son has one and the same will and operation as the Father. In the first causes, therefore, all things are eternal in the Father's Wisdom, yet they are not coeternal with it. For the cause precedes its effects just as the artisan's understanding precedes his art.

M: We discussed these questions with true reasoning and deduced them by firm authority, establishing an unshakable habit of mind.

D: Don't you see that I am rightly shaken and dashed between floods of mutually exclusive thoughts? For how can these arguments be reconciled? If all things that exist in the creative Wisdom are eternal, how were they made from nothing? And how can anything that was made in time and along with time be eternal?

Suppose someone were to say that the primordial causes are forever eternal in the Father's Wisdom, yet the formless matter in and through which they come forth in their effects through generation, producing the genera and species that fill the world, is not eternal. That person would be compelled to admit that matter, which was made from nothing, cannot be numbered causally among the eternal causes of things. And if he conceded this, he would necessarily have to conclude that not all things exist in the Father's Wisdom, but only some. But no right-thinking philosopher would deny that formless matter should be counted in the number of all things made by God in his Wisdom. For who can say that the causes of all things were eternally created in the Word of God, yet formless matter lacks its own cause? I can by no means discover this. Hence, if matter is included in the number of the created universe, it necessarily follows that its cause cannot be excluded from the number of causes eternally created in the Wisdom of God.

### 130. *That matter is created*

M: Concerning formless matter, which the Greeks call *hyle,* no one who thinks rightly about the creation of natures has any doubt that it was created by the Creator of all, both causally among the causes and also among their effects, according to their proportions. For he who made the world from formless matter[22] himself made that formless matter from absolutely nothing.[23] There is not one author of the world made from formless matter and another of the matter previously created from nothing, but one and the same Creator of both. For all things that exist, whether formless or formed, proceed from one Beginning. The universe was created by the One, just as all numbers break out of the monad and all lines derive from the center.[24]

The secular philosophers are convicted of a great error in this, for they said that formless matter is coeternal with God, who took command of his works from it, as if using something that existed outside himself and was coeternal with him.[25] It seemed to them unworthy that formless matter should have been created by God, who is the form of all things,[26] invariable and immutable. But they were blinded by clouds of false reasoning. We, however, following the truth of holy Scripture, believe by faith that both the formlessness and the forms of all things, and everything that is in them according to essence or accident, were created by the one cause of all. We believe this by faith and contemplate it by intellect, so far as is given to us.

### 131. *God creates like and unlike things*

The almighty Creator, who is deficient in nothing and extends to infinity, was able to create—and did create—not only things like himself, but also those unlike. For if he had created

22. Wis 11.18; cf. Augustine, *De Genesi ad litteram* 1.14 (CSEL 28.1, 21).
23. Augustine, *De vera religione* 18.36 (CCSL 32, 209).
24. Dionysius, *De divinis nominibus* 5.6 (PG 3: 820d–821a).
25. Augustine, *Contra Faustum* 11.1 (PL 42: 387–89).
26. Augustine, *De vera religione* 55.113 (CCSL 32, 259); *Sermones* 117 (PL 38: 662–63).

only things like himself—truly existing, eternal, unchangeable, incorruptible, immortal, and intellectual—he would have seemed to fall short in the creation of unlike and opposite things. Then he would not have been judged to be the maker of absolutely everything that reason finds capable of coming to be. The things unlike and opposite to him are said to be (and are) all that oppose the aforesaid qualities, not by negation or privation, but by unlikeness and opposition of nature. Indeed, mobility and matter, which is still imperfectly formed, are opposed to perfect being. Temporal things are opposed to eternal, changeable to changeless, and compound to simple, standing in a diametrically, mutually opposed relation. Yet all these like and unlike things have one and the same Artisan, whose omnipotence fails in no operation of nature.

Thus the beauty of the whole created universe is established by a wonderful harmony of like and unlike, gathered into a certain ineffable unity out of the diverse genera, varied forms, and different orders of substances and accidents. Musical harmony[27] is created from diverse vocal qualities and intervals, differing proportionally, but rendering a sweet accord through natural aptitude in the art of music. In the same way, the harmony of the universe derives from the diverse subdivisions of a single nature, which seem dissonant when they are considered individually, but are united in accord with the uniform will of the Creator. All things that are and that are not, therefore, flow from one Beginning of all—whether in the primordial causes, which were eternally made once and for all in the Word of God; or in the formless matter from which those causes found occasion to make the visible creation appear through generation; or in their effects, by which this world completes its course from beginning to end in its natural order, under the guidance of divine Providence.

27. *Organicum melos,* probably referring to *organum,* in which men's and boys' voices chanted the same vocal line at an interval, often a fourth. Full polyphony still lay centuries in the future. Honorius uses a more elaborate version of this analogy in a famous passage from his *Liber XII quaestionum,* c. 2 (PL 172: 1179b).

### 132. *That all things are both created and eternal*

D: For seekers of truth, I think no question is deeper than this one: how can all things be simultaneously eternal and created? For created things are opposed to eternal ones: if they were made, they are not eternal, and if they are eternal, they were not made. I cannot find an argument by which anyone could teach that the same things are simultaneously eternal and created.

M: The dazzling subtlety of this question nearly repels the gaze of our contemplation. Yet, illumined by God, let us not hesitate to investigate it, lest we incur the fault of idleness or inertia. Nothing is accidental to God, and if nothing is accidental to him, it is not by means of an accident that he created the universe. Scripture is not silent about this, but openly proclaims, "In the beginning God made heaven and earth," and so forth.[28]

D: God created the universe, and creating it was not accidental to him.

M: Then he did not exist before he created the universe, for if he had, the creation of things would be accidental to him.

D: God precedes the universe not in time, but solely because he is understood to be the cause of all things. For if he preceded it in time, it would be accidental to him to create the universe in time.

M: If, then, God precedes the universe he created in no other respect than as its cause, being a causal agent is not accidental to God, for he is always a cause. But the universe subsists eternally in its cause. It is manifest, then, that the whole created universe is eternal in the Word of God.

D: I cannot deny this conclusion when I consider that all numbers eternally and uniformly exist in the monad, and all lines in the center. Although they may be formed into various kinds of numbers and figures by someone who is counting or drawing, yet they always remain uniformly in their beginnings, that is, the monad and the center. We understand that their beginnings were never without them, nor did their becoming have a starting point in those beginnings. While they flow out of

28. Gn 1.1.

them in multiples, yet by a uniform reason, they do not cease to be within them in an eternal, unchangeable state.[29]

### 133. *All things are eternal in the Word of God*

M: The testimonies of Scripture and the holy fathers likewise affirm that all things are eternal in God. The Apostle says, "In him we live and move and have our being."[30] We have our being in God through the reason of our being, which exists in him. We move in God through the virtues of good action. We live in God according to the aforesaid reason of living well and existing in him.[31] Lest anyone should think that we are one thing and our reasons another, the Apostle did not say, "in him our reasons live and move and have their being." Rather, he said "in him *we* live and move and have our being." For us to have being, insofar as we have it, means nothing but this: our reasons themselves eternally subsist in God.

St. Augustine also affirms that the ages are "not made, but eternal in the dispensation of God's Word."[32] Again, he says that "all things unchangeably live in the Word of God, through which all things were made—not only those that have been, but also those that will be. Yet in him they neither were nor will be, but simply *are*. And all are one, or rather, all *is* one."[33] Concerning the Word of God, he says, "In one way the things that were made through him are beneath him. But in another way they are in him, as things that he himself is."[34] Those creatures that are in God, and are said to *be* God, are not other than those that come into the world through generation. Rather, one and the same nature of things is considered one way in the eternity of the Word of God, another way in the temporality of the created world. St. Dionysius also says, "He is called the One, for he is all things in general."[35] Through these and similar testimonies, we

29. Dionysius, *De divinis nominibus* 5.6 (PG 3: 820d–821a).

30. Acts 17.28.

31. Maximus, *Ambigua* 3 (PG 91: 1084bc); 6.3 (PG 91: 1116b); 38 (PG 91: 1329b); 61 (PG 91: 1392a).

32. Bede, *De natura rerum* 1 (PL 90: 188a).

33. Augustine, *De Trinitate* 4.1 (CCSL 50, 162).

34. Augustine, *De Genesi ad litteram* 2.6 (CSEL 28.1, 41).

35. Dionysius, *De divinis nominibus* 13.2 (PG 3: 977c).

are given to understand not only that all things are eternal in the Word of God, but also that they are the Word itself.

### 134. *All things are created in the Word of God*

The testimonies of holy Scripture declare very clearly that all things are simultaneously created and eternal in the Word of God. John the Evangelist says, "All things were made through him, and without him nothing was made."[36] See how plainly he says that all things were made in the Word! But lest anyone should think they were only created and not eternal, there follows, "What was made in him was life."[37] It is as if he said, "What was made" (either in the principal causes or in their effects) "in him" (the Word, in which the reasons of all things are eternal) "was life."[38] Again, the Apostle says, "In him were created all things in heaven and on earth, whether visible or invisible; all things were created by him, through him, and in him."[39] "The causes of things that exist," as Maximus says, "were foreordained before the ages in the will of God, according to which he fashioned the visible and invisible creation out of non-existence. By reason and wisdom, he made and makes all things at an opportune time, both in general and as individuals."[40]

None of the faithful should doubt that all things are simultaneously eternal in the Word of God and created. For both true reasoning and the authority of holy Scripture unanimously agree on this. The eternal things are not other than those that were made, but the same things are simultaneously both eternal and created.

### 135. *That the Son of God is Word, reason, and cause*

D: I ask you to explain how eternal things are created and how created things are eternal.

M: The reasons of all things, which are understood to be

36. Jn 1.3.
37. Jn 1.3–4.
38. Augustine, *De Genesi ad litteram* 5.14 (CSEL 28.1, 157).
39. Col 1.16; Maximus, *Ambigua* 3 (PG 91: 1077c–1080a).
40. Maximus, *Ambigua* 3 (PG 91: 1080a).

in the very nature of the superessential Word, are eternal. For whatever substantially exists in God the Word is necessarily eternal because it is nothing other than the Word itself. From this it follows that the Word itself is the manifold, most primordial reason of the whole created universe. We can also say that God the Word is the simple, manifold, and primordial reason of all things.

The Greeks call him Logos, which means "word," "reason," or "cause." He is indeed the Word because through him God the Father spoke all things into being. Or rather, he is himself the Father's speech, utterance, and expression, as he said: "The word that I have spoken to you is not mine, but the word of him who sent me."[41] In other words, I am the Word of the Father who has spoken to you. He is reason because he is the principal exemplar of all visible and invisible things. Therefore, the Greeks call him *idea,* which means "species" or "form," for in him the Father saw everything he wished to make before it came into being. He is also the cause, for the occasions of all things subsist in him eternally and unchangeably. He is simple because in him the whole universe is one, undivided, and inseparable. Indeed, the Word of God is the undivided, inseparable unity of all things, for he *is* all things.

Yet he is manifold because he is diffused through all things to infinity, and that diffusion is the subsistence of them all. "For he reaches from end to end mightily and orders all things sweetly."[42] Again in the Psalm: "His word runs swiftly."[43] The Father's Word runs swiftly through all things so that they might all exist, for his course through all things is the manifold, infinite subsistence of them all. Dionysius testifies that he abides in himself universally and simply, for in him are all things. "He reaches from end to end" and "runs swiftly" through all things, that is, without delay he makes all things and becomes all in all. And while he subsists in himself as one, perfect and more-than-perfect, separate from all things, he extends himself into all things, and that extension *is* all things.[44] Hence the

41. Jn 12.48–49.
42. Wis 8.1.
43. Ps 147.15.
44. Dionysius, *De divinis nominibus* 13.1 (PG 3: 977bc).

word "cherubim" means "outpouring of wisdom."[45] Indeed, the outpouring, extension, or course of the Father's wisdom precedes all things; it is the cause of their existence and is itself all things.

Who that considers the truth would believe or think that God prepared himself places through which he could diffuse himself—he who is contained in no place, but is the common place of all (and therefore the place of places, captured by no place)? Who would think that he prepared himself local or temporal spaces through which he might extend himself and run his course—he who lacks all space and in his eternity transcends all times? Not only to say, but even to think such things about the ineffable, superessential nature is to invent false imaginings. It is most absurd and most pernicious.

### 136. *Error is the death of the soul*

There is no worse, more shameful death of the rational soul than to imagine such monstrous, abominable idolatries about the Creator of all. To intellects that piously seek the Creator, this is what Truth itself proclaims universally, with intelligible voice: For all things that are and that are not—that is, for those that can be comprehended by sense or intellect, and those that transcend sense and intellect—subsistence is nothing but participation in the one and only Cause of all. Everything that is participated-in precedes both its participation and the things that participate in it. God therefore precedes all things that participate in him, whose being is their participation. Hence Dionysius the Areopagite writes in *The Celestial Hierarchy* (that is, *The Supreme Sovereignty*):[46] "The superessential divinity, subtending the essences of the things that are, draws them into being. For the being of all things is the super-being of divinity. By existence, therefore, all things participate in being."[47]

Participation in the divine being is assumption. But assumption is the outpouring of divine Wisdom, which is the substance

45. Dionysius, *De caelesti hierarchia* 7.1 (PG 3: 205b).
46. *Summo principatu.*
47. Dionysius, *De celesti hierarchia* 4.1 (PG 3: 177cd).

and essence of all things and whatever is naturally understood to be in them. The abiding of divine Goodness is the changeless cause of all things, but its procession and ineffable motion accomplish the effects of all. So participation and assumption are nothing but the being of all things. God therefore is "the most perfect providence, the causal agent of being and well-being for all things."[48] The providence of all things is not different from the cause of all, but it is one and the same God who "proceeds into all and becomes in all" (that is, in the universe that he makes), "and contains all things."[49]

## 137. *God becomes in all things*

We therefore understand that the Wisdom of God the Father, of whom such things are predicated, is not only the creative Cause of all things, but is also created and comes to be in all that she creates, and contains all things in which she becomes. For whatever is truly understood to exist in all things is nothing but the manifold virtue of creative Wisdom, which subsists in all things. If you were mentally to take creative Wisdom away from all the things she creates, they would be utterly reduced to nothing. No being, no life, no sense, no reason, no intellect, and absolutely no good would remain. Augustine also testifies that the whole creation, considered in itself, is absolutely nothing. Whatever is understood to subsist in it, subsists by participation in creative Truth.[50] If every true thing is true by participation in Truth, and Truth alone abides, other things can be removed because they verge on nothing. Truth alone, therefore, subsists in all true things. If the Word of God both makes all things and becomes in them all,[51] then we have proven that everything we understand to subsist in the Word is simultaneously eternal and created. The Wisdom that creates all things becomes in them all; and the cause in and through which they are both eternal and created, is itself both eternal and created in them.

48. Dionysius, *Epistola* 9.3 (PG 3:1109c).
49. Ibid.
50. Augustine, *Confessions* 7.11.
51. Dionysius, *Epistola* 9.3 (PG 3: 1109c).

### 138. *The world was made from formless matter*

D: I marvel greatly and come to a standstill, stupefied and out of breath. For I am attracted by these arguments, which are plausible and corroborated by the testimonies of the holy fathers and holy Scripture. Yet again, I falter and draw back, quickly slipping back into the thick darkness of my thoughts. The keen gaze of my mind is not sufficient to examine and fully penetrate the depth of the present question.

Hearing the verse, "you who made the world from formless matter,"[52] I used to think it meant that the visible and invisible world was made from formless matter, which God created out of absolutely nothing as a kind of omen of his operation. There was a time when the whole universe did not exist. Therefore, in the first beginnings of its creation from absolutely nothing, it proceeded into formless matter, and consequently arrived through genera, forms, and other natural numbers at a perfection known to the Creator alone.

St. Augustine argues that it was not made through intervals of time, for formlessness precedes form not in time, but in the natural order by which a cause comes before its effect. By analogy, a voice and a word come forth at the same time from the mouth of a speaker, yet the voice comes before the word, not in time but in cause. For the word is produced by the voice; by no means does the voice come from the word. In the same way, the formless state of all things as well as their formation and perfection were brought out of nothing into being, once and for all, by the Creator's will—according to a natural procession and sequence, but not in distinct intervals of time.[53] This was my faith and my understanding, however slight.

### 139. *The world is eternal*

But now I hear you say different things that greatly trouble me, recalling me firmly but unwillingly, as it seems to me, from the views I have held until now. Your present argument, I think,

52. Wis 11.18.

53. Augustine, *De Genesi ad litteram* 1.14–15 (CSEL 28.1, 20–22).

wants to persuade me that the things I used to think were created from nothing, and by no means eternal, are simultaneously eternal and created. I believe this is a great contradiction, for eternal things seem opposed to the created and the created to the eternal. Eternal things never begin and never cease to exist; there was never a time when they were not, for they have always existed. But those that were created had a beginning when they were made. They began to be, for there was a time when they were not; and they will cease to be what they have begun to possess.

### 140. *The world will pass away*

If we consult true reasoning, nothing that begins to exist in time is allowed to remain forever. It necessarily comes to an end; whatever begins in time is compelled to perish. But let no one think that I mean to argue that things that come into being in the world in time, from matter, through generation, are reduced to nothing. That would be a supreme evil. I mean, rather, that they dissolve into [the elements] from which they are composed and in which they subsist. For the bodies of human beings and other animals are said to perish when they are dissolved, yet they are not reduced to nothing; they return to the whole. We understand this in general, aptly enough, to concern the whole of this visible world. Because its existence had a beginning, its being will inevitably come to an end. As it was when it was not, so it will be when it is no longer. This is what the Psalmist testifies, proclaiming to the eternal Creator of things: "The heavens are the works of your hands; they will perish, but you will remain forever."[54] The Creator of all says himself, "Heaven and earth will pass away."[55]

But this is the part greatest in size, with the magnificent sublimity of the constellations and the purest subtlety of nature, strewn with the fixed stars, musical in their courses, forever filled with light. If even that part of the world is to perish, as Scripture testifies, should we think that its inner parts, which are

54. Ps 101.26–27.
55. Mk 13.31.

far inferior, will remain? No, if the better parts must pass away, it is impossible that the inferior will not also perish. When the container is taken away, true reason does not allow what is contained in it to remain.

We say all this to contrast things that are eternal with those that are made. For there is no small difference between those things that never began and never cease to exist, and those that begin to exist and cannot remain forever. It is not without cause that the mind's eye recoils from the argument that eternal things are created and created things eternal.

I would not easily believe you to agree with those who understand that many (or almost all) of the things that are made will remain forever and thus become eternal. For example, they say that "this universe, which consists of heaven and earth, massed together from the four elements in the form of a sphere,"[56] which is called the world and made out of nothing, will remain eternally except for certain small parts of it—the corruptible bodies subject to generation and corruption. For they cannot deny that those will perish. But the heaven with its constellations will remain forever, whether it continues to rotate or its movement ceases. On that point their opinions vary. Some affirm the future stability of mutable things, but others say the natural movement of the elements will never cease. The former follow the scriptural verse, "All things will be at rest,"[57] understanding it to concern the future stability of mutable things. But others cite this verse: "Who can silence the harmony of heaven?"[58] They think it was said about the eternal motion of mutable things. Indeed, how could the celestial harmony resound without the movement of the ethereal sphere and all the constellations? Music is always in motion, just as geometry is in stasis. They also affirm that this earthly globe will doubtless always have its own quantity, following the verse: "A generation comes, a generation goes, but the earth remains forever."[59] But they make this exception: its surface will be leveled on all sides,

56. Bede, *De natura rerum* 3 (PL 90: 192a).
57. Wis 18.14.
58. Jb 38.37.
59. Eccl 1.4.

so it will become more beautiful than it is now and will be renewed with a new equality of its parts. It is not that the present earth will perish, but it will abide, with its quantity and equality changed for the better. They want the heaven to be understood in the same way: its beauty, which even now smiles on the bodily senses, will increase at the end of the world, yet without destruction of its spherical form and painted, star-spangled surface. For it is written, as they say, "There will be a new heaven and a new earth."[60]

They understand the saying that the heavens will perish to concern not the upper parts of the world, but the space of this atmosphere below the moon. Just as this air was turned into water in the Flood, at the end of the world it will be turned into flame. Not only do they not deny, but also they openly affirm, that the waxing and waning of all things within the moon's orbit will cease their regular changes. Again, they believe that the spaces of the air and the ether are to be divided. The ether will become the eternal possession of the blessed angels and human beings who are like them. But the lower atmosphere surrounding the earth will become an eternal prison, with eternal flames locally and visibly burning to torture the devil with his members, that is, fallen angels and wicked humans who are like them.[61] Because they think that the whole creation both is and will continue to be local and temporal, that is, the world's dimensions and motion are marked by intervals of time, they do not doubt that it will remain forever.

With these and similar false opinions, they try to assert that things that were not and began to exist can be called simultaneously created and eternal. For they will always remain in the same state in which they were created in time. They believe that things which do not lack a beginning will lack an end, so they are both created because they began to exist, and eternal because they will never cease to exist. Nevertheless, I cannot imagine that you agree with such opinions, which true reason mocks. Nor do I think that in your previous arguments, you made the

60. Is 65.17; Is 66.22; 2 Pt 3.13; Rv 21.1.

61. Augustine, *De Genesi ad litteram* 3.9 (CSEL 28.1, 71–72); 3.10 (CSEL 28.1, 73–74); 11.26 (CSEL 28.1, 359).

case for such an eternity (or to speak more truly, semi-eternity), or taught that things are simultaneously created and eternal in this way. Rather, I believe you penetrate the hidden divine mysteries with a deeper gaze into their natures, beyond human opinions, using a method still unknown to us and following in the footsteps of the fathers, who explored such things deeply.

### 141. *The archetypal world will remain*

They say that the nature of this world will remain forever because it is incorporeal and incorruptible. But the other things of which it consists will perish—that is, everything in it that is composite. Because there is no body in the world that is not composite, and every compound will be dissolved into the things that compose it, this whole visible, corporeal, composite world will be dissolved. Only its simple nature will remain.

M: I cannot deny that I was once deceived by the false reasoning of human opinions, far removed from the truth. Indeed, I was deceived! For in my ignorance, I assented to all or almost all of this rubbish, seduced by a certain analogy to the truth and by my carnal senses. This happens to many people. But now, following the footsteps of the holy fathers, I withdraw my foot a little as a ray of divine light recalls me from my errors (and those of others) and leads me into the right path. Indeed, divine mercy does not allow those who humbly, piously seek the truth in the darkness of ignorance to go astray, fall into the pit of false opinions, and perish there. For no death is worse than ignorance of the truth, no abyss more profound than to take falsehood for truth, which is the property of error. It is clear from these things that I fabricated the most foul, abominable monstrosities in human thinking. When the carnal soul loves and follows such things as if they were true, turning its back on the true light as it wishes to comprehend fugitive shadows, yet cannot, it normally falls into an abyss of misery.

D: It remains to mention something that greatly troubles me. Namely, how can all things be both eternal and created, and how can things that have no beginning or end be circumscribed by a beginning and an end? These positions are mutually contradictory. What seems to me incomparably deeper and more wonderful than everything is that you assert, on the authority of St. Dionysius the Areopagite, that God himself is both the Creator of all and created in all things. This teaching is still unheard-of and unknown, not only to me but to many, in fact almost everyone.[62] For if it is so, who will not at once burst out and proclaim, "Then God is everything and everything is God"? This will be thought monstrous even by those who are held to be wise, given the manifold variety of visible and invisible things. Yet God is one! Unless you can prove these points by a natural example, you will be accused of great heresy.[63]

### 142. *All numbers are in the monad*

M: Is arithmetic a natural art?

D: None is more natural.

M: In arithmetic, therefore, the monad or unity is the beginning, middle, and end of all numbers. It is the whole, the part, and every quantity of all limits.

D: Whoever doubts this is ignorant of arithmetic.

M: Tell me, then: do all numbers, which reason can multiply as much as it wishes, exist in the monad causally and eternally?

D: True reason does not teach otherwise. For they exist in it causally because it subsists as the beginning of all numbers. There they are all undivided, simply and universally; they are multiple in reason alone, but not in act and operation. The monad is the cause and substance of all numbers. They all eternally subsist in it and do not begin to exist in time.

M: So if the monad, or unity, is the beginning, middle, and end of all numbers, then all numbers subsist eternally in the monad. When they flow forth from it, they do not cease to be in it, for they cannot abandon their natural state. By analogy, then, as numbers are eternal in the monad but come into being by multiplication, the universe is eternal in the Word of God, but comes into being temporally in its effects.

62. Dionysius, *Epistola* 9.3 (PG 3: 1109c).

63. Prophetic words. Eriugena was condemned for heresy (pantheism) in 1210 and again in 1225.

D: I fully see that numbers cannot come into being except by multiplication, for they are eternal in the monad. But I still do not see how, whence, or where they come from.

M: All numbers forever exist causally in the monad, that is, in force and potency. But the monad subsists eternally in wisdom and knowledge. It is not that some numbers are established by force and potency in the monad, while others exist in act and operation in the genera and species of intelligible numbers. Rather, it is the same numbers that flow forth.

D: They are in the monad by force and potency, but the same numbers exist in act and operation in genera and forms.

M: Do you see, then, that the same numbers are eternal where they are causally present in force and potency, that is, in the monad, but where they are understood in act and operation, they are created?

### 143. *What force and potency are*

D: I see. But I ask what the force and potency of numbers in the monad are, and what their act and operation are in genera and forms.

M: Force is their substantial virtue, by which they subsist eternally and immutably in the monad. Potency is the possibility by which they can be multiplied in genera and species. Act is the movement of the mind as it contemplates the purest numbers in their nature, without imagination. Operation is the movement of the same mind as it commends the numbers (which it contemplates in itself) to memory, coarsened by phantasms as if by bodies.

Intellect and reason do not create the intellectual numbers in themselves. Rather, they come into being in human and angelic intellects from the one Creator of all, by whom they are eternally established. Through the intellect, they descend into ideas. Any art passes from the knowledge in which it subsists by way of the intellect into reason. It makes a second descent from reason into memory, where it declares itself more openly in phantasms as if in certain forms. By a third descent, it diffuses itself to the corporeal senses, where it reveals its power by sensible signs through genera and species. Thus the intellectual numbers diffuse themselves from the monad to shine out in the mind in a certain way. Then, flowing from the mind into reason, they reveal themselves more openly. Quickly descending from reason into memory, from the nature of the memory they receive fantastic appearances, in which they clearly reveal the powers of their multiple forms to those who inquire about them. Next they descend into the senses, and finally into figures.

Now do you see those three points that you asked about—how, where, and whence?

Whence? From the monad.

Where? In the intellect.

How? By different degrees. Numbers descend first from themselves into the intellect, then from the intellect into reason, from reason into memory, and from memory into the bodily senses. In the last stage, if it is necessary for the benefit of learners, they descend from the senses to visible figures.

### 144. *What a fantasy and a phantasm are*

D: I see now that numbers are both eternal and created: eternal in the monad, but created as they are formed in multiples when they descend in fantasies. But I ask, what is the difference between a fantasy and a phantasm?[64]

M: Images that come outwardly through the bodily senses are properly called fantasies, while those that come from memory are phantasms. For example, a fantasy is an image of a certain body I have seen, whether in color or in dimensions, and imprint on the memory through sensation. But a phantasm is the image I fashion of something I have never seen. Either it does not exist at all or, if it does, it is not as I imagine it.[65]

64. *Inter fantasiam et fantasma*—a distinction that does not recur. I have generally preferred the term "phantasm" because the English meanings of "fantasy," either as a psychological phenomenon or an artistic genre, are so far from what Honorius has in mind. What he defines here as a "phantasm" is closer to what we mean by a "fantasy."

65. Augustine, *De Genesi ad litteram* 12.6 (CSEL 28.1, 386–87); 12.23 (CSEL 28.1, 414–15); *De musica* 6.11.32 (PL 32: 1180–81).

### 145. *Numbers come into being in two ways*

D: It seems that numbers, eternally subsistent in the monad, are created in two ways: either in the mind and reason through understanding, without imagination, or in the memory and bodily senses through imagination, fattened as it were, as if made from matter.

M: This is so, but they do not come into being from matter. Rather, they are born incorporeal from incorporeal things, namely from form, which is incorporeal, and colors, which are not bodies but understood around bodies. So just as all numbers are eternal in the monad, they come into being in the intellect and reason or else in memory and sensation. Or rather, Unity itself, which is in itself eternal, comes into being in them all. In the same way, all things which are from God are simultaneously eternal and created. Or rather, God himself is both the Creator of all things and comes into being in all.[66]

D: In my opinion, all numbers flow from the monad as from a fountain, just as two rivers arising from one source seem to flow within two separate beds. One is through the inner pores of nature, that is, through intellect and reason. The other runs through the outer forms of visible things and through the senses, until the two flow together in memory, where they are formed in manifold ways.

But I still do not see how incorporeal things, which are remote not only from the senses but even from memory, can appear in memory and the senses—that is, in images and visible figures, as if in bodies.

### 146. *The soul of Moses*

M: In the nature of spiritual things, many apparitions do not occur according to the known or unknown laws of nature, but they come about in a marvelous, ineffable way beyond all laws, by the will of God unconstrained by law. Who can account for the way the soul of Moses visibly appeared at the Lord's Transfiguration?[67] We should pay no heed to those who think he

66. Dionysius, *Epistola* 9.3 (PG 3: 1109c).
67. Mt 17.3.

was raised in the body at that time and visibly appeared on the mountain with Elijah, not as a soul but in his body, and returned again to the tomb. Who then will say how a soul, which is incorporeal and invisible, was seen visibly and corporeally when it appeared neither in its body, nor in sensible matter taken from anywhere else? But by some ineffable power known to God alone, the invisible spirit was made visible in itself.

### 147. *The soul of Samuel*

What will you say about the soul of Samuel? We should not believe those who say it was not he that appeared, but some figment in his likeness. They think it unworthy that the incantations of the Pythoness should have recalled a holy soul from the underworld.[68] But they take no account of divine providence, nor of the fact that through impure spirits as well as pure ones it governs the nature of things. On the testimony of Augustine, we agree that the soul of Samuel itself, not in its body or in any likeness, visibly prophesied to the king who consulted him.[69] But let us return to the manifest examples of nature, which no right-thinking philosopher contests.

### 148. *Incorporeal forms*

D: What are they?

M: The wise say they are the incorporeal forms of things. Consulting true reason, they pronounce the same opinion they have about colors, which are incorporeal.

D: Whoever doubts this has no place among philosophers.

M: Then if forms and colors are reckoned in the number of incorporeal things, explain, if you can, why they are accessible to the bodily senses. For everything that is perceived can be perceived only as a colored form.

D: I think that forms and colors cannot appear in themselves, but they appear in some kind of matter that is subject to them.

M: Matter without form and color is entirely invisible and

68. 1 Sm 28.7–20.

69. Augustine, *De cura pro mortuis gerenda* 15.18 (CSEL 41, 651–52).

incorporeal. So you could more reasonably say that formless matter appears to the senses in colors and forms, rather than that forms and colors appear in matter. For matter comes into being from a joining of intelligible things. Quantities and qualities, while they are incorporeal in themselves, produce formless matter when they come together in one. By the addition of forms and incorporeal colors, this matter is changed into different bodies.[70] Bodies, then, are born of incorporeal things, for they do not come from nothing but from something. For who would say that their aforesaid occasions are nothing—that is, quantities and qualities, forms and species, colors, the dimensions of length, breadth, and height, and together with these, places and times? If you take these away, there will be no bodies. But if you join them, bodies soon come into being—whether universal, like the four greatest bodies in the world, or individual bodies distributed to the most specific things. I believe you will not deny that all these bodies are composed of the four simple elements because they are dissolved into them.

D: I will not deny it. But I would say that those elements, which are simple in themselves and produce all bodies through their composition, are made out of nothing.

### 149. *All things are in the cause*

M: What then will you say about the primordial causes? If all bodies come from the elements, but the elements come from nothing, then their cause will seem to be nothing. It necessarily follows that either the Word of God, in which the Father made all things, is nothing—or else we must posit some cause called "nothing" outside of the Word, a cause from which God made all things and in which he established them before they came to be. Either it is not a cause, or, if it is, I do not see why it is called "nothing." In fact, I would sooner say that the cause is everything than that it is nothing. For all things subsist causally and primordially in their proper cause.

D: I am compelled to admit that the four elements of the world subsist in the primordial causes. For these are the causes

70. Gregory of Nyssa, *De hominis opificio* 24 (PG 44: 212d–213b).

not only of the elements, but universally of all things visible and invisible. Nothing is perceived in all the orders of nature, whether by sense, reason, or intellect, that does not proceed from them and subsist in them causally.

### 150. *All bodies come from the four elements*

M: If I am not mistaken, you will not deny that all bodies, which occupy the lowest place among all natures, are composite and subject to dissolution. They exist from something, not from nothing.

D: I will not deny it. They are produced from the qualities and quantities of simple, invisible bodies that are not comprehensible to the senses. These are called "elements" because the investigators of nature say that all bodies are composed by their combination,[71] dissolved into them, and preserved in them. They are also commonly called "universal" because all individual bodies come from them. Again, I confess that the elements were not made from nothing, but they proceed from the primordial causes. None of the faithful doubt that these causes were made once for all in the Word of God, hearing the prophet who says to God, "In wisdom you have made all things."[72] And at the very start of holy Scripture it is written, "In the beginning God made heaven and earth."[73]

### 151. *Where the primordial causes come from*

M: It remains, then, for us to ask about the primordial causes. Were they made from nothing in the Word of God, or were they always in him? If they were always in him, there never was when they were not, just as there was never a time when the Word was not, in whom they existed.[74] And if they were always in him, how were they made from nothing in him? For it is not reasonable to

71. Plato, *Timaeus* 48b–c.

72. Ps 103.24.

73. Gn 1.1.

74. "There never was when he was not": a phrase commonly used to assert the eternity of the Word and oppose christological heresies in the fourth century.

say that things that have always existed had their beginning from nothing. If anyone were to say, "That 'nothing' from which they were made always existed, and they were always made from it," we should ask him, "Where did that 'nothing' always exist—in the Word of God in which all things subsist, or in itself outside the Word?" If he replies, "It was always in the Word," let him be opposed in this way: "Then it was not nothing, but something great." For all things that subsist in the Word of God subsist truly and naturally. What was thought to be nothing (but from which we believe all things were made) will be counted in the order of primordial causes. But if he thinks the "nothing" existed in itself outside the Word, he will seem to imagine two mutually opposing principles as a Manichaean does.

In fact, many secular philosophers thought that the formless matter from which God made all his works was coeternal with him.[75] They called that matter "nothing" because, before it received forms and species, it did not appear at all, as if it were absolutely nothing. For whatever is completely without form and species can rightly be called "nothing."[76] But the light of truth has expelled all these delusions, proclaiming that all things come from one beginning. In the nature of visible and invisible things, we cannot discover the mode of generation by which whatever has subsisted eternally in the only-begotten Word of God breaks out in its own species. In the Word of God all things are one, and God took no matter or cause outside of himself for the universe he created in his wisdom. For outside of him there is nothing, and within him, that from which he made everything he wished to make in his wisdom is found to be coessential with him.

## 152. *What "from nothing" means*

Thus there is no place for "nothing" either within or outside of God, yet we do not believe in vain that he made all things from nothing. So when we hear that all things were created from nothing, we should understand only this: there was a time

75. Augustine, *Contra Faustum* 11.1 (PL 42: 387–89).
76. Augustine, *De Genesi ad litteram* 5.18 (CSEL 28.1, 161).

when they were not. So it is not unfittingly said, "They always were—yet they were not always. There never was when they were not—yet there was a time when they were not." Indeed, "they always were" in the Word of God causally, by force and potential, beyond all times and places, beyond all generation accomplished in place and time, beyond every form and species known by sense or intellect, beyond every quality, quantity, and other accidents by which we understand the substance of every creature to exist (though not what it is). And "they were not always" because, before they flowed forth through generation into forms and species, places and times, and all the accidents that befall their eternal, changeless subsistence in the Word of God, "they were not" in generation. They did not exist locally, temporally, or in their proper forms and species, which are subject to accidents. Therefore, it is said of them, not unreasonably, "There never was when they were not," because they subsist forever in the Word of God, in which they have no beginning. For eternity is infinite. And yet "there was a time when they were not," for through generation, they began in time to become what they were not, that is, to appear in forms and species.[77]

If anyone attentively considers the nature of things, they will find no nature subject to sense and intellect of which it cannot truly be said, "It always was, is, and shall be—yet it was not, is not, and shall not be always." Its first constitution in the wisdom of God, through the primordial causes, was and is and ever shall be without change. But because that constitution is known to God alone and transcends the senses and intellect of every creature, what it is cannot be known to any created intellect. Through generation, it begins in time to acquire quantities and qualities, through which its existence (though not what it is) can be openly revealed as if by clothing. Therefore, in some sense it begins to exist—not insofar as it subsists in the primordial causes, but insofar as it begins to appear from temporal causes. By temporal causes I mean qualities, quantities, and the other accidents that befall substances through their generation in time. Therefore, it is said of them, "There was a time when they were not," because they did not always appear in their accidents.

77. Augustine, *De Genesi ad litteram* 5.18 (CSEL 28.1, 161).

### 153. *All things are eternal in their causes and temporal in their effects*

By the same reasoning, they are now said to exist; and they truly are and will remain forever insofar as they subsist in their causes. But insofar as they exist with the accidents that befall them from without, they are said to exist, yet they do not exist truly and forever, for they will be dissolved into the components from which they were taken. Nor do they exist truly and forever, given that every substance will be purified of all corruptible accidents and delivered from all that does not pertain to the state of its proper nature. Creation will exist with its natural virtues alone, beautiful, in indissoluble simplicity. And in those who are good it will be adorned with the gifts of grace, glorified by the contemplation of eternal beatitude beyond every nature (including its own), and changed into God himself—having become God not by nature, but by grace. After considering these arguments, who but an extremely slow-witted or contentious person would not grant that all things that come from God are simultaneously eternal and created?

D: Even now, not all doubt has been driven from me. I perceive that all things that come from God are both eternal and created: eternal in the Word of God, but created in their forms, species, and accidents. Yet I cannot fully see how this accords with reason.

M: Then do you think I meant to teach that all things are eternal in the Word of God insofar as they are eternal, but created outside the Word insofar as they are created? For you do not think it accords with truthful reasoning that the whole universe of created nature should be simultaneously eternal and created in the Word.

D: I did not think that was your teaching. For I do not believe any right-thinking philosopher would imagine that an eternal part of the universe subsists in the Word of God, but a created part was formed in time outside the Word. Holy Scripture does not allow us to think such things, for it says, "In wisdom you have made all things,"[78] and again, "In the beginning God made

78. Ps 103.24.

heaven and earth."[79] The Apostle says, "In him all things were created—in heaven and on earth, visible and invisible."[80] And in the Gospel we read, "All things were made by him, and without him nothing was made."[81] Nor can reason find anything outside the Word, either substantially or according to accidents. For it cries out that all things that are and that are not are comprehended in the Word of God. But John the theologian testifies that in the Word of God all things are simultaneously eternal and created by saying, "What was made in him was life."[82] This means that "what was made in him" temporally and spatially through generation "was life" eternally through reason.

M: Do not doubt, then, that all the causes and all their effects are both eternal and created in the Word—and do not imagine that I have taught anything different.

### 154. *God's works are his only will*

D: I have no doubt about the eternity of all things and their creation in the Word, nor do I think you have taught otherwise. But I ask only how all things can be simultaneously eternal and created in the coeternal Word of the Father. For it is against reason, I think, for created things to be eternal and eternal things created.

M: I wonder why you seek a reason in these matters where all reason fails, or understanding in things that surpass all understanding. Concerning divine providence and its operation, we should think of the divine will alone, which "does all things as it wishes" because it is omnipotent.[83] It implants natural reasons, hidden and unsearchable, in all things because it is the supernatural reason of all, for "there is nothing more secret, nothing more present. It is difficult to know where it is and more difficult to know where it is not."[84] It is the ineffable light, ever-present to all intellectual eyes, and no intellect knows what

79. Gn 1.1.
80. Col 1.16; Maximus, *Ambigua* 3 (PG 91: 1077cd).
81. Jn 1.3.
82. Jn 1.3–4.
83. 1 Cor 12.11.
84. Augustine, *De quantitate animae* 34.77 (PL 32: 1077).

it is. It is diffused through all things to infinity; it becomes all in all and nothing in nothing. Let us believe, then, and insofar as it is given to us, let us gaze with the mind's eye on all things visible and invisible, eternal and temporal. Let us speak universally on whatever the whole created universe contains—eternity and time, places and spaces and everything that is named according to substance and accident; and [we will see] that everything is at once eternal and created in the only-begotten Word of God. Its eternity does not precede its creation, nor its creation its eternity. Indeed, the eternity of things is created, their creation eternal, in the dispensation of the Word. For all things that are seen to have arisen in time and place in the order of the ages, through generation, were created eternally once for all in the Word of God. We should not believe that anything began to be when it was perceived to arise in the world. All things have always existed substantially in the Word of God, and their rising and setting in the order of time and space through generation, that is, through the assumption of accidents, has always existed in the Word of God, where future things have already happened.

Indeed, divine Wisdom circumscribes all times, and all things that arise in time in the nature of things precede and subsist eternally in her. She is the measureless measure of all things, their numberless number, and their weightless weight or order.[85] She is time and the world; she is past, present, and future. She creates and circumscribes all times in herself while being above all times—preceding, encompassing, and enclosing all the intervals of time in her eternity. Let none of the faithful be unaware that all things are at once eternal and created in Wisdom, although no one can understand how eternal things are created or created things are eternal. For that is known to the Word alone, in whom they are both created and eternal.

### 155. *No one knows the mode of creation*

D: No rational or intellectual creature can know the mode of creation of things in the Word. But can we find out why we are

85. Wis 11.21; Augustine, *De Genesi ad litteram* 4.3–4 (CSEL 28.1, 99–100).

compelled to say that eternal things are created in the Word of God? For it would seem that the present question could be solved if we could adopt this teaching: Insofar as all things subsist in the Word of God in their beginnings, we must understand them as eternal, but insofar as they proceed into their effects through generation in the order of time, they are created. In this way, their eternity in the Word of God would precede their creation in the order of the ages. Yet true reason does not allow us to say such things, for it cries out most truthfully that not only the primordial causes, but also their effects—along with places, times, essences, substances, and every created thing—are both eternal and created in the Word of God, once and for all. Nothing remains, then, except to ask not *how* they are both eternal and created, but *why* they must be called both created and eternal.

M: Divine authority pronounces that all things are created, saying, "In the beginning God made heaven and earth,"[86] "In wisdom you have made all things,"[87] and "All things were made by him."[88] Let anyone who can, explain the mode and reason of the creation of all things in the Word of God. As for me, I confess that I do not know, hearing the Apostle say, "He alone has immortality and dwells in unapproachable light."[89] And reason itself leads us to understand not only that all things are both eternal and created in the Word of God, but also that the Word himself makes all things and is made in all. It is no wonder if the Word of God flees from our mind's eye in all things that were made in him, when even in sensible things, no one could say how the force in a seed breaks out and becomes apparent to our senses in the visible species and forms of things, their various colors, and their different sweet fragrances. Even as it is manifest, it does not cease to be hidden, and whether it is manifest or hidden, it is never forsaken by its natural virtues. It remains whole in all parts and in itself; it does not grow when it seems to be multiplied, nor diminish when it is thought to be contracted in little space, but remains immutably in the same natural state.

86. Gn 1.1.
87. Ps 103.24.
88. Jn 1.3.
89. 1 Tm 6.16.

For example, it is no less in a grain of wheat than when the harvest is multiplied, and what is more wonderful, it is no greater in the whole than in a particle of grain. For it is multiple in a single grain and single in many.

Thus the unshaken authority of divine Scripture compels us to believe that the whole created universe was fashioned in the Word of God. But the reason of its creation transcends all intellects and is known only to the Word in which they were created.

### 156. *The will of God is his work*

D: But I would like to hear what you think about the eternity of the universe in the Word of God.

M: Do you think the Word of God, in whom all things were made, saw everything that was made in himself?

D: I do indeed.

M: How did he see—with bodily senses or with intellect?

D: I would say that God saw what he made neither with the senses nor with intellect. For he is incorporeal and lacks bodily senses, and he who "transcends every intellect" is not properly called intellect.[90] But he knows the things that exist as his volitions.[91]

M: So just as God sees his volitions, he sees the things that he made.

D: But I beg you, say whether the divine volitions that God sees are different from the created things that he sees as his volitions.

M: The will of God is his action, and the same is also his vision. He made his volitions; the things he made are his volitions, and he sees what he made.[92]

D: If the will of God and his vision are nothing other than God himself, and God made his volitions, which he saw, then God made himself. And if it is so, who would doubt the eternity of all things that were made in God when they are understood to be not only created and eternal, but even God himself?

90. Phil 4.7; cf. Augustine, *De civitate Dei* 22.29 (CCSL 48, 856).

91. *Voluntates.*

92. Maximus, *Ambigua* 3 (PG 91: 1085ab).

M: Walk step by step to avoid stumbling.

D: Go before me, and I will follow.

### 157. *The will of God is eternal*

M: Do you think that God was ever without his volitions?

D: By no means. Everything God has, he has unchangeably and forever, for he is not subject to accidents.

M: Then God always had his volitions and always saw them?

D: It would be madness to think that God did not always have and always see his volitions.

M: Therefore, the divine volitions are eternal, for he himself is eternal.

D: I fully grant this.

M: What then? Did he always have and always see the things he willed? For nothing is future for God, who contains in himself all times and everything in them. Indeed, he is the beginning, middle, and end of all things—their full circuit, progress, and return.

D: I do not doubt that nothing is future for God.

M: Everything that he wished to make, therefore, he always had in his volitions; and what he had, he always saw—not outside himself but within himself. So if everything that God wishes to be made and sees that he will make, he wills and sees not outside himself but within himself, then there is nothing in God that is not himself. It follows that everything he sees and wills should be understood as coeternal with him.

D: If the will of God, his vision, and his essence are one, I am compelled to admit that all things whatsoever, eternal and created, are said to be God. For if to be, to will, and to see are not different for him, but one and the same, it remains the case without contest that the one God is said to be all in all. And if this is so, no pious philosopher should be unaware of the eternity of all things that are in God, or rather, that *are* God.

But I still do not fully see how the divine nature—outside of which nothing exists, and within which all things subsist—receives nothing within itself that is not coessential with itself.

### 158. *There is nothing outside of God*

M: You do not doubt, I suppose, that no nature subsists except for God and creation. When you said, "outside of which nothing exists," I think you meant that the creative nature allows nothing outside herself, because outside of her nothing can exist. She created and creates the whole to be contained within herself, yet in such a way that she is herself different (being superessential) from what she created in herself. For it seems unlikely to you that she created herself.

D: You have perceived my whole mental conception of God and creation. Indeed, until now I have held that the fullness of the universe consists in these two parts, God and creation. But now my faith seems to be shaken, weakened by what you have said.

M: I see that your faith is stabilized and fortified by true reasoning, since you believe there is nothing outside of God. But turn your mind's eye more keenly toward the things that you believe to be in God.

### 159. *Within God there is nothing but God*

D: I sense that in God there is nothing but himself and the creation fashioned by him.

M: In God, therefore, you see what is not God.

D: I see what is from God, yet created.

M: How then does it seem to you? Did God see everything he made before it came to be?

D: I believe he saw everything before it came to be.

M: Then he saw the things he wished to make; he saw nothing other than the things he made; and he saw what he made before he made them.

D: So I believe.

M: Tell me, then, what are the things God saw before they came to be? Either he saw himself before he made what he made, or else he saw creation when it was not yet created. For everything that exists is either God or creation. But how did he see what did not yet exist? If what he saw was in him and appeared because it existed, then it existed before creation, because creation did not yet exist. But if God alone is allowed to exist before all creation, nothing else preceded creation. So either what God saw before he made the creation was himself, or else creation is eternal in itself and coeternal with God. For it is agreed that God saw the things that were to be made. He did not make them in ignorance without foreseeing what he wished to make.

D: I see that I am walled in on all sides, and there is no escape. For if God saw everything that was to be made in himself before it came to be, true reason will teach that he necessarily saw himself—and he will be everything that he made. And if he made the things he saw in himself, he will be both the Maker and what was made. But if he saw the creation about to be made before it came to be, then creation existed before it was made, for God does not see anything false because he is unchangeable truth. Everything in that truth is true and unchangeable. And if God saw creation in himself before it came to be, then he always saw what he saw, and what he saw always existed; for everything God sees is true and eternal. Creation, therefore, was in God before it came to exist in itself, and it is understood in two senses: creation is eternal in divine knowledge, but temporal afterwards in its own condition. If this is the case, either the same creation is better than itself insofar as it subsists eternally in God, and inferior insofar as it is created in itself—and the act of its creation occurs not in God, but outside of God in itself, as it were. But that would contradict the verse, "In wisdom you have made all things."[93]

Alternatively, it is not the same nature that existed eternally in the knowledge of God and was created afterwards, so to speak, in itself. On this account, God did not see the things that were made before they came to be, but he saw only those that are eternal in himself. Holy wisdom, however, professes that God did not see certain things in himself and afterwards make other things in themselves. Rather, the same things were eternally seen and eternally created. All this exists in God and nothing is outside of God. But if the nature of divine Goodness is one

93. Ps 103.24.

thing, while another is what God saw would be made, then made (and saw and made in himself), then the simplicity of the divine nature is ruptured because something is understood to be in it that is not itself—and that is absolutely impossible.

## 160. *God is all things*

Yet suppose the divine Goodness is nothing other than what she saw in herself to be made, but all is one and the same nature whose simplicity is inviolable, whose unity is inseparable. In that case, it will be given that all things everywhere are God: the whole in the whole, the Creator and the created, the seer and the seen, time and place and the being, substance, and accidents of all things—and to speak simply, all that truly is and all that is not, superessential in essences, supersubstantial in substances, Creator above every creature, created within every creature, subsisting beneath every creature, beginning to exist from itself, moving itself through itself, moved toward itself and resting in itself, infinitely multiplied in itself through genera and species, yet not forsaking the simplicity of its nature, but recalling its infinite multiplication back to itself. For in it all things are one.

## 161. *God and creation are the same*

M: You will not hesitate any longer, I think, to confess that all things are both created and eternal, and all that is in them is truly understood to subsist.

D: I see that nothing exists except the ineffable nature of divine Goodness, for that is the substantial Good and "no one is good except God alone."[94]

M: Then we should not understand God and creation to be two different things, but one and the same. For creation subsists in God and, at the same time, God is created in creation in a marvelous, ineffable way as he makes himself manifest. The invisible makes himself visible, and the incomprehensible, comprehensible. He both creates all things and is created in all; he

94. Lk 18.19.

is the maker of all, yet is made in all. Though eternal, he began to be, and though immobile, he is moved into all and becomes all in all.[95] By an ineffable condescension, the Trinity itself is in the things that exist in order that they might exist, or rather, that it might itself be in all things, from the highest to the lowest. Forever eternal, it is created by itself in itself, needing no material other than itself in which to create itself. From himself, therefore, God receives the occasions of his theophanies, or divine appearances, "for from him and through him and in him and to him are all things."[96] Even that material from which we read that he made the world[97] is from him and in him—and insofar as it is understood to exist, it is himself.

This is no wonder, given that the souls of Moses and Samuel, which are by nature invisible and incorporeal, appeared as if they were visible and corporeal, not fantastically but truly—not in some matter taken from outside, but in themselves, without intermediary—in order to accomplish mysteries.[98] By this miracle we should understand that the divine power is above all things yet comes to be in all things. It does not take matter from elsewhere, nor does it make from nothing the matter in which it comes to be and makes itself manifest. In the same way the virtue of seeds, which in itself is invisible and incomprehensible, multiplies itself in infinite forms and species and becomes subject to the bodily senses; but when it is sought, it flees from the mind's eye. No place, therefore, is left for that "nothing" (that is, the privation of every condition and essence) from which those who lack understanding imagine that all things were made. For they do not know what sacred theology signifies by that name.

D: True reason proclaims that these things are most true, even though they are inaccessible to many and far removed from those who seem to philosophize. The authority of holy Scripture confirms this, saying, "In the beginning God made heaven and earth,"[99] that is, the Father fashioned the whole

95. 1 Cor 15.28.
96. Rom 11.36; Dionysius, *De divinis nominibus* 4.10 (PG 3: 708a).
97. Wis 11.18.
98. Mt 17.3; 1 Sm 28.7–20.
99. Gn 1.1.

created universe in the Son. And what did the Father create in the Son that was not the Son himself? Otherwise, he would have created not *in* him, but outside of him, anything that he received from elsewhere or made out of nothing. Or how would the Word suffer anything that was not consubstantial with him to come into being in him? For light does not allow darkness to exist in itself, nor does truth accept fiction. Nothing can be true that has not been forever eternal; but nothing is eternal that was made from the privation of all eternity and being. Or what else did the Father make in his Wisdom if not his Wisdom itself? As it is written, "In wisdom you have made all things,"[100] that is, you have made your wisdom as all things. Did God fashion some building in his wisdom in another place or space—not so that his wisdom might substantially become all things, but so that it might merely contain all things, and all things might come to be in it as if it were something completely different? That is not what reason teaches.

### 162. *The sun is in all things through its light and heat*

For even this visible sun, which in itself is simple fire and receives no admixture of anything that is not consubstantial with it, contains and comprehends in itself the nature of all sensible things. It is not that it contains within it anything other than itself, but it is substantially everything it contains in itself. For the substance of all visible things is created in it, and it governs all bodies that are born in the world and nourished by its hidden operations. It becomes whole in all places; from itself and in itself, it is created in all things, bursting forth visibly in them all and consuming them all, though invisible in itself.

But I ask you to explain what is signified by the word "nothing."

### 163. *That "nothing" is God*

M: That name signifies the ineffable, incomprehensible, divine, inaccessible radiance that is unknown to all intellects,

100. Ps 103.24.

human or angelic, because it is superessential and supernatural. Considered in itself, it neither is nor was nor shall be. It is understood in no existing being, for it transcends them all. But when the mind's eye beholds it in the things that exist, through a certain ineffable condescension, it alone is found to exist in them all—and it is and was and shall be. When therefore it is understood to be incomprehensible because of its excellence, it is rightly called "nothing." But when it begins to appear in its theophanies, something is said to come forth from nothing (as it were), and that which is properly thought to be above every being is also properly recognized within every being. Thus every visible and invisible creature can be called a theophany, which means a divine appearance. Every order in nature from the highest to the lowest—that is, from the heavenly beings down to the utmost limit of the visible world—the more secretly it is understood, the more it is seen to approach the divine radiance. But the further it descends here below, the more manifestly it reveals itself to the gaze of contemplatives. Therefore, the forms and species of sensible things receive the name of the most manifest theophanies.

So the divine Goodness, which is called "nothing" because it is found in no being (for it lies beyond all things that are and that are not), descends from itself, in itself, from the negation of all beings into the affirmation of the whole universe of being, as if descending from nothing into something. Scripture calls its progression from inessentiality into the things in which it comes to be by the name of "formless matter."[101] It is matter because it is the beginning of the being of things, but formless because it is closest to the formlessness of divine Wisdom. Divine Wisdom is called "formless" because it is changed into no form above itself, for it is the infinite exemplar of all forms; and when it descends into the different forms of visible things, it has regard to itself as if to its own formation. Thus the divine Goodness, contemplated above all things, is said not to exist and to be absolutely nothing. Yet it is also said to be in all things and even to be all things—for it is the being and substance of the whole universe, its genus and species, its quantity and quality, the bond

101. Wis 11.18; Augustine, *De Genesi ad litteram* 1.14 (CSEL 28.1, 21).

of all things, the position and condition, the place and time, the action and passivity, and everything whatsoever that can be understood by any intellect at all in the whole creation.

### 164. *God as Being (ΩN)*

Hence St. Dionysius says, "He is above all and before all, superessentially, superΩN." For so he names God, that is, "the being of the whole."[102] He is the maker of all things and he is made in all. When he is sought above all, he is found in no being. But when he is understood to be in all, nothing subsists in them except him alone; for he is all.[103]

### 165. *The mode of creation*

D: It remains for you to discuss the eternal creation of all things in God, insofar as the ray of divine virtue allows the mind's eye to ascend to the divine mysteries.

M: When God first descends from the superessentiality of his nature, in which he is said not to be, he is created by himself in the primordial causes. Thus he becomes the beginning of all being, all life, all intelligence, and all that gnostic theory contemplates in the primordial causes. Then he descends from the primordial causes, which occupy the midpoint between God and creation, that is, between that ineffable superessentiality above every intellect and the substantially manifest nature beheld by pure minds. He comes into being in their effects and is manifestly revealed in his theophanies. Next he proceeds through the multiple forms of these effects down to the lowest order of all nature, which includes bodies. And thus, proceeding into all things in an orderly fashion, he makes them all and becomes all in all. Returning to himself, he calls all things back to himself; and even as he comes into being in all, he does not cease to be above all. In this way he makes all things from nothing. That is,

102. Dionysius, *De divinis nominibus* 5.8 (PG 3: 824b); 5.4 (PG 3: 817c). ΩN is the Greek participle for Being, commonly used for the divine name "He who is" (cf. Ex 3.14).

103. Dionysius, *De divinis nominibus* 5.4–5 (PG 3: 817c–820a); 5.8 (PG 3: 821d–824b).

he produces beings from his superessentiality, creates lives from his supervitality, and intellects from his superintellectuality. In short, from the negation of all things that are and that are not, he produces affirmations of all things that are and that are not.

This manifestly teaches the return of all things to the cause from which they proceeded, when all things will be changed into God as air is changed into light,[104] and God will be all in all.[105] Indeed, even now he is all in all. But after the fall of human nature and its expulsion from the seat of paradise, that is, when man was thrust from the height of spiritual life and knowledge of the most radiant wisdom into the most profound darkness of ignorance, no one has been able to see with the gaze of true intelligence how God is all in all—unless he is illumined by divine grace and rapt with Paul into the heaven of divine mysteries.[106] The cloud of carnal thoughts and the darkness of vain fantasies stand in the way, and the mind's eye is weakened by irrational passions. Repelled from the splendors of pure light, it is confined within the accustomed bodily shadows.

### 166. *The angels see nothing in creation except God*

But the heavenly beings, who never abandoned the stability of eternal bliss, perceive nothing else in the whole creation except God himself, for they see all things in God and in the primordial causes, above all sense and intellect. Needing no works of nature to recognize the truth, they enjoy only the ineffable grace of eternal light.[107] The incarnate Word of God came down to lead human nature back to that vision, receiving it as it was before it fell in order to summon it back to its original state—healing the wounds of sin, extinguishing the shadows of false fantasies, opening the eyes of the mind, and revealing himself in all who are worthy of such a vision.

104. Maximus, *Ambigua* 3 (PG 91: 1073d–1076a and 1088d); 6.19 (PG 91: 1137bc); 6.20 (PG 91: 1140c).

105. 1 Cor 15.28.

106. 2 Cor 12.2.

107. Augustine, *De Genesi ad litteram* 4.24 (CSEL 28.1, 123–24).

### 167. *There is nothing shameful in creation*

D: These matters are very difficult and far removed from the senses of those who think of corporeal and visible things. But for those who ascend spiritually above visible and temporal things toward knowledge of the truth, they shine most truly and sweetly. Among those who live carnally and do not wish to discern the clear light of wisdom, who could hear such things and not at once burst out and declare, "The people who say this are insane! For how can God, who is above all things—invisible, incorporeal, and incorruptible—descend from himself and create himself in all things 'so that God may be all in all'?[108] How can he proceed down to the very lowest parts of this world, to what is visibly shameful and corruptible, to the vilest forms and species, so that he might be present even in these—if he is all in all?"

M: Those who say such things do not know that there can be nothing shameful in the whole created universe. No evil can cause harm; no error can deceive or seduce. In fact, to those who live shamefully and wickedly, honorable things seem to be shameful; what is good seems evil; what is correct seems erring; what is righteous seems depraved. But if their own shame, malice, and error were taken away, then to those who understand piously, all things remain pure, perfect, unpolluted, and very good, free of all error. Such people do not understand what holy Scripture proclaims: "Every good gift and every perfect gift comes down from above, from the Father of lights."[109] By "good gift" it declares the substantial existence of all things, and by "perfect gift," the virtues by which all nature is adorned. And all of this, both substance and virtue, comes down from the Father of lights, that is, from God, the source of all goods. Flowing into all things that are and that are not, he comes into being in them all, and without him nothing can exist.

108. 1 Cor 15.28.
109. Jas 1.17.

### 168. *The Word of God is the nature of all things*

D: We have said enough about the "nothing" from which God made all things.

M: Yes, enough. But we do not say these things to refute the view of those who think God made all things from "nothing," meaning the privation of every condition. What theologians denote by "nothing" is the superessentiality and supernatural nature of divine Goodness. By the authority of St. Dionysius, we know that when we investigate the divine nature, negation has more value than affirmation.[110] That is why God in the Scriptures is often called "nothing." Indeed, Scripture testifies that all things were made from nothing,[111] and all participate in a single nature that is common to all. God created this nature of all things once and for all, and all come into being by participation in it. This nature was not born of "nothing" but of the Father. St. Basil affirms that the Word of God is the nature of all things, which were made in him and through him.[112] It is by being the Word that all things come to be, for the Word itself is all. He is also the Wisdom of God, as the Apostle testifies: "Christ the power of God and the wisdom of God."[113] In this wisdom, as the Psalmist says, the Father made all things in heaven and on earth: "In wisdom you have made them all."[114] Wisdom is consubstantial with the Father before all things, as Ecclesiasticus says: "Who has searched out the wisdom that is before all things?"[115] The same text says it was made in the primordial causes: "Wisdom was created as the first of all things."[116] And Wisdom says of herself, "The Lord created me at the beginning of his ways."[117] To show that the Word was created in its effects, that is in creatures,

110. Dionysius, *De caelesti hierarchia* 2.3 (PG 3: 140c–141a); *De mystica theologia* 1.2 (PG 3: 1000b).

111. 2 Mc 7.28.

112. Basil, *Hexaemeron* 8.1 (PG 29: 164d).

113. 1 Cor 1.24.

114. Ps 103.24.

115. Sir 1.3.

116. Sir 1.4.

117. Prv 8.22 LXX; Augustine, *Confessions* 7.21.

listen to the Gospel: "What was made in him was life."[118] Behold the "nothing" from which all things were made.

### 169. *Two senses of "nothing"*

As for those who think the world was made from a "nothing" that signifies the privation or absence of all being, I don't know what to say. In fact, there can be no privation where there was no prior condition, and where no condition preceded, no privation can follow. If the world was made from privation, then it had some condition before it came into being, which is absurd. But if it lacked all conditions, it could by no means come into being from the privation of any condition because it never had one. The same argument applies to absence, for absence is the removal from the senses of some present object, or an object that is capable of being present. So if the world was made from absence, it was preceded by some nature whose absence was the occasion for creating it; and that nature had to be either God or a creature. If it was God, then the world was made from God's absence. But if it was a creature, it was necessarily either visible or invisible. If it was visible, then another visible world preceded this one. If it was invisible, then this world was made from the absence of some invisible nature. But if no nature other than God preceded the whole created universe, how could the world have been made from the absence or privation of things that did not exist?

If anyone were to say the world was made from a "nothing" that is simply the negation of all things that can be named or understood, then let them reach this conclusion. Such a "nothing" should necessarily denote God, who alone is exalted above everything that is named and understood. "He who is known best by not knowing" is none of those things that are or that are not.[119] But if by "nothing" such a philosopher denies both God and creation, he will necessarily confess what he is trying to deny, namely that the world was made from the privative negation of both God and creation. For I think he will not dare to say: "Everything that exists is either God or a creature, or

118. Jn 1.3–4.
119. Augustine, *De ordine* 2.16.44 (CCSL 29, 131).

else neither God nor a creature." If he said that, he would be counted among those who say the matter from which they think God created the world is coeternal with him. But if everything that exists is either God or a creature, and no sane philosopher would imagine that the world was made from the negation of both, only one kind of negation remains as the cause for making the world. By the removal of every creature, such negation exalts God above all that is named and understood, proclaiming him to be none of those things that are or that are not.

### 170. *There is one principle, not two*

But here is the strongest argument concerning this matter. If God and creation are two different things, then they are either from one principle and therefore of the same nature; or they are two mutually opposing principles; or they are equal, and neither is from the other. If God is from no one, but creation is from God, then one will be from the other and they are not equal, for one thing is not begotten by another that is equal to it. But if creation is from God, then God will be the cause, and creation the effect. But if creation is the effect of a cause, it follows that God as cause comes into being in his effects, for nothing that is alien to its own nature proceeds from a cause into its effects. For example, nothing is produced in heat and light but the same fiery force.

If anyone were to say, "But one does beget one that is equal to it, for God the Father, being one, begets God the Son as one who is equal to him," he should know he has made a serious error. For the supreme and holy Trinity is not one plus one plus one. Rather, it is a simple, indivisible One in three inseparable hypostases, and that One is multiple in virtue, not in number. It is not one "something," but universally and infinitely One, above every one that can be named and understood.

Do you see, then, what is signified by that word "nothing," from which God is believed to have made the world?

D: I see that all things are from God and God is in all things, and they were made from nothing but himself, for "from him and through him and in him, all things were made."[120]

120. Rom 11.36.

But I ask you to recapitulate, clearly and briefly, how the fourfold division of all nature is appropriate to God.

### 171. *Fourfold nature*

M. I think we have agreed that God is the beginning, middle, and end of the whole created universe. He is the beginning because all things proceed from him, the middle because all run through him and in him, and the end because all things desire him in whom they rest, for they seek nothing further. These three things are one in him, although they differ in the minds of contemplatives. First of all is creative nature. God creates the nature of all things, whose cause and beginning he is, and is himself created by nothing. In the middle, he is created by himself and creates in the primordial causes. In their effects, he is created and does not create. In the end he neither creates nor is created, when "God shall be all in all"[121] and all creation will be overshadowed and changed into God, like a star at sunrise.[122] Every contemplative mind is allowed to behold this divine nature, like a kind of Moses ascending to the summit of contemplation.[123] Yet it still can scarcely be discerned in its purity even by the wise, given the smoke of earthly fantasies, the clamor of things mutable, the glimmer of things suddenly born, and the obstacle of things suddenly passing away. For it is given to very few, utterly removed from earthly thoughts, and purified by virtue and knowledge, to know God in these visible creatures—just as Abraham knew him before the Law in the movement of the stars,[124] and Moses knew him under the Law in the burning bush and on the mountaintop.[125] Under grace, the Apostles knew Christ when they were introduced into divine mysteries through visible symbols on the mountain. For "his garments, white as snow"[126] signified the visible creation, in and through which

121. 1 Cor 15.28.

122. Maximus, *Ambigua* 3 (PG 91: 1077a). This chapter is illustrated by the frontispiece.

123. Ex 19.20; Maximus, *Ambigua* 6.5 (PG 91: 1117bc).

124. Gn 15.5–6.

125. Ex 3.2, 19.20.

126. Mt 17.2.

we understand the Word of God that subsists in all things.[127] As the Apostle testifies, "the invisible things of God are perceived through the created world."[128]

D: I can now very clearly see the fourfold division of universal nature, and I know beyond all doubt that it must be understood concerning God and in God. But I think we should return to our purpose.

### 172. *In the beginning God made*

M: You are right, but first I think we should touch on a few things concerning the six intelligible days in which we read that God performed his works. The divine prophet Moses briefly writes about the creation, once and for all, of the primordial causes of visible and invisible things when he says, "In the beginning God made heaven and earth."[129] By "heaven" he means the causes of spiritual things, by "earth" those of bodily things. Because they had not yet flowed forth into forms and species, there follows: "The earth was empty and void," or "invisible and uncomposed."[130] And because they were hidden and incomprehensible in the divine counsel, he adds, "And there was darkness on the face of the abyss." He continues with the beginning of procreation in its effects: "And the Spirit of God was warming the waters" or "moving over the waters."[131]

### 173. *What "let there be light" means*

Next he moves on to explain the mystical meaning of the number six, saying, "And God said, Let there be light."[132] That is, let the primordial causes proceed from the incomprehensible mystery of their nature into forms and species that will be

127. Maximus, *Ambigua* 6.17 (PG 91: 1128b–d); 6.18 (PG 91: 1132c); 6.31 (PG 91: 1168b).

128. Rom 1.20.

129. Gn 1.1. A lengthy hexaemeral commentary begins with this chapter.

130. Gn 1.2; the second reading follows the LXX. Cf. Augustine, *De Genesi ad litteram* 1.1 (CSEL 28.1, 5).

131. Ibid.; Basil, *Hexaemeron* 2.6 (PG 29: 44ab); Augustine, *De Genesi ad litteram* 1.18 (CSEL 28.1, 26–27).

132. Gn 1.3.

comprehensible and manifest to the intellects of those who contemplate them. "And there was light,"[133] that is, at God's command the obscurity of the primordial causes proceeded into manifest forms and species. "And he divided the light from the darkness,"[134] that is, he separated the knowledge of the effects from the obscurity of their principal causes. The division of light from darkness is the discernment of things that appear in forms and species from their principles, in which they transcend every intellect. "And God saw the light, that it was good."[135] That is, it pleased God that the original causes, formed before all creation and above every intellect, should be revealed to human and angelic intellects by the outpouring of a light of understanding. "And he called the light day and the darkness night."[136] That is, he gave contemplative minds the power to call the revelation of visible and invisible things through their forms and species "day," but to name as "night" their incomprehensible depth in their principles, a depth unknown to every created intellect. "And there was evening and morning, one day."[137] Although we may understand a division and a difference between the obscurity of the causes and the clarity of their effects, yet to the intellect they are one and the same. For we do not understand one creation to be made in the causes and another to be formed in their effects, but one and the same creation exists in the eternal reasons. Creation is produced in the darkness of the most secret wisdom, remote from every intellect, but it is made subject to intellects by the procession of the reasons into their effects, as if revealed in a day of perfect knowledge.

### 174. *How Augustine interprets "Let there be light"*

St. Augustine holds that the verse "Let there be light" signifies the creation of angelic, intellectual, heavenly being.[138] By

133. Ibid.
134. Gn 1.4.
135. Ibid.
136. Gn 1.5.
137. Ibid.
138. Augustine, *De civitate Dei* 11.9 (CCSL 48, 328–30); 11.19 (CCSL 48, 338); 11.32 (CCSL 48, 351).

the division of light from darkness, he understands either the separation of formless matter from the formed creation (light denotes the perfection of form, darkness the confusion of formlessness),[139] or else the double contemplation of the heavenly beings. On the one hand, they contemplate the creation in its eternal reasons in God, according to which it was created. On the other, they perceive it in itself, under God, insofar as it is a creature.[140] The first contemplation is signified by the term "light," and the second by "darkness." For just as light has greater dignity than darkness, so the radiance of the eternal reasons, according to which every creature was made, is nobler than the obscurity of creation contemplated in itself.[141]

### 175. *On the first day*

Therefore, God called the light day (that is, the splendor of the divine reasons) and the darkness night (that is, the more obscure species of created nature in itself). By "evening" he wished to signify the end of his completed activity, and by "morning" the beginning of what follows. Therefore, the first day, whose morning (or beginning) had preceded with the creation of light, ends with evening.[142]

### 176. *What Basil thinks about this*

But St. Basil understands "Let there be light" to denote the nature of this visible light, namely fire, which was still incomprehensible and invisible when it was created. Afterwards, as if emerging in its wellsprings, it shone in the ethereal bodies. Over the space of three days it was poured out and traversed the abyss of the earth's surface in its hidden course, shedding light everywhere.[143] Because the world is thought to have been

139. Augustine, *De Genesi ad litteram* 1.17 (CSEL 28.1, 25); 4.1 (CSEL 28.1, 93).

140. Augustine, *De Genesi ad litteram* 2.6 (CSEL 28.1, 41).

141. Augustine, *De Genesi ad litteram* 4.23 (CSEL 28.1, 122–23); *De civitate Dei* 11.7 (CCSL 48, 327).

142. Augustine, *De Genesi ad litteram* 1.17 (CSEL 28.1, 26); 4.1 (CSEL 28.1, 93–94); 4.18 (CSEL 28.1, 115).

143. Basil, *Hexaemeron* 2.7 (PG 29: 44c–45b); 6.2 (PG 29: 121ab).

created at the vernal equinox, when the sun spends equal periods of twelve hours above the earth and twelve beneath the earth, that is how Basil interprets "God divided the light from the darkness."[144] It means he divided the whole space of one day, that is twenty-four hours, equally between day and night. When the text says, "He called the light day and the darkness night," this refers, he thinks, to the intervals of time by which light and shade complete their alternating course around the earth.[145]

## 177. *The second day. What the firmament signifies*

D: It seems we have said enough about the first day.

M: So let us move on to consider the second day. But first let me say that I have no intention to present an allegorical understanding. With God's guidance, I will try only to explain a few things about the creation according to the literal sense.

D: I do not ask for more, for the holy fathers have said enough about the allegorical sense.

M: "And God said, Let there be a firmament in the midst of the waters, and let it separate the waters from the waters."[146] All agree with one accord that the firmament signifies nothing but the visible sky. But some assert that the term "firmament" denotes only the outermost revolving sphere, encompassing the whole world and adorned with the choirs of stars. Others think it denotes the whole of space beyond the moon, where the planets and their orbits are believed to lie, along with the outermost sphere of stars. Still others maintain that it signifies the whole empty space that revolves around the earth, that is, the air, the ether, and that most lofty sphere, for they say we do not read anywhere else about the creation of air and ether.

Everyone has explained why it should be called by the name "firmament" as seems best to them. Some say it is because it supports the upper waters, as if there were physical waters above it.[147] Some think it supports the choirs of stars as if these were

144. Gn 1.4.
145. Gn 1.5; Basil, *Hexaemeron* 2.8 (PG 29: 48bc).
146. Gn 1.6.
147. Augustine, *De Genesi ad litteram* 2.10 (CSEL 28.1, 48).

heavy bodies, and some that it contains and supports the whole visible world within itself. There are also some who want to designate the realm of this heavier air by the proper name "firmament" because they think that, by the firm corpulence of its nature, it supports within itself everything that is born of earthly vapors in it—such as clouds, rain, showers, snow, and hail—insofar as it can, as if the name distinguished the whole from the part, that is, from other realms of visible nature that are lighter and higher. As for me, though, I think it is called "firmament" because the site of the whole bodily creation is stabilized and bounded by it. We understand that nothing sensible, corporeal, spatial, or temporal exists beyond it. In fact, the boundary of all visible things is supported in it. That is why in Greek it is called *stereoma,* which means "solid," because everything solid (that is, bodily) is simultaneously bounded and stabilized by it.

### 178. *What the waters signify*

I do not find much to say about the waters amid which God said the firmament should be made, though I am not unaware of what many of the holy fathers thought about them. St. Basil says that the waters called the "abyss," diffused everywhere around the earth, were of a very thin, rarefied texture. At first there was darkness, then the Spirit of God moved over them, and the primeval light, circling over the course of three days, shone on the earthly mass when it was still formless. On the third day the waters were condensed and gathered into a single place so that the dry land might appear. In this place, in the midst of the waters, God is said to have made the firmament.[148]

St. Augustine strongly opposed this reading, yet he did not have much to say about those waters between which God made the firmament. He introduced the opinions of others but did not reveal what he himself understood, on I-know-not-what occasion. Yet he preferred those views to the opinion of others who contend that the firmament designates the region of the

148. Basil, *Hexaemeron* 2.4 (PG 29: 37a); 2.5 (PG 29: 41b); 3.5 (PG 29: 64ab); 4.3–4 (PG 29: 84b–85a).

air, set between the water of the seas and rivers below it and water in the clouds suspended above it.[149]

Without refuting anyone else's opinion, I will explain in a few words what I think about these waters.

## 179. *A threefold division of nature*

D: This is quite necessary, for no one has yet given a satisfactory answer to this question.

M: There is a threefold division of the whole of created nature. Everything created is either entirely body, like the earthly and aquatic realms; or entirely spirit, like the reasons of things; or something in between, like the four elements.

The lower parts of the world are called "lower waters" because everything born in this world grows and is nourished by moisture. If the moisture is taken away from bodies, they at once decay, diminish, and are reduced to almost nothing. But the spiritual reasons of all visible things are called "upper waters" because all the elements, whether simple or compound, flow down from them as from great fountains, and are governed by them as if watered by a certain intelligible virtue. The firmament set in the midst of these waters is the nature of the simple elements, which transcends visible bodies as much as it is transcended by their invisible reasons. As much as it receives from the reasons above it, it distributes to the bodies below it, and as much as it receives from the bodies below, it restores to the reasons above, bringing back to them all that flowed down from them. By its firm simplicity, the firmament sustains the abyss of intelligible reasons above it and guards the flux of mutable bodies beneath it to keep them from perishing. For as philosophers say, the causes descend into the elements, and the elements into bodies, and when bodies are dissolved, they return through the elements into their causes. Bodies themselves also change into one another, for in the Flood the air was turned into water, and when it receded, water was turned back into air.[150]

149. Augustine, *De Genesi ad litteram* 2.4 (CSEL 28.1, 36–37).
150. Gn 7.10–8.14.

"So God said, Let there be a firmament in the midst of the waters."[151] That is, let the solidity of the simple elements come into being between the depth of their reasons and the mutable flux of bodies composed from their combinations. "And let it divide the waters from the waters,"[152] that is, let it separate compound bodies from simple reasons. Bodies are scattered through space, mutable in time, and subject to generation and corruption, while the reasons have no variation in space and time. They are free from generation and corruption and stabilized by immutable law.

### 180. *The difference between causes and elements*

D: What is the difference between the simplicity of the causes and that of the elements?

M: The simplicity of the causes is understood to lack the nature of places and times, but that of the elements cannot lack places and times, for it is contained in them. The causes are always entirely free from accidents, but the elements sometimes take on accidents and sometimes lay them down. They lay them down in universals and take them on in particulars.

### 181. *What is general and what is special in creation*

In all the works of the first six days, wherever Scripture mentions, "God said, Let there be light," "Let there be a firmament,"[153] and so forth on the remaining days, it should generally be understood to signify the special creation of the primordial causes, whose creation is universally placed first under the names of heaven and earth. But wherever it says, "And there was light," "And God made the firmament," "And it was so,"[154] it signifies the procession of the same primordial causes into their effects through genera and species.[155]

151. Gn 1.6.
152. Ibid.
153. Gn 1.3, 1.6.
154. Gn 1.3, 1.7.
155. Augustine, *De Genesi ad litteram* 2.6 (CSEL 28.1, 42).

### 182. *What the sky is*

D: Move on to what follows.

M: "And God called the firmament sky."[156] As Pliny has it, it is called "sky" from the painting of the stars, like an engraving.[157] But in Greek it is called *uranos,* which means "vision from above," because the loftiness of its nature rises above every bodily creature. There are some who think there are very thin waters above the firmament, that is, above the choirs of stars. But both the argument from weight and the order of the elements refute them. Others argue from the paleness of the stars that the waters above the sky are like steam, almost incorporeal, for they say the stars are cold and therefore pale. But the coldness is not because the waters lack substance, as they claim without thinking about what they are saying.[158] For where fire substantially exists, there is also cold. No wise person would say that a crystal, though its nature is cold, lacks the fiery virtue that penetrates all bodies. Where the fiery force burns, there is heat; where it does not burn, there is cold. But it only burns where it has material fuel to consume.

### 183. *That the sun in the ether is not hot*

That is why the sun's rays spreading through the realm of ether do not burn, for they find no fuel to burn in its extremely subtle, spiritual nature. But when they descend to the realm of heavy air, having found fuel for their activity, they begin to blaze. The coarser the bodies they touch, the more they exercise their burning force on objects that dissolve, or can be dissolved, in the power of heat. But when they return above, lifted toward the outermost region of the world that is closest to the most refined, spiritual nature, they find no fuel to burn and they generate no heat, showing only their activity of illumination.

156. Gn 1.8. *Celum* can be translated as either "sky" or "heaven," but the literal sense predominates here.

157. *Celum from celatum.* Pliny, *Natural History* 2.4.8.

158. Augustine, *De Genesi ad litteram* 2.1–5 (CSEL 28.1, 32–39).

### 184. *Why the stars are pale*

That is why the ethereal, pure, and spiritual heavenly bodies are always luminous, but lacking in heat. For this reason they are believed to be both cold and pale. Consequently, the planet called Saturn is said to be cold and pale because it is close to the choirs of stars.[159] But the solar body, which occupies the midpoint of the world, has a splendid color midway between pale and ruddy. To produce this balanced splendor, it receives one part of its color from the paleness of the frigid stars above, the other part from the redness of the warm bodies beneath.

As philosophers say, the distance from the earth to the sun is the same as the distance from the sun to the stars, so the sun occupies a kind of midpoint.[160] For its subsistence, it receives a certain heaviness from the lower natures and a spiritual subtlety from the upper ones, gathering in itself the opposing qualities of both parts of the world (upper and lower). As if weighed in a balance by their contention, it is not permitted to abandon its natural position. The gravity of the lower part does not permit it to rise higher, nor does the lightness of the upper part allow it to sink lower. The planets that revolve around it change their colors according to the qualities of the realms through which they move.[161] I refer to Jupiter, Mars, Venus, and Mercury, which, as Plato teaches in the *Timaeus,* always pursue their orbits around the sun. So when they are above the sun, they show their bright faces, and when they are below it, red faces.[162] The pallor of the stars, therefore, does not require us to understand the element of water to be present in any form above the sky, for that pallor arises from the absence of heat.

But let us return to our purpose. "And there was evening and morning, the second day."[163] Wherever this verse is inserted, we are given one and the same understanding of the whole

159. Pliny, *Natural History* 2.8.

160. Pliny, *Natural History* 2.21.

161. Pliny, *Natural History* 2.15, 2.18; Bede, *De natura rerum* 15 (PL 90: 230a–231a).

162. Calcidius, *Commentum in Timaeum* 108–10; Martianus Capella, *De nuptiis Philologiae et Mercurii* 8.857.

163. Gn 1.8.

universe, even though one kind of contemplation is suited to the spiritual reasons of the world in the primordial causes, another to the simple, universal elements, and still another to compound, particular bodies.

## 185. *On the third day*

D: We spoke briefly about the second day because this is unknown to almost everyone. It follows that you should make some cursory remarks about the third day.

M: "And God said, Let the waters beneath the sky be gathered into one place, and let the dry land appear. And it was so."[164] St. Basil, bishop of Caesarea in Cappadocia, asserts that a boundless quantity of waters—very thin, almost like vapor—was diffused on all sides around the mass of the earth, which was still formless and invisible. They still filled the realms of air and ether and shone within the compass of the primal light, and on the third day they were gathered into one place. He holds that the firmament, made on the second day, was in the midst of them. Above it the upper portion of the waters was suspended, while the lower waters spread out in the abyss were collected into one place, that is, gathered in the compass of the ocean enclosed by its shores, so that the dry land might appear and a place be given to the air and ether.[165] But when we consult the truth, this opinion seems to be overturned by many arguments. It is illogical and results in utterly false imaginings.

As Augustine affirms, we do not believe that the earthly mass was created first of all, with the abyss spread around it on all sides; next, the firmament was made in the midst of the waters; and then the lower waters remaining beneath the sky were gathered into one place. No, not one of these events preceded another in place and time. In fact, all of them, with the natures of other visible things, were created all at once and ordained and established in their times and places. The generation of anything in its forms and species, quantities and qualities, did not

164. Gn 1.9.

165. Basil, *Hexaemeron* 2.4 (PG 29: 37a); 2.5 (PG 29: 41b); 3.5 (PG 29: 64ab); 4.3–4 (PG 29: 84b–85a).

precede the generation of anything else by an interval of time. Rather, all things proceeded at once from their eternal reasons, in which they subsist essentially in the Word of God, each according to its own genus, species, and individual numbers.[166]

Through the prophet, the Holy Spirit indicates by the perfection of the number six that the Creator made the world all at once. By virtue of this number, the Spirit indicates the perfection of the divine activity—making not a temporal but an intelligible distinction.[167] For this number is the sum of its factors; the whole does not exceed the parts nor the parts the whole. Six equals six times one, or twice three, or thrice two.[168] For just as a voice precedes a word not in time, but as its cause, so the creation of all visible things from still unknown causes occurred without time.[169]

### 186. *All things were made in the twinkling of an eye*

For all things were made at once "in a moment, in the twinkling of an eye."[170] Things that are distinct in the course of time—those that have been born, are being born, and are yet to be born—were made all at once in him in whom past, present, and future are one, once and for all.

### 187. *On the waters*

Having refuted the aforesaid opinion, we must ask what kind of waters beneath the sky were gathered into one place, and what that one place is. As soon as the sensible waters, which in the vernacular are called the sea, the abyss, or the ocean, had

166. Augustine, *De Genesi ad litteram* 4.33 (CSEL 28.1, 131–32).

167. Augustine, *De Genesi ad litteram* 5.5 (CSEL 28.1, 145–46); 4.7 (CSEL 28.1, 103); *De civitate Dei* 11.30 (CCSL 48, 350).

168. Augustine, *De civitate Dei* 11.30 (CCSL 48, 350); *De Genesi ad litteram* 4.2 (CSEL 28.1, 94–96); *De Trinitate* 4.4 (CCSL 50, 169); Martianus Capella, *De nuptiis* 7.736; Boethius, *De institutione arithmetica* 1.19; Maximus, *Quaestiones ad Thalassium* 40 (PG 90: 396c).

169. Augustine, *De Genesi ad litteram* 1.15 (CSEL 28.1, 21).

170. 1 Cor 15.52.

broken out of their hidden places, they appeared in their proper species, quantity, and quality in their own place, that is, between the earth and the air that is closest to the earth, bounded by their shores. One part of them flowed secretly in the bosom of the earth, as if in the pores of some great body, and another part openly covered its surface. They had been scattered in these regions when they had no single place of their own. Since then, they have been confined in that place and do not transgress their definite boundaries.

There are four principal bodies in this world composed from the four simple elements: earth, water, air, and ether,[171] with all that is in them and all that is made from them. They received their species all at once, along with their places, numbers, times, intervals, differences, properties, measures, and weights, and everything that is either perceived and understood in them, or else surpasses perception and flees from understanding. But if anyone were to give a physical account of such things which the bodily senses cannot comprehend, he would either be spurned by those who think only of sensible things, just as if he had said nothing at all, or else he would be thought by those who cannot distinguish nature from its motions to be speaking allegorically. Indeed, physics considers the substantial reasons of nature, and ethics its rational and irrational motions.[172]

### 188. *What the waters beneath the sky signify*

D: Explain, I beg, whatever seems to you a probable solution to this question. Do not be afraid of how anyone will take it—whether they do not understand what you say because they recoil from the light of truth or they spurn it because they are corrupted by the poison of envy or filled with contentious zeal for old opinions.

M: The sky or firmament signifies the four pure elements. The waters beneath the sky stand for the matter, form, species, and flux of all bodies that flow from the elements in any way

171. Honorius uses "ether" and "fire" interchangeably for this element.

172. Physics, ethics, and logic are the traditional branches of Stoic philosophy.

and, once dissolved, flow back into them. These waters are gathered into one place in the understanding when all corporeal things are included in the scope of one and the same definition: "Everything whatsoever, understood or perceived around its own substance, is variable and mutable."

The dry land is the substantial form or species, unchangeably subsisting, in which being, virtue, and operation exist inseparably. They can neither be corrupted nor changed by the proper supports of their own nature.[173] A substantial form is the form by participating in which every individual species is formed. It is one in all and all in one; it is neither increased in many nor diminished in few. It is no greater in all humankind than in the first man, nor any less in one person than in all together. This dry land appears when it is separated from the flux of accidents and shines nakedly before the intellectual eyes. A qualitative form is the form that produces a body when it is joined to matter. For when quality and quantity come together, they constitute visible bodies, which vary due to the quality and quantity of their nourishment, and the regions and climates in which they are born and nourished.

"And God called the dry land earth, and the gathering of the waters he called seas."[174] By earth he denotes the stability of the substantial form; by waters or seas, the flux and bitterness of corporeal accidents. "And God saw that it was good."[175] The vision of God is the creation of the whole universe. For God, it is not one thing to see and another to create, but his vision is his will and his will is his action.[176] The goodness of God is the cause of all goods, or rather, it is itself all goods. Therefore, "God saw that it was good," that is, he saw himself as good in all things. God sees nothing but himself because there is nothing outside of him, and everything that is in him, he himself is. "And he said: Let the earth bring forth green plants bearing seed, and fruit-bearing trees on the earth bearing fruit according to their

173. Dionysius, *De caelesti hierarchia* 11.2 (PG 3: 284d); *De divinis nominibus* 4.23 (PG 3: 724c–725a).

174. Gn 1.10.

175. Ibid.

176. Maximus, *Ambigua* 3 (PG 91: 1085ab).

kind, whose seed is in the fruit."[177] That is, let the seminal power of plants and trees, which was created causally in the inner reasons of their substances, come forth through generation in sensible forms and species. "And it was so," that is, the primordial causes proceeded into their effects. "And the earth brought forth green plants" and so forth.[178] That is, those creatures that subsist invisibly in their causes burst forth visibly through generation.

## 189. *The fourfold division of wisdom*

If any think this explanation is not literal but allegorical, let them attentively consider the fourfold division of wisdom. The first part is practical or active; the second part, physical or natural; the third part, theological, pertaining to God. The fourth part is logical or rational; it shows what rules to follow in disputations about the other three parts of wisdom. The first investigates the virtues, by which vices are supplanted and utterly rooted out. The second considers the reasons of nature in the causes and their effects. The third determines what we should piously think about God, the one cause of all things. But the fourth teaches how we should rationally discuss virtue, nature, and God. A literal narrative about the creation of things will be associated with physics. Therefore, I maintain that nothing I have said is allegorical.

On the first day, we said that the creation of light signifies the procession of the primordial causes into their effects. On the second, I think we judged that the complete threefold constitution of the world—from its reasons, from the simple elements, and from composite bodies—is fittingly described by the term "waters" and the firmament created in the midst of them. On the third we decided that, by the gathering of the waters and the appearance of the earth, divine Scripture implies the separation of all mutable accidents, by rational insight, from the changeless solidity of the substantial forms. For holy Scripture very often signifies bodily and sensible things metaphorically by

177. Gn 1.11.
178. Gn 1.12.

the names of spiritual and invisible ones. Conversely, it signifies spiritual things by the names of bodily ones. All visible bodies are formed by the combination of elements. Therefore, the elements are called "letters" because by their conjunction, an articulate voice is produced.[179] When the elements are considered in themselves, they seem to be contrary, for cold is opposed to heat and moisture to dryness. But when they are mingled together, they create the composite forms of all visible things by a certain marvelous, ineffable harmony. (In reality it is not the substance of the elements, but only their qualities that conflict.) Because these composite forms can be dissolved and returned to the elements, they are denoted by the term "waters beneath the sky."

In all these matters we have not discussed allegory, but only pure physics.

### 190. *On the understanding of the saints*

D: We should by no means neglect or dismiss the understanding of the divine fathers, especially since we know they very often discussed matters simply to accommodate the capacity of their hearers, who did not possess deep knowledge of natural reasoning. So I would not rashly say that the God-bearing Basil, illumined by celestial grace, too simply expounded the works of the first six intelligible days as he had understood them, but rather that he adapted his speech to the simplicity of his audience. Speaking to the people, he explained the creation that God had made all at once, as he deeply knew, as if it had been distributed across intervals of time, for the sake of hearers whose perception could not surpass intervals of time and distances in space. We can see that the most sublime prophet Moses himself did the same thing, for he could not narrate all at once what God was able to make all at once. We too, who try to gaze on the light of truth while we still blink in the darkness of ignorance, cannot simultaneously explain in words all that we behold at once in our minds. For every art, though conceived in its entirety in the mind of the knower, is necessarily conveyed to the ears

179. Plato, *Timaeus* 48bc. Honorius may connect these "letters" with the literal sense, though the term he uses for it is *hystoria*.

of students in a particular, orderly fashion, in accord with the diverse lapses of time produced by letters, syllables, and words.

We should not, therefore, think the aforesaid father understood simply what he seems to have expounded simply. Who will dare to blame the divine lantern without knowing how brightly it could shine in itself—and how much it wished to temper its light for the less capable? In fact, Basil himself affirms that God made everything all at once when he says, "The Word of God runs through all things from the beginning of creation until the end of the universe, always accomplishing and moving all things. With a single commandment, he moves the nature of all that exists, created all at once, into genera and species, like a sphere that never ceases to turn as if it were rolling downhill until the end of the universe, when it will arrive at a kind of peace."[180] Thus the one Word, with one commandment, bade the one nature of existing things to come into being. All at once he created it and brought forth its proper species. Just as God created the nature of all things simultaneously by a single command, even though the theologian [Moses] repeats it six times, the same nature simultaneously began to run through all creatures. One did not precede another in the accounting of time or the dimensions of space.

### 191. *Genera and species in a substance*

M: This and not otherwise is the way we should think about the holy fathers.

There follows: "And the earth brought forth green plants and fruit-bearing trees."[181] Once the mutability of accidents has been separated from the stability of a substance, its manifold power as it breaks forth visibly in diverse species is signified by plants and trees. Every species is naturally contained in a genus, every genus in a substance. Conversely, every substance reveals its power through genera in its proper forms and species. And the life that is active in seeds, bidden by virtue of the divine command, governs all this. So natural philosophers, not without reason,

180. Basil, *Hexaemeron* 9.2 (PG 29: 189bc).
181. Gn 1.12.

call plants and trees "living creatures[182] fixed in a place." For they are animate bodies growing in the intervals of space and time and fixed in the places where they grow.[183]

We should note that, just as the gathering of waters cannot stand by itself unless it is supported by the mass of the earth, neither can the flood of accidents hold together except in an underlying substance—whether they are hidden in its bosom, the way qualities and quantities are hidden causally, or erupt outwardly and appear in matter, like bodily masses suffused with various colors. Or they may be stable, like the species and figures that, when added to mutable matter, produce visible bodies with a certain special stability. They gather into one lest they be suddenly dissolved and, abandoning the species that contains them, slip and flow back into the flux of their mutability.

But let us pass on to the fourth day.

D: The order of our discussion requires this.

### 192. *On the fourth day*

M: "And God said, Let there be lights in the firmament of the sky, and let them divide the day and the night. And it was so."[184] You have heard about the general creation of all the lights in the heavenly firmament in the primordial causes, before every day, time, and place. Now hear about their procession into their effects: multiplied into their proper species, separated by intervals of space, revolving over the course of time, arranged with stable motion and mobile stability.[185] "And God made the two great lights: the greater light to rule the day, and the lesser light to rule the night, and the stars"—and so forth.[186] Of the three greatest bodies in the world, philosophers say, the lowest one is the midpoint of the whole world, like the center of a circle or a sphere. Divine authority called it the dry land or the earth, which God clothed with plants and trees after separating the

182. *Animalia.*

183. Plato, *Timaeus* 77c; Augustine, *De Genesi ad litteram* 2.13 (CSEL 28.1, 53).

184. Gn 1.14–15.

185. Maximus, *Ambigua* 67 (PG 91: 1412bc).

186. Gn 1.16.

waters. Having described this, the prophet's attention turned to contemplate the other two greatest bodies in the world: "Let there be lights in the firmament of the sky." I think you remember what I observed about the firmament?

## 193. *On the four elements*

D: I do indeed, unless memory deceives me. We had agreed that the name "firmament" probably signifies the universe of the four simple elements. In themselves they are most pure, incomprehensible to every bodily sense, and diffused everywhere throughout the universe. But by their invisible course and their proportional union with one another, they produce all sensible bodies—celestial, airy, watery, and earthy—whether huge, tiny, or of moderate size. To speak in general, the whole heavenly sphere and all that is contained in it, from the highest to the lowest, are produced by the conjunction of elements. Whatever is born in the order of ages, through the exchanges of corruptible things, proceeds from these elements and is resolved into them. The Greeks call them *pyr, aer, ydor,* and *ge*—that is, fire, air, water, and earth—from the names of the largest bodies composed from them. We should note that sensible bodies are not made from the union of the substantial elements themselves, for they are incorruptible and indissoluble, but from their qualities joined together in proportion.

## 194. *The four qualities of the elements*

Four qualities of the elements are most notable: heat, moisture, cold, and dryness. Natural philosophy maintains that all material bodies are composed of these qualities added to forms. Philosophers say that two of the qualities are active, heat and cold; and two passive, moisture and dryness. For when heat mingles with moisture, and cold with dryness, in a certain natural union, everything that is born on earth and in the sea is procreated. If anyone should wonder why cold, which is proper to water, descends from the upper regions of the air "into the lap" of earthly dryness,[187] it is because the waters suspended in the

187. Virgil, *Georgics* 2.326.

clouds are colder than those that flow in seas and rivers. And if anyone asks why many philosophers affirm that fire and air are active, but water and earth passive,[188] even though cold water mixed with the dryness of earth is active in seeds, not passive, here is the explanation. Water is cold and moist, but it receives moisture from the air and cold from itself. By the quality it takes on from the neighboring element, it passively receives the action of heat; but the quality that is its own is always active in seeds.

The four elements, therefore, occupying a middle place between the primordial causes and composite bodies, have received the name of "firmament."

### 195. *All bodies come from the elements*

M: You see rightly. So if the four simplest, most universal elements of the world are called by the name of firmament, do you think those four are connected and diffused everywhere in all bodies—ethereal,[189] airy, watery, and earthly—so that one can find no sensible body lacking the combination of all four? Or do certain elements flow together from others, but not all of them from all?

D: Philosophers say that within the compass of this sensible world, no body can exist in the dimensions of length, breadth, and height, in which the nature of the four elements cannot be understood, even though they are invisible. Just as everything that bodily perception discovers in the world receives the material of its composition from nowhere except mutual exchange of the qualities of the four elements, so in everything in this world (that is, all bodies), rational investigation finds nothing but the uniform combination of those simple, inseparable elements. Although some qualities may appear more prominent to the senses in some bodies, others less so, yet the assembly of those general elements[190] is uniformly commensurable, one

188. Augustine, *De Genesi ad litteram* 3.10 (CSEL 28.1, 73); 7.19 (CSEL 28.1, 215).

189. "Ethereal" refers to the stars, or bodies of fire.

190. Honorius's language is strangely ecclesiastical: *synodus ipsorum catholicorum elementorum.*

and the same in them all. Indeed, the divine mind balanced the equilibrium of the whole body of this world on an even scale between two extremes, which are mutually opposed. I refer to heaviness and lightness; between these two, every intermediate visible body is weighed. Insofar as all bodies participate in heaviness, they are able to receive earthly qualities, that is, solidity and stability. Insofar as they draw upon lightness, they participate in heavenly qualities, that is, emptiness and mutability.[191] Those in the middle, equally balanced between the extremes, participate equally in their qualities. But in all things there is one and the same movement, stability, capacity, and possession of the four universal elements.[192]

M: All natural philosophers agree on these points. So everywhere, throughout the entire visible world, there is an equal measurement and concourse of the four purest elements, which divine authority calls the firmament.

## 196. *On fire*

D: This has already been discovered by reason. The meaning of Greek nouns is a witness, for fire is called *pyr* because it penetrates all things through their pores, that is, hidden courses. There is no body from which fire cannot be shaken out if it is drawn by some collision. For even the friction of the waves shimmers, and they would not run as they do if they were entirely lacking in heat. What shall I say about colors, which undoubtedly proceed from the nature of light? Do we not see all bodies suffused with them?

## 197. *On air*

Air is called "spirit," or breath, because it breathes through all things. There is no sensible nature that the most subtle air cannot penetrate, as we can argue from scents and sounds. For you will not find a body that does not yield some odor to those who smell it or some sound to those who strike it.

191. A surprising turn since mutability is normally associated with earth, not heaven.

192. Gregory of Nyssa, *De hominis opificio* 1 (PG 44: 128c–132a).

### 198. *On water*

Water is called *ydor,* which means "a perceived image." There is no corporeal object from whose surface, if it is polished by some friction, an image cannot be reflected.

### 199. *On earth*

Earth is called *actos* from heaviness. There is no body that does not seek its natural place in proportion to its weight, whether it inclines toward the center of the world or the extremes. Or else earth is called *ge,* which properly signifies "valley." The valley of every creature is the place where it is circumscribed by its own definition.

So when you see any body, if you perceive the light of color in it, it partakes of the fiery element. If you hear a sound, whether spontaneous or artificial, it is airy. If its image is reflected in a flat surface by nature or art, it is watery (but where there is no reflection this is not a defect of nature, but of diligence). Where it tends upward or downward out of a desire for its natural station, understand that it partakes of the earthy element. There are many other natural proofs by which we know beyond doubt that the inseparable conjunction of the four elements is present, always and everywhere, in all composite bodies.

### 200. *On the stars*

M: These things seem right to me. So it is said, "Let there be lights in the firmament of the sky,"[193] that is, let the stars be made—bright, shining bodies composed from the qualities of the four elements, which are diffused in all places. We understand the underlying bodies of the stars in their courses in one way, and the brightness that shines from them through all the world's climatic regions in another. For "white" is one thing and "whiteness" another, nor are "bright" and "brightness" the same. One denotes a subject, the other an accident. By a divine com-

193. Gn 1.14.

mand, as Basil says, vessels for light were made to carry it around the compass of the world at fixed intervals of time.[194]

### 201. *On the moon*

The verse "Let there be lights" expresses in general the creation of all heavenly bodies that shine on the earth. Some of them are not far from the earth, like the moon, which Pythagoras says is 126,000 stades above the earthly globe.[195] So it is called close to the earth and often falls under its shadow. When it does not receive the sun's light, the moon suffers an eclipse. Philosophers call the distance between the moon and the earth a "tone," that is, an interval with a proportional quantity.[196] Experts in sounds say that tones have two modes of harmony. They call these *diastemata,* which are intervals between sounds, and analogies, which are their proportional ratios. Some are located in the middle of the world, like the sun and all the planets that revolve around it. Others are in the upper regions of the world, like the choirs of fixed stars.

D: Concerning the orbits and the distances between the most luminous heavenly bodies, wise men in the world have many varied opinions—and as far as I can tell, they have reached no certain conclusion. So, I beg you, do not hesitate to explain whatever seems to you most likely and reasonable about such matters.

M: As for the questions you now raise, scarcely any opinion is supported by reason or fully elaborated by any philosopher. I think this is not because they fail to understand them—otherwise, they would not rightly be called physicists or philosophers. But none of those whom we have read so far seem to explain their reasoning clearly, beyond a doubt. Nevertheless, using what they have written in scattered places and proved by experiment and definite arguments, I will not refuse to explain

194. Basil, *Hexaemeron* 6.2–3 (PG 29: 121a–c, 124b).

195. The length of a stade was disputed (chap. 202 below), but one of the most common figures was 185 meters, or one-eighth of a mile. Scientists today give the distance between the earth and the moon as an average of 238,855 miles.

196. Pliny, *Natural History* 2.21–22; Martianus Capella, *De nuptiis* 2.169.

to you what seems most likely about the distance between the earth and the moon. It has been ascertained without error that the moon is 126,000 stades from the earth at the time of its eclipse. Nature itself causes the shadow of the earth, which they call night, to touch the orb of the moon,[197] for the lunar globe would suffer no loss of its light if it were not deprived of the sun's rays when it falls into this region of shadow. That is why, without ambiguity, reason teaches that the shadow of night extends exactly as far as the moon is distant from the earth. The shadow of night extends to the orbit of the moon. Night, therefore, proves beyond doubt that the moon is 126,000 stades from the earth. From gnomic or horological speculation,[198] philosophers have subtly sought that distance and discovered it without ambiguity. It is handed down that the most learned in all geometrical and astronomical calculations was Eratosthenes.[199]

### 202. *On sundials*

"Sundials (*scaphia*) are bronze hemispherical bowls which measure the passage of the hours by means of a tall stylus standing at the center of the bottom of the bowl. This stylus is called a *gnomon*."[200] Lines are drawn from it as from the center to the outer rim of the basin. These lines divide the whole circumference of the sundial into twenty-four sections corresponding to the twenty-four hours of the day. In these intervals of time, the whole celestial sphere revolves until it returns to the same position on the natural horizon that it had reached on the day before. Eratosthenes, by carefully observing the movement of the gnomon's shadow through the sections of the sundial, came

197. Pliny, *Natural History* 2.10.

198. That is, calculations based on measurement from sundials (*horologia*). "Gnomic" refers to the *gnomon* or stylus of a sundial.

199. Eratosthenes, born in Cyrene (Libya) ca. 276 BCE, was a polymath who became head of the library at Alexandria. His experiment to calculate the circumference of the earth was recorded by Cleomedes in *De motu circulari corporum caelestium*, 1.10. But Eriugena, and Honorius after him, received this account in translation through multiple intermediaries and did not understand the experiment, so the account is garbled. One of Eriugena's sources, Martianus Capella's *De nuptiis Philologiae et Mercurii*, was a late antique textbook of the liberal arts.

200. Martianus, *De nuptiis* 6.597.

to understand clearly that as this shadow traverses the hourly intervals around the gnomon, its motion is proportional to the circuit of the night around the earth through the same hourly intervals. For this reason, whatever is observed in the basin of the sundial, representing the zodiac, can be understood by a similar observation to describe the motion of the heavenly bodies. At the vernal equinox, the length of the gnomon's shadow equals half the length of the gnomon in Meroë, an island in the Nile, and Syene, a city in Egypt.[201] But half the [length of the] gnomon is the diameter of the circle formed by whole sundial. Therefore, the shadow of the gnomon at the equinox equals the diameter of the sundial.[202] Because every diameter is doubled by the sphere or circle whose diameter it is, the gnomon's shadow must describe a circle that is twice its length, being doubled by the circle or sphere whose center it is. For example, if the number of a circle is ten, its diameter is five.[203]

By this clever reasoning based on the sundial, the ingenious Eratosthenes calculated the circumference of the whole earth with a subtle experiment. He first recognized that the circumference of the equinoctial circle, which divides the whole earth and the whole celestial sphere into two equal halves, consists of 360 degrees; and he understood without doubt that it takes one-twelfth (or 30 degrees) of this sphere two hours to rise or set from the place through which they move.[204] So reason proves that the unceasing movement of the heavenly bodies causes what the shadow in the sundial indicates to the senses. For the shadow of the gnomon would not move through the intervals of the sundial if the ethereal body that contains the stars were

201. Eratosthenes actually made his calculations at the summer solstice, basing them on the distance between Alexandria (not Meroë) and Syene (modern Aswan).

202. This could possibly be true at the winter solstice, but not at the equinox. The experiment requires two observers to take measurements in diverse locations at the same time of the day, which is not specified here.

203. The circumference of a circle is of course pi times its diameter, not twice the diameter. Since this formula discovered by Archimedes was well known to ancient mathematicians, it is hard to know what Eriugena intended.

204. This observation was made not by Eratosthenes, but by his Alexandrian successor Hypsicles, in *On Ascensions.*

not revolving around the earth. Therefore, whatever the mass of the earth accomplishes in the middle of the cosmos, the gnomon accomplishes in the middle of the sundial. And just as the shadow of the gnomon traces a course around itself through the circumference of the sundial, the night (which is the earth's shadow) describes a course around the earth itself on all sides,[205] through the space of the atmosphere that separates the moon from the earth. But the sun casts the same shadow from the bodies of the earth and the gnomon. Thus, with the help of the geometers of King Ptolemy, Eratosthenes discovered without error that the circumference of the whole earth is 252,000 stades.[206]

D: Pliny Secundus, Ptolemy in the *Geography,* and Eratosthenes seem to disagree about the measurement of the earth.

M: It seems unlikely that the supreme authorities in worldly wisdom would disagree so widely as for some to argue that the circumference of the earth is 252,000 stades, while others say it is 180,000.[207] It is possible that two people taking measurements, one taller and one shorter, measured a stade with longer and shorter steps, so that greater and lesser stades were used to calculate the measurement of a single part. Both parties confirm that the measurement of a stade is 125 steps.[208] It is reported that Hercules was the first to measure a stade near Mount Olympus.[209] But according to the Greek reckoning, a stade equals 6 iugera,[210] 100 cubits, 240 steps, 400 ells, or 600 feet.

D: I would like to know the measurement of the lunar body.

M: Many say that the globe of the moon is equal in size to the earth. But because every body is three times larger than its con-

205. That is, even when the sun is not visible.

206. Pliny, *Natural History* 2.108.247; Martianus, *De nuptiis* 6.598. Because several values for the length of a stade were in use, as explained below, this figure cannot be converted precisely into any modern unit of measurement. But astronomers agree that Eratosthenes's estimate had no more than a 10 percent margin of error, depending on the length of the stade used. The premises of his experiment were sound.

207. For Ptolemy see Martianus, *De nuptiis* 6.609–10.

208. Pliny, *Natural History* 2.23.85; Martianus, *De nuptiis* 6.610.

209. The "Olympic stade" was a fairly standard value.

210. A measurement of area comparable to an acre; the other units all measure length.

ical shadow,[211] the moon's shadow during an eclipse of the sun hides one-eighteenth part of the earth. This figure is 14,000 stades, which when tripled equals a sixth part of the earth. So they gather that the lunar body is one-sixth as large as the earth.[212] Therefore, they understand the size of the moon as 42,000 stades, for it equals a sixth part of the earth as measured in thousands of stades.

### 203. *On the mystery of numbers*

You will notice that the size of the moon and the earth are comprehended in the reciprocal values of the numbers six and seven. Six times seven or seven times six (42) embraces the orb of the moon, and again, six times forty-two (252) encompasses the size of the earth. Reason requires that all these numbers should be computed in thousands of stades, to reveal the crown of the most perfect constitution of natural bodies in the world. In fact, the cubic and solid shape of the number 1,000 signifies all perfection. The stability of nature is signified by the number six, its movement by seven, and the immutable proportion of both by a thousand. The mobile stability and stable motion of all things are established most perfectly by eternal ratios.[213]

Not without reason did the philosophers make all these measurements in stades. For the number five returns to itself: the first cube of five completes the stability of motion. For 5 x 5 x 5 yields 125 paces, which make up one stade. Hence, not without reason, both the movement of worldly bodies and their stability are summed up in the same number, which is both cubic and voluble and returns to itself.

### 204. *On the sun*

D: I would like to hear briefly about the ethereal regions.

M: The orb of the sun, balanced halfway between the heaviest

211. This is not accurate.

212. Martianus Capella, *De nuptiis* 8.859. The ultimate source of this calculation is Aristarchus of Samos (ca. 310–230 BCE), *On Sizes and Distances*. Aristarchus was the first to propose a heliocentric model of the solar system.

213. Maximus, *Ambigua* 13 (PG 91: 1228bc).

and the lightest nature, is eternally borne in a circular motion along the celestial equator, around the lower regions of the world. Neither scholars of secular literature nor exegetes of the divine Scriptures permit its size to be established by a fixed definition. For both Pliny the Elder in the *Natural History* and St. Basil in his *Hexaemeron* absolutely forbid the size of the sun to be defined.[214] Because the solar body permits no shadow to extend into infinity, but encloses the shadows of bodies within fixed dimensions, it plainly reveals its own boundless size. Pythagoras reports that the sun is distant from the moon by a double proportion.[215] You will find, therefore, that from the earth to the outermost sphere there is a distance of 756,000 stades, and you will marvel at the harmony of nature. For there are just as many thousand stades in the length of the moon's orbit as there are in the distance from the earth to the signs of the zodiac in the celestial realm. In both, the measurement is 756,000 stades. Therefore, the circumference of the universe is measured at 3,276,000 stades, so that the whole world may be enclosed in the perfection of the number six.

Let no one blame us if these measurements are not corroborated by the witness of holy Scripture. For an opponent cannot prove that they are not the case, just as we cannot confirm that they are.

### 205. *On philosophers*

D: How shall we respond if someone faults us for using philosophical reasoning?

M: Say this. When the people of God fled from Egypt, they were admonished by divine counsel to carry spoils, and they used those spoils blamelessly.[216] Likewise, experts in worldly wisdom have not earned blame as if they erred by reasoning about the visible creation, but rather because they did not seek its Au-

214. Pliny, *Natural History* 2.11; Basil, *Hexaemeron* 6.9–10 (PG 29: 137c–141b).

215. That is, double the distance from the earth to the moon. Pliny, *Natural History* 2.21.

216. Ex 3.21–22, 11.2, 12.35–36.

thor sufficiently beyond it. For they should have discovered the Creator from the creation, as we read that Plato did.

Christ at the time of his Transfiguration appeared in two snow-white garments shining like the sun, for his majesty is recognized in both Scripture and the visible creation.[217] "His invisible things," the Apostle says, "are seen and understood from the creation of the world."[218] Indeed, the knowledge of sensible things is a great and very useful step toward understanding of intelligible things. For just as we come through sense perception to understanding, so we return through the creation to God. It is not fitting for us to look only at the surface of visible things, as irrational animals do, but to contemplate the hidden reasons in them. An eagle sees the form of the sun more keenly; a wise human being sees its position and its movement through space and time more keenly.

If man had not sinned, he would not have been ignorant of the perfect boundaries of his possession of this world. He would have been another angel praising God in sensible creatures, and even after the Fall he has not altogether lost the dignity of his nature. There remains in him a rational movement by which he desires knowledge of things and does not wish to be deceived. Although he may in fact be deceived in many things, yet he is not deceived in all.

## 206. *What a cubit is*

D: Because we are discussing measurements, I would like to know what a cubit is, since many people have different opinions about it.

M: Noah's ark, the ark of the Covenant, the tabernacle, and other mystical works of the Old Testament are measured in cubits. St. Augustine says that a cubit is a measure of no more than two and a half palms.[219] The palm itself is measured from the tip of the thumb to the tip of the little finger.

217. Maximus, *Ambigua* 6.17 (PG 91: 1128b–d); 6.18 (PG 91: 1132c); 6.31 (PG 91: 1168b).

218. Rom 1.20.

219. Source unidentified.

### 207. *On geometers*

D: What do you think about those who measure the earth by degrees, stades, and other units of measurement—those whom the Greeks call geometers?

M: Do you think they measured the earth in feet, paces, cubits, or similar measures?

D: I would not easily believe this could be done, given the great diversity of mountains and valleys. Not even the level ground of the plains is so even that it could be measured with steps of equal length.

M: Then perhaps they measured by bodily sight?

D: Impossible—for perception deceives and nothing should be trusted to its judgment. The eye is deceived when an oar appears broken in water, or when it perceives a double image of the moon, a candle, or anything else through a deviation of sense, that is, splitting of the rays emitted by the pupils of the eyes, and interprets it as duplication.[220]

M: How then did they measure?

D: They first used a geometrical rod, as they say, which the Greeks call a ray. Multiplying five paces by its cube, that is, 5 x 5 x 5, they measured one stade. Having discovered one stade, it was easy to find many stades in the plains of Egypt, which is said to be the mother of such measurements.

M: Outside of Egypt, how did they explore the parts of the earth that are difficult to measure because of their great irregularity?

D: Neither by feet nor by rays, but by the argumentation of reason alone. They used sundials infallibly, discovering the intervals between degrees by the analogy of their shadows. For as far as one degree, that is, the daily progress of the sun through the zodiac, extends on the earth, its shadow on the sundial occupies the same proportional distance.

M: So they deduced the breadth of the degrees and stades by measuring where they reach the earth?

220. Augustine, *De Genesi ad litteram* 12.25 (CSEL 28.1, 417–18). This is the optical theory of extramission, according to which the eye itself emits rays that touch the object of perception.

D: They did not estimate in this way, but first they measured the highest mountains, determining how many thousand stades they rise above the surface of the earth. For example, they assert that the peak of Mount Olympus has an elevation of 10,000 stades, and they measured the heights of the Pindus, Rhodope, Ceraunian, and Atlas mountains. They began to extend a mental line from the peaks of the mountains into the aerial regions, always drawing it at an equal distance from the earth like a perfect circle, until it reached the place where it started. Thus they perceived with the mind's eye that the circumference of the earth is equal in all places.

M: This is how geometrical measurement was first discovered. Pliny estimates the size of the earth, measured by the peaks of the highest mountains, by drawing a mental line through geographical speculation.[221] Otherwise, the circular measurement of the earth could not succeed.

D: Go back to Scripture.

## 208. *Day and night*

M: "Let there be lights in the firmament of the sky, and let them divide the day and the night."[222] That is, the lights created in the sky separate day from night. Day and night always exist around the circumference of the earth. Wherever the sun is present, it illumines that region. Where it is absent, the brightness of the moon and stars supplies a kind of lamplight in the shadowy darkness, lest it be completely impenetrable to the gaze of animals.[223]

## 209. *Signs*

"And let them be for signs and for seasons and days and years."[224] By signs we understand not the stars, but omens of fair or stormy weather to come, which we experience especially from the colors of the celestial lights.[225]

221. Pliny, *Natural History* 2.108.
222. Gn 1.14.
223. Augustine, *De Genesi ad litteram* 2.13 (CSEL 28.1, 53).
224. Gn 1.14.
225. Augustine, *De Genesi ad litteram* 2.14 (CSEL 28.1, 54).

### 210. *Seasons*

The verse uses the general term "seasons," or times, for the journey and return of the stars, which are recalled by divine providence to the same movement and position in space at fixed intervals of time in the natural revolution of days and years.[226] "And let them shine in the firmament of the sky":[227] no star suffers an eclipse of its light, but they all shine in the ethereal regions at all times, with no overshadowing—except for the moon, which, when it descends into the region of shadow, loses the sun's rays and appears darkened. Thus it follows: "And let them illumine the earth. And it was so."[228] That is, it was so in the original causes, from which they proceeded into their own species, quantities, intervals, movements, and degrees of splendor. Hence the procession of the causes into species follows: "And God made two great lights, the greater light to rule the day" (the sun, whose presence produces day) "and the lesser light" (the moon, whose size and light are incomparably surpassed by the sun) "to rule the night, and the stars. And he set them" (that is, he fixed the stars) "in the firmament of the sky, that they might shine upon the earth."[229] Although the choirs of stars revolve with the world, they nevertheless remain fixed in their positions at all times. Reasoning about the cosmos infallibly teaches that no nature can be lower than the earth, which occupies the midpoint and the lowest place in the arrangement of the universe. For this reason, it is understood that no bodily creature is beneath it. So all the regions of the world and the bodies that surround the earth on all sides, whether mobile or stationary, were naturally created above it. Therefore, it says, "that they might shine upon the earth." For wherever they shine, whether below the horizon in the southern hemisphere (as human opinion estimates) or above the horizon in the northern hemisphere, they shine on the earth by their natural position. So the region above the earth is called a "hemisphere" because the stars appear to people in it.

226. Augustine, *De Genesi ad litteram* 2.14 (CSEL 28.1, 54–55).
227. Gn 1.15.
228. Ibid.
229. Gn 1.16–17.

"And let them rule the day and night and divide the light from the darkness."[230] That is, let them separate night and day, so that it will be day when the sun appears and night when the moon and stars appear. We should note that this division of light and darkness is not in the heavenly lights themselves but exists for those who dwell on the earth.[231] For the heavenly bodies always shine; for them it is always day, and they suffer no night. Their seats are continually radiant with their own light, as well as the sun's light, and they distribute the grace of their brightness to the world no less by day than by night. But for those who dwell on earth, for whom the days and nights alternate, the heavenly lights divide the light from the darkness. For day is nothing but the presence of light, and night is nothing but its absence.

## 211. *On the fifth day*

D: I think we should move on to the works of the fifth intelligible day.

M: So the order of things requires. "And God said: Let the waters bring forth creeping things with a living soul."[232] It is asked why the account of a living soul is introduced here. Some say that heaven with its stars, the ether with its planets, the air with its clouds, the water with its waves, and the earth with its plants and trees altogether lack not only a soul, but any kind of life. Therefore, in the works of the first four days, no mention of a soul or life is introduced. But others, including Plato, say that no body is deprived of life.[233] The greatest interpreters of holy Scripture agree with them, affirming that plants and trees are alive.

The nature of things does not allow it to be otherwise. For no matter can produce a body without a form; no form subsists without its own substance; and no substance can lack the vital motion that holds it together and causes it to subsist (for every-

230. Gn 1.18.
231. Augustine, *De Genesi ad litteram* 1.10 (CSEL 28.1, 15).
232. *Reptile anime viventis.* Gn 1.20.
233. Plato, *Timaeus* 30b, 37d.

thing that is naturally moved takes the beginning of its motion from some kind of life). It necessarily follows that every creature is alive in some way—either as Life in itself or as a participant in life, whether or not the movement of life manifestly appears in it. Every body is lesser than any life.[234] However little may be the time it remains in its form, it remains alive, whether through the life that governs each individual animal or the Life that administers the whole nature of the world. For just as there is no body that is not included in its own species, there is no species that is not governed by virtue of some kind of life. Therefore, if all naturally constituted bodies are governed by some species of life; every species seeks its own genus; and every genus takes its origin from the most universal substance, then it is necessary that every living species, which contains a multitude of diverse bodies, should revert to the most general form of life. By participating in this Life, it becomes a species. Worldly philosophers call this most general life "the most universal soul," which through its species administers all that is encompassed by the celestial sphere.[235] But those who contemplate divine wisdom call it "common life." Participating in that one Life that is substantial in itself, the source and creatrix of all life, by its divisions [the Soul] distributes the lives of visible and invisible creatures according to the divine ordinance, just as the sun known to our senses spreads its rays everywhere.

### 212. *No creature is without life*

Yet life does not reach into all things in the same way as the sun's rays do, for sunlight does not penetrate everything. For instance, it does not pass through the interior of many bodies. But no creature, whether sensible or intelligible, can be without life. Even bodies that appear dead to our senses are not entirely abandoned by life. Just as their composition and formation come about through the ministration of their proper

234. Augustine, *De Trinitate* 9.4 (CCSL 50, 297). Honorius uses "life" and "soul" interchangeably.

235. This is the *Anima mundi* or World Soul identified by Abelard and some philosophers of Chartres with the Holy Spirit, though Honorius avoids that implication. Manuscript P includes a drawing of it (fol. 1v).

life, so too their dissolution, loss of form, and return to the elements from which they were taken are accomplished by its service. Seeds committed to the earth do not return to life unless they first die,[236] and their death is the separation of matter and form. The same life that vivifies the seminal power, and by it, the seeds themselves before they are dissolved, does not abandon them in their dissolution; it always adheres to them. Or rather, it even dissolves them and at once begins to bring them back to life, that is, recall them to the same form, without delay. Where was that life at the time of the body's dissolution, except in the dissolved body itself? For just as life is not assembled when the body is assembled, nor dissolved when it is dissolved, neither is it reborn when the body is reborn. It does not invigorate the whole when it is joined together any more than when it is divided into parts. It is no greater or more powerful in the whole than in the part, and no less or weaker in the part than in the whole; for in all things it has the same control.

## 213. *What death is*

Dissolution itself, which is called the death of the body, is dissolution to our senses and to matter, but not to that nature that is inseparable and always exists in itself, and is not separated by distances in space and time. In fact, a human being does not cease to be human. A man consists of body and soul, but if he is always a man, he is always soul and body. Although the parts of a human being are separated from each other when they return to their proper elements, yet it is necessary by nature for them always to subsist inseparably. A human body, whether alive or dead, remains a human body. Likewise, a human soul, whether it governs its body connected to it or ceases to govern it when it dissolves into parts (as it appears to the senses), still does not cease to be a human soul. It administers the body dispersed among the elements no less than when it is united by the framework of its limbs, as true reason teaches beyond any doubt.

236. Jn 12.24.

### 214. *Dissolved bodies pass into qualities*

If the soul is a spirit that in itself lacks any bodily thickness, so too the elements into which the body dissolves are close to the spiritual nature. So it is no wonder if the incorporeal soul can rule the parts of its body that are preserved in natures resembling it; for it can more easily affect things like it than those unlike. But dense, corruptible bodies are unlike it, while very fine bodies, not at all subject to corruption, are like it. When parts of the dense body dissolve from its structure, they pass into very light, spiritual qualities—not to cease being bodies altogether, but to become spiritual bodies like the elements themselves.

This is also proven by an argument from the living body. Some parts of it are heavy and dense, such as the bones, flesh, nerves, and veins, and all the humors that moisten, nourish, and build up the whole mass. All these parts are taken into the body's constitution from watery and earthy qualities. But other parts are very light, such as vision and hearing. These parts of the body are drawn from fire and air, for there is "something luminous in the eyes, something airy in the ears."[237]

### 215. *What vision is*

Vision, as Augustine testifies, is a light that is first born from the fire of the heart. Then, ascending to the top of the head (to the part called the little membrane, which surrounds and protects the brain), it is drawn through certain channels to the eyebrows and pupils of the eyes. From there, bursting out with an impetus as swift as the sun's rays, it touches places and bodies that are nearby or even at a great distance, reaching them just as quickly as it touches the eyelids.[238]

### 216. *What hearing is*

Hearing is a very subtle kind of ringing. Proceeding first from the breath of the lungs and rising to the aforesaid part of the

237. Augustine, *De musica* 6.5.10 (PL 32: 1169).

238. Augustine, *De Genesi ad litteram* 1.16 (CSEL 28.1, 23); 4.34 (CSEL 28.1, 135); 7.13 (CSEL 28.1, 212); 12.16 (CSEL 28.1, 401).

head, it spreads through its hidden channels into the spiral cavities of the ears. As it bursts out and mingles with regions of the air, nearby or distant, it hastens to receive whatever sounds are in the air without delay.

These subtle parts of the body, which are closely related to spiritual natures, draw their origin from the interior of the dense mass, but are separated from it and extend far outward. For vision extends to receive the colored forms of visible things, and hearing to produce inner images of the accents of voices or other sounds produced by striking the air, which we call the forms and colors of voices. The other three senses seem to be contained within the boundaries of the body, although the sense of smell is not unfittingly thought to extend outward.

### 217. *On the human soul*

All this is accomplished by the soul (which in itself is simple and lacks corporeal quantity and spatial dimensions) in the body it controls by its presence. Although the soul is not contained in any place, it quickens and governs the local parts of its body wherever they may be. It is not enclosed locally in the mass of carnal members, nor does it act locally by extending outward, like the senses. But it is potentially present to receive the phantasms that are formed in the instruments of its senses, wherever they may be. Its greatness can be recognized by this proof of its natural virtue and freedom from place.

Indeed, at one and the same moment it senses the phantasms, or images, of the stars with eyebeams scattered through the ether, of sounds with hearing diffused in the air, of odors within or outside the body with the sense of smell, of flavors with the sense of taste, and of everything that can be felt with the sense of touch. The soul first perceives these phantasms, formed from bodily numbers in the sense organs, with amazing swiftness and without delay. It receives them through numbers that meet, introduces them through numbers that advance, commends them to memory through recordable numbers, organizes them through rational numbers, and approves or disapproves them through intellectual numbers, according to the rules of the divine numbers that are above it, whose exemplars it perceives.[239] It makes judgments concerning the numbers established within itself and the bodily and sensual numbers which are both outside it.[240]

## 218. *On the eight numbers*

Reason has discovered eight orders of numbers, of which the first and highest is above the intellect in the eternal causes. According to it the rational soul discerns all things, as the Apostle says: "The spiritual man judges all things, but he himself is judged by no one."[241] Two others exist fully outside as well as within the soul. One of these, the outermost, is in bodies from which the bodily senses are formed, where the phantasms are created. The other is formed in the bodily senses themselves; it is set up to be the first order of phantasms in the instruments of the senses (I mean the eyes, ears, and other sense organs). In the soul itself, five numbers are considered to be innate. First are the *occursores,* which go to meet the phantasms and receive them. After these, the *progressores* are like guides to the city of memory. When the phantasms reach it, they are introduced by the *recordabiles.* Then the *rationales* distribute them through the city just as the *intellectuales* command. The throng of phantasms coming in through vision occupy a special place in the memory. Likewise, those that enter through hearing and the other senses are received in their own seats in the same city.

It is no wonder, then, if after the dissolution of the body, the rational soul acts within its parts diffused among the elements by a hidden, natural ministration that is removed from all bodily sense—given that even while the body is still alive and in one piece (as far as it appears to the senses), the soul exercises the power of its governance not only in the mass of members, but also in the senses that are extended far from the body.

239. The different kinds of "numbers" employed in this theory of perception are called *corporales, occursores, progressores, recordabiles, rationales,* and *intellectuales* (see chap. 218). They are loosely connected with different cells of the brain.

240. Augustine, *De musica* 6.6.16–6.9.24 (PL 32: 1171–77); 6.13.42 (PL 32: 1185).

241. 1 Cor 2.15.

### 219. *The most universal life*

D: Return to the most universal life.

M: There is a twofold division of the most universal life: rational and irrational. It is rational in angels and humans, but irrational in all animals that have the power of sensation as well as in material things without sensation, such as plants and trees.[242] The cause of difference is called intellectual in angels but rational in humans. Thus the four different kinds of created life are gathered in four species: intellectual in angels, rational in human beings, sensual in beasts, and insensible in plants and other bodies such as the four elements, whether simple or compound. I refer to earth, water, air, and ether.

### 220. *The human being is all creation*

For this reason the human being is justly called the workshop of all creatures, for in man is contained the whole creation.[243] He has intelligence like an angel, reasoning like a human being, sensation like an irrational animal, and subsists in body and soul like a plant; he lacks nothing that belongs to any creature. For you find no creature outside of these things.

### 221. *The angels are above the senses*

D: Aren't all these things also contained in the angel?

M: By no means. The power of sensation distributed to animals cannot subsist except in a body composed of the four elements. There will be no vision where there is no fire, nor hearing if air is absent. Take away moisture, and neither smell nor taste will remain. In the absence of earth, all touch is removed. But angelic bodies are simple and spiritual, lacking all the external senses.[244] They do not receive knowledge of sensible things

242. The figure of Anima Mundi (the World Soul) in the famous P drawing, fol. 1v, holds a scroll that reads, "Vegetabilis in arboribus, sensibilis in pecoribus, racionabilis in hominibus" (vegetative in trees, sensitive in beasts, rational in humans).

243. Maximus, *Ambigua* 37 (PG 91: 1305a).

244. Augustine, *De diversis quaestionibus* 47 (PL 40: 31); *Epistola* 9.3 (CSEL 34.2, 21).

through the phantasms of bodies. Rather, they perceive every bodily creature spiritually in its spiritual causes, just as we ourselves will see when we are transmuted to equality with their nature.[245] The angels therefore lack bodily sensation, for they are above it. And for this reason they lack all irrational life, whether sensory or deprived of sensation; they are not weighed down by composite, corruptible bodies. Hence you will find many things in a human being that angelic nature by no means receives. But nothing subsists in an angel or any other creature that does not naturally inhere in man.

### 222. *The power of the soul*

D: So if every kind of life exists in man, he contains not a single life but many different ones, possessing at the same time irrational and rational life, sensory life and the life of plants.

M: Look attentively at the powers of the human soul. Although it has one and the same subsistence, power, and operation, both in all human bodies taken together and in particular individuals, it can nevertheless accomplish all its vital motions and ministries in its body, both within and beyond it. In fact, beyond the corporeal senses it reasons and understands like angelic life. Within the bodily senses, it exercises the power of sensation like irrational animals, yet without forsaking its rationality. It nourishes its body and promotes growth like the life that lacks sensation, but penetrates plants and trees. It is everywhere whole in itself and in all its members, and the whole soul guards all its senses. In the bones, nails, and hair it reveals the power of a life like that of plants, for these parts of our body, being impermeable to air, do not participate in sensation. In the fivefold instrument of the senses, it shares in the irrational life of animals that lack the power of reason. In all these things, although it may often be moved irrationally, nature does not allow it to lack its own proper reason. But in everything it can do beyond the aforesaid powers—that is, the powers of quickening, nourishing, and perceiving through the senses—whether it acts

245. Augustine, *De Genesi ad litteram* 4.24 (CSEL 28.1, 123–24).

or is acted on, it is known by right reason to act or be acted on outside of its body.

## 223. *The life of plants*

D: Now that we have said these useful things about life or the soul, I would like to know why mention of a "living soul" is made on the fifth day.[246]

M: Because on the fifth day, the creation of animals that flourish with five senses is first mentioned. The life of plants and other insensible things, entirely without intellect and reason, is counted more among bodily numbers than among vital numbers. So in the works of the first four days, when the species of heavenly and earthly beings are brought forth openly from the primordial causes and receive their perfect formation, nothing that signifies vital motion is mentioned. A soul that has no sensation seems also to be completely without vital motion. For this reason it is called simply a soul, but not a *living* soul. It can do nothing outside of its body, and therefore it is counted among the numbers of bodily nature rather than the species of universal life. This is no wonder, for if such a soul is judged to lack reason and intelligence in infants conceived in the womb or newly born (for even though it is rational and intellectual, it cannot yet manifest the signs of reason and intelligence in the very young, still imperfect parts of its little body),[247] how much more should a soul that is naturally deprived of the powers of intelligence, reason, and sensation also be deprived in Scripture of the term "living soul"?

## 224. *All bodies are contained in life*

D: I approve this opinion. But since many contend that plants and trees have no vital motion at all, saying they thrive through the moisture that makes them green, but with no other life, I would like some serious authority to support those who say that plants are governed by some kind of life.

246. Gn 1.20.

247. Gregory of Nyssa, *De hominis opificio* 29 (PG 44: 236b–d).

M: You are not unaware, I think, that all philosophers who argue about the world hold a unanimous opinion about this portion of nature. They say that all bodies contained within this sensible world are contained by vital motion, whether they are stationary or moving.[248] Basil, the most noble bishop of Cappadocia, says, "Plants and trees may be said to be alive because they participate in the power of nutrition and growth, even though they are not animals or ensouled."[249] Gregory of Nyssa, the brother of this Basil, says that the vital and animal virtue is contemplated in three differences. The first, called germinal, concerns plants; the second or irrational concerns animals; the third is called rational and concerns human nature.[250] Augustine too says, "Let not our religion be the worship of that life by which trees are said to live, for it has no sensation. From that genus comes the life that maintains the harmony of our body. With this life even our hair and bones are alive, though they are cut without sensation."[251] In my opinion, these testimonies of the fathers suffice to corroborate what we have said.

## 225. *On the soul of irrational animals*

D: As for the soul of irrational animals, I am eager to know why many of the holy fathers affirm that it perishes with their bodies and cannot survive longer. Basil says, "The soul of every animal is its blood.[252] Congealed blood normally turns into flesh, but corrupted flesh is resolved into earth. Consequently, the soul of beasts is some kind of earthly substance. Do not think, therefore, that it is older than the substance of their bodies or survives after the dissolution of the flesh."[253] Gregory of Nyssa too says that in beasts "there can be an ambiguous kind of soul, but it is not truly a soul. Rather, it is a certain vital operation that goes by the name of soul."[254]

248. Plato, *Timaeus* 30b, 37d; Pliny, *Natural History* 2.1.1–2; 2.5–7; 2.7.27.
249. Basil, *Hexaemeron* 7.1 (PG 29: 148c).
250. Gregory of Nyssa, *De hominis opificio* 8 (PG 44: 144d–145a).
251. Augustine, *De vera religione* 55.109 (CCSL 32, 257).
252. Lv 17.11; Dt 12.23.
253. Basil, *Hexaemeron* 8.2 (PG 29: 168a).
254. Gregory of Nyssa, *De hominis opificio* 15 (PG 44: 177a).

M: If this is as they claim, why does the first division of universal life separate the rational, intellectual soul from the soul that lacks reason and intellect? Why are two species of the single genus of life set up as contraries? For the rational and the irrational are not mutually opposed; they express the different species of one genus. But to live and to die are absolutely opposed to each other; one signifies a condition, the other its privation. Condition and privation contradict each other. So if one species survives after the body's dissolution but the other perishes, how will their genus preserve its wholeness? When a genus perishes, all its species must perish too. Conversely, when the species perish, reason requires that their genus should also perish, for a genus is saved in its species and a species in its genus. And if, as Dionysius says, all the species in a genus are one,[255] how will that one partly perish and partly survive? For there is a single genus of all things composed of body and soul, which is called "animal" because all animals substantially subsist in it. In this genus a man, a lion, an ox, and a horse are one, and one substantial thing. And if that one is one substantial thing, how will it perish when these three—substance, power, and operation—survive incorruptibly in every creature, with no increase or decrease?[256]

The bodies of all animals are not reduced to nothing when they are dissolved. Rather, they return to the qualities of the elements whose combination materially forms them, as natural reason clearly asserts. How then can their souls perish utterly when the soul is the better nature (for no one with wisdom denies that any soul is superior to every body)? How unreasonable it would be for the worse part to survive and be saved, while the better part is corrupted and perishes! And if what is compound is preserved, though separated into its parts, how can what is simple and lacks composition be dissolved when it cannot be destroyed? What student of wisdom does not know that every body is compound while every soul is simple? Some assert that irrational souls perish after the body's dissolution because, as they say, they were taken from the earth and are resolved into

255. Dionysius, *De divinis nominibus* 13.2 (PG 3: 977d–980a).

256. Dionysius, *De caelesti hierarchia* 11.2 (PG 3: 284d); *De divinis nominibus* 4.23 (PG 3: 724c–725a).

earth. Why then do they exalt the power of the irrational soul in the senses with great praise, even preferring it to the power of the rational soul in the bodily senses?

### 226. *On the goods of the irrational soul*

What human being sees as keenly as an eagle or a gazelle? What man can smell as well as a dog? What shall I say about the long memory of irrational animals? Ulysses's dog recognized its master after twenty years.[257] A camel that suffers an injury from its masters seeks a fitting opportunity for its revenge after many years, for it always remembers the injury. And what shall I say about their natural virtues? They say the griffin is so chaste that after losing its conjugal partner, it preserves inviolate chastity forever, remembering its prior marriage; and the same is said about the turtledove. Concerning the great filial piety of storks, it is written, "When their father is old and loses his plumage from old age, his offspring surround him on all sides and keep him warm with their own feathers. They prepare food in abundance and even offer powerful help in flight, lifting the quiet bird on both sides,"[258] and thus they help him in every way.

I cannot figure out how all these natural virtues could exist in an irrational soul if, as they say, it were earth born of earth and resolved into earth, or if it were not truly a substantial soul. And if the soul is earth and earth is a body, why is the body called a soul when, because of their natural difference, these are quite unlike each other? And if the soul is a body, it will necessarily have a life that quickens it, for there is no body without life and form. Otherwise, it would not be a body. For that reason, it would be the soul of a soul or the life of a life. Without refuting the opinion of the saints, therefore, we will seek to the best of our ability to find what we should more reasonably hold. And we hold the unshaken view that every life or soul that governs a body subsists by participation in the one primordial life or soul. Natural reason does not allow the soul utterly to abandon the life it received by participation in life, whether or not

257. Augustine, *De quantitate animae* 26.50 (PL 32: 1064).
258. Basil, *Hexaemeron* 8.5 (PG 29: 176c).

it is controlling a body. But when bodies are dissolved, souls are preserved in their genera, abandoning the governance of their bodies.

### 227. *On fish and birds*

D: Let us pass on to the verses that remain.

M: "Let the waters bring forth creeping things with a living soul, and birds on the earth beneath the firmament of the sky."[259] As the creeping things have a living soul, we understand that this also applies to birds,[260] for more signs of a living soul are distinguished in the senses of birds than of fish. "The hearing of fish is sluggish, and they see with blurred vision because of the water. Nor do they have much memory, and they possess neither imagination nor knowledge of what ordinarily happens."[261] But all these capacities flourish in birds no less than in human beings, or even more so.

It is asked why birds are said to have been produced from water. For it would seem more credible if, just as animals that dwell on land are said to have been created from earth, only fish as the possessors of water were created from water, but birds were created from air, since they fly through the air. We should know, however, that there are two kinds of water. One kind, found in seas and rivers, is of a denser quality; the other kind is vaporous, cloudy, and lighter. The denser kind is supported by the solidity of earth, the lighter kind upheld in the serenity of air. The creeping things with a living soul—that is, the genera and species of all fish—are believed to have been created from the denser kind of water; but the birds in their genera and species, from the lighter kind. Now the atmosphere between the moon and the earth is divided into two parts. The upper part is serene; it is not subject to disturbances born in the air from earthly and aquatic vapors. But the lower part is moist and of a more corpulent character; it is affected by the movement of winds, the massing of clouds, and other phenomena produced by the nearness

259. *Reptile anime viventis.* Gn 1.20.
260. Augustine, *De Genesi ad litteram* 3.8 (CSEL 28.1, 70).
261. Basil, *Hexaemeron* 8.1 (PG 29: 165a).

of earth and water. Whatever is born from that lower part of the air is of a moist, watery quality, and is not unfittingly believed to be created from the air.[262] Birds could not cross the part of the air that is closest to the earth and the waters if they altogether lacked an airy nature. But since they are distinguished by the lightness of their feathers, the hollowness of their bones, and their ease in flight, it can be clearly understood that they were created not only from water but also from air.

## 228. *Amphibians*

This is easily seen as well from the nature of amphibians that live in both water and air, or else in water and on land. There are certain birds that dwell alternately in the air and the water. While they live in water, they take the form of fish; but in air, the form of birds. And they do this for six months at a time, changing their form: for six months they swim in the water, and for six they fly in the air and descend to the earth like other birds. Birds of this species always travel in flocks, whether in air or water. They are called flying fish.[263] From this we understand that birds participate in the substance of both elements, air and water. There are also amphibians that live double lives on land and in water—seals, crocodiles, and many similar creatures.

Here is another argument to show why birds are believed to be made from moist air. They breathe in and out, so they dwell both on land and in the air. But they suffocate in water, which is why they always swim on its surface, except for those amphibians that freely immerse themselves in the waves. But fish, because they were created only from the dense form of water, cannot breathe in and out like earthly and airy animals. They quickly die from contact with earth and air, yet they are not entirely deprived of breathing and respiration. If they were, they would be unable to sleep. Yet as Pliny says, fish do sleep. So they have lungs that breathe in and out, but they do not draw their breath from the more corpulent air. Rather, they draw it from that very

262. Augustine, *De Genesi ad litteram* 3.3 (CSEL 28.1, 65–66); 3.6–7 (CSEL 28.1, 68–69).

263. *Luligo,* an obscure term that can also refer to a dolphin or porpoise.

thin air that penetrates all bodies.[264] Because fish and birds are of a moister nature than other animals, their qualities manifestly declare that they are created from water alone, for they are moist and cold. Therefore, divine Scripture relates that they are brought forth from the waters: "Let the waters bring forth creeping things with a living soul, and birds on the earth."[265] This is as if it plainly said that one kind of water is denser, so let it bring forth fish; let the other, lighter kind bring forth birds.

This difference can also be discerned from their bodies, for we see fish encumbered by the heaviness of denser bodies, while birds are lifted on high by the lightness of wings. When it says, "on earth beneath the firmament of the sky," this clearly means that birds' bodies are not at all burdened by earthly weight, but borne above the earth in the air, from whose moist quality they were created, beneath the firmament. No other species of animals approaches the subtlety and spirituality of the simple elements by a natural likeness as birds do. They were rightly bidden to come into being beneath the firmament, that is, in proximity to the elements whose quality is purest, almost incorporeal. In short, the bird is created beneath the firmament of the sky, which is near to and yet beneath the extremely light, tenuous quality of spiritual bodies.

These things are said about the creation of fish and birds in the primordial causes. Their procession into genera and species follows: "And God created great whales and every living soul," and the rest.[266] A whale is a monster; by it all the others are implied.

Having said these things about the fifth day, let us now move on to the return of all things into that nature that neither creates nor is created.[267]

264. Pliny, *Natural History* 9.7.16–19.

265. Gn 1.20.

266. Gn 1.21.

267. The return (*reditus*) is the theme of *Periphyseon,* Book 5, which Honorius transcribed in its entirety. But in fact, he moves on at this point to Book 4, which deals with human nature and the Fall.

# BOOK IV

## 229. *On the sixth day*

D: FIRST I would like you to expound something succinctly concerning the sixth day.

M: "And God said, Let the earth bring forth a living soul."[1] That is, let the earth bring forth a living animal. The text signifies the whole animal by its better part, the soul.[2] Because the lesser part—the body—is taken from the earth, the whole animal (body and soul) is commanded to come forth from the earth, according to that trope by which the whole is understood from a part.[3] The soul is absolutely not earth, just as the body is not a soul. Yet, because the soul clings to the body in the unity of animal nature, Scripture says it came into being from the earth at the same time.

## 230. *What "earth" means*

Alternatively, the word "earth" implies the changeless solidity of the whole substantial nature of things, visible and invisible. Hence the Apostle says, "Mortify your members that are on the earth."[4] This means: mortify the members of evil (which are "yours" because they were made by you, not God), which you have built on the earth, that is, on the solidity of the nature created by God. Set up instead the members of righteousness, which are the virtues. So, just as you have constructed a temple to the devil by various sins, build a precious house for God with

1. Gn 1.24.
2. Augustine, *De Trinitate* 7.4 (CCSL 50, 255).
3. Synecdoche.
4. Col 3.5.

the stones of virtues. Hence the Psalmist says, "Let sinners be consumed from the earth, and let the wicked be no more."[5] That is, when the earth of nature is delivered from all evil, sins and iniquities will be consumed so they will be no more. For as long as they seem to exist, even though they are nothing, let them be confined by the nature that is their subject. But when nature is purified, sins and iniquities, which cannot subsist by themselves, will be utterly reduced to nothing so they will be no more. Of this earth it is written, "Not so are the wicked, but they are like dust that the wind drives off the face of the earth."[6] This means that the wind (the discernment of God's just judgment) will drive the dust of all evil off the surface of the earth, that is, off the substantial beauty of nature.

Once again, it is written concerning this earth that "His spirit will go forth and return to his earth."[7] Whose spirit? The spirit of him who, in suffering for us, "bowed his head and gave up his spirit."[8] Where will it go? It descended to hell to bring back human nature, which was held captive there.[9] But since death could not hold captive the one in whom it had found no crime, "he will return to his earth," that is, to his nature that he made, redeemed, and assumed, in an immortal body. Indeed, he will return in the original state of human nature, and beyond even that in the glory of the Resurrection. His spirit went forth alone, yet did not return alone but with the whole of human nature, as he said: "If a grain of wheat dies, it brings forth much fruit."[10] "You will send forth your spirit," says the Psalmist, "and renew the face of the earth";[11] that is, you will restore the wholeness of nature.

The soul of Christ was given up for the salvation of the world with bowed head, that is, with the compassion of his divinity;[12] it went forth and returned to the nature he redeemed by his mis-

5. Ps 103.35.
6. Ps 1.4.
7. Ps 145.4.
8. Jn 19.30.
9. Eph 4.8–9.
10. Jn 12.24–25.
11. Ps 103.30.
12. Phil 2.30; 1 Jn 3.16.

sion. It was also sent forth to restore the beauty of nature, which had been destroyed. Or the spirit of Christ, with his head (which is Christ) bowed in humility, was given over to a momentary death of the flesh "for the whole creation."[13] The firstborn of creation is the one whose spirit went forth and will return to his earth, that is, to the nature he had forsaken because of the first man's sin. That nature belonged to Christ before it abandoned the sinner, but for the sake of Christ, whose spirit it is and who suffered for it, he will return to that [original] nature.[14] And he will return and be sent out more fully at the time of the resurrection so that, by his power, the face of all nature may be restored to its original beauty.

Therefore, because all animals were created causally and primordially in body and soul on this earth, which is common to them all, and all were created in honor, what wonder is it if by a divine command, the earth is bidden to bring forth a living soul, that is, a living animal, so that it might openly bring forth in genera and species what it held causally and secretly in the causes and reasons? And see how the divine word reveals to us the natural order of things, for it says, "Let the earth bring forth a living soul in its genus."[15] It posits the genus first, for all species are contained in the genus, and in it all are one;[16] and in them it is divided and multiplied through the general and the most specialized of forms. Scripture reveals this also when it says, "cattle and creeping things and beasts of the earth, according to their species."[17]

### 231. *Where dialectic comes from*

For this reason we understand that the art called dialectic, which divides genera into species and resolves species into genera, was not devised by human invention, but created in the nature of things by the author of all arts, provided that they are

13. Col 1.15.

14. This ambiguous sentence is clearer in Eriugena, where it refers to the Holy Spirit.

15. Gn 1.24.

16. Dionysius, *De divinis nominibus* 13.2 (PG 3: 977d–980a).

17. Gn 1.24.

truly arts. It was discovered by the wise and is usefully employed in the skilled investigation of reality.

### 232. *Why animals were created on the sixth day*

D: From the things you have reasonably said as well as what we discussed above, if I am not mistaken, fish and birds were created from this visible, tangible, moist, cold element of water. We can take this to mean that they were brought forth from the mysterious and hidden depths of nature, in which they were causally and primordially made, into genera and species. Just as the word "earth" signifies the solidity and fruitfulness of nature, the same nature's hidden depth can be understood in the meaning of "waters." Thus one and the same source of all animals can be recognized, whether we read that they were created from earth or from the waters, though our contemplation of them is divided. One mode of prophetic contemplation is said to have been created on the fifth day, another on the sixth. This is not without reason, for the earthly animals that were bidden to come forth from the earth on the sixth day, when the human being was made, seem to have a greater similarity to man in their nature. Indeed, the speculation of natural philosophy finds that everything we recognize in the nature of the human animal, except intellect and reason, inheres in them by nature.

### 233. *On the power of seeds*

M: Just as we see the marvelous, beautiful variety of innumerable colors in a single peacock feather, so we recognize the multiple, infinite understanding of the divine Scriptures. Indeed, the very nature of things draws us to this understanding. For this sensible earth and water are bodies composed from the qualities of the four elements. Nothing is born of itself, and no species of nature seems to be born from them directly. But the power of seeds, by the activity of the life called "nutritive," bursts forth into different species of plants, shoots, and animals through genera and forms drawn from the secret bosom of creation, according to their innate laws and reasons, as far as divine providence permits. Through this process by which the visible, tangible earth and water proceed into their natural species, qualities, and quantities, all things that seem to be born of them receive their source of generation. For there is a universal nature common to all things, created from the one principle of them all. They derive from it like streams flowing from an ample fountain through the hidden channels of the bodily creation, breaking forth into the various forms of individual creatures. The aforesaid power, proceeding from diverse seeds in the hidden recesses of nature and bursting forth at first in the seeds themselves, then mingles with diverse humors and bubbles up in individual, sensible species.

### 234. *That man is an animal*

D: These things seem certain. Now man, created on the sixth day, is counted among the animals that are included in a single genus. So I would like to hear from you whether or not we should understand him as included in that divine command that commanded the earth to bring forth a living soul.

M: Scripture says, "Let the earth bring forth a living soul in its genus,"[18] so it has very plainly shown that all animals are included in this command. For there is no species that is not fully contained in its genus. Yet, through the dignity of reason and understanding, this animal form, ordained in the human being, surpasses the nature of other animals belonging to the same genus. Hence the prophet's contemplation prudently wished to distinguish human nature from other animals in order to relate the human being's creation more fully and thoroughly as the last of all God's works, in keeping with the excellence of human nature. Therefore, the greatest, most precious animal species is mentioned twice in the works of the sixth speculative day. He is mentioned first in his genus when the earth is commanded to bring forth an animal. Then a bit later, after a very brief division of the other animals, his creation in the image and likeness of God is introduced.

D: So a single species is brought forth from the earth among other animals, and at once he is said to be made in the image

18. Gn 1.24.

of God! This rightly troubles me. If that whole genus called "animal," with all its species, were made in the image and likeness of God, perhaps I would not be disturbed by what you teach—namely, that man was both brought forth from the earth along with other animals and afterwards fashioned in the image and likeness of God. But the divine history relates that man alone and no other animal was created in God's image. I am amazed at how man is brought forth from the earth among "cattle and creeping things and beasts of the earth,"[19] yet he alone is formed in the image of God, incomparably far beyond all other animals, just as Scripture says: "Let us make man in our image and likeness."[20] What is yet more wonderful, how can he be brought forth from the earth among those creatures over whom he is commanded to have dominion? For Scripture adds, "And let him have dominion over the fish of the sea, the birds of the sky, and the beasts of all creation, and over every creeping thing that moves upon the earth."[21]

## 235. *The three movements of man*

M: You are rightly troubled. In fact, the threefold division of this genus into "cattle (or quadrupeds), creeping things, and beasts"[22] was not made without cause. For on the other days in which genera and species are mentioned, namely the third and fifth, no division of a genus into species is introduced. Either the genus alone is mentioned simply, with no distinction into species of plants (on the third day), or else the genus alone and a single species of fish are mentioned (on the fifth day). But on the sixth day, not only is the creation of the genus recounted, but also its threefold division into species—cattle, creeping things, and beasts. This threefold division implies a threefold movement that is understood to exist only in man, the sole rational animal.

19. Ibid.

20. Gn 1.26.

21. Ibid.

22. *Iumenta—vel quadrupedia—et reptilia bestiasque.* Gn 1.24. The reading *quadrupedia* comes from the LXX. See Augustine, *De Genesi ad litteram* 3.11 (CSEL 28.1, 74).

The first movement, called "cattle," is that by which the five senses of the body move in a disciplined way[23] toward the knowledge of sensible things, in a skillful effort to understand them. This bodily perception is called "quadruped" because we perceive that everything it shows us about the nature of sensible things is composed of the four elements. The second movement, derived from irrational nature, resists reason—such as rage, greed, or the craving for sensible goods. This is signified by the term "beasts." The third movement occurs in the part of the soul that controls growth and nourishment. Pervading the harmonious body through a silent channel, it is called by the name of "creeping things." Only two of these three movements are found in animals other than man. The one that exists in the senses lacks the control of reason and is therefore bestial. The second, which belongs to the life of nourishment, is like a creeping thing. Man participates in these along with other animals, and reciprocally, other animals participate along with man. Do you see, then, how man is in all animals and all are in man, and yet man is above them all?

### 236. *That the human being is both an animal and not an animal*

And if anyone looks more attentively at the marvelous, wholly ineffable creation of his nature, he will clearly find that the same human being is at once a particular species within the genus "animal," yet subsists above every animal species. For this reason he can receive both affirmation and negation,[24] and both can rightly be predicated of him: "Man is an animal; man is not an animal." For when he is considered with regard to the body, nutritive life, sense perception, memory of sensible things, and every irrational appetite, such as rage and greed, he is altogether an animal, for he has all of these in common with other animals. But when reason and intellect are weighed along with the interior senses and all their rational movements, known as virtues, together with the memory of divine and eternal things,

23. *Disciplinabiliter.*

24. An aspect of the divine image; compare chaps. 25 and 243.

he is altogether not an animal. For all these are innate in man along with the heavenly beings, who by the excellence of their substance incomparably surpass everything that is found in the nature of animals.

### 237. *The human being as double*

Hence the Apostle divides the human being in two, as it were, of which one part is called animal and the other spiritual: "The animal man does not perceive the things that belong to the Spirit of God," and again, "The spiritual man judges all things."[25] Again the Apostle says, "The outer man is corrupted, but the inner man is renewed from day to day,"[26] that is, he will ascend "from virtue to virtue."[27] The nature that man shares with animals is called flesh, and the nature by which he participates in heavenly being is called mind, spirit, or intellect. Therefore, the creation of man is double:[28] what is animal is created with the animals, and what is spiritual with the spiritual beings. So do not be troubled that I said man was brought forth from the earth with the other animals in one and the same genus, but also made in the image and likeness of God, beyond the nature of all animals.[29]

D: Perhaps it would not trouble me if I could clearly discern how man was created in one and the same genus as all animals, yet subsists in his better part above all animal nature.

M: Insofar as he is an animal, man was made among the animals in a single genus. But insofar as he is not animal, he was made outside every animal genus.

### 238. *A human being does not have two souls*

D: Now a greater, far more difficult question has arisen. For you seem, in my opinion, to think that two souls exist in a single human being. One governs, quickens, and nourishes the body,

25. 1 Cor 2.14–15.
26. 2 Cor 4.16.
27. Ps 83.8.
28. Gregory of Nyssa, *De hominis opificio* 16 (PG 44: 181b).
29. Gn 1.24, 26.

makes it grow, perceives sensible things through the bodily senses, stores their phantasms in its memory, and does everything else that the souls of other animals are known to do in their bodies. But the other subsists in reason and intellect and is made in the image and likeness of God. This seems quite absurd!

M: Neither reason nor divine authority permits me to think there are two souls in one human being. Rather, they prohibit this, nor is it lawful for any right-thinking philosopher to hold that view. I assert rather that man consists of one and the same rational soul, joined to the human body in an ineffable way. By a wondrous and intelligible division, man has no share in animality in the part made in the Creator's image and likeness; he is utterly free of it. But in the part that shares in animality, the same man was brought forth from the earth within the universal genus of animals—that is, the nature common to all.

### 239. *That the soul is simple*

D: What then shall we say? Should we believe that the human soul is simple in nature, devoid of all composition, or that it consists of certain parts joined in a kind of unity?

M: There is one belief that I firmly hold, namely that the soul is simple; in no way does it consist of parts joined together. I totally reject the alternative, the view that it takes any compound nature from mutually differing parts. For it is whole in itself and everywhere exists as a whole. The whole soul is life; the whole is intellect; the whole is reason, sensation, and memory. The whole soul quickens, nourishes, and controls the body and gives it growth. The whole soul perceives the forms of sensible things with all the senses. Beyond all bodily sensation, the whole soul considers, distinguishes, combines, and judges the nature and order of the cosmos. Above and beyond all creation and its own self, the whole soul, when it is purged of all vices, revolves around its Creator with an eternal, intelligible motion. Yet, although it subsists naturally in such simplicity, it is analytically divided into its intelligible and substantial differences as a whole is divided into parts, according to the abundance of its motions. For this reason it is designated by many names.

## 240. *On the names of the soul*

When it revolves around the divine being, it is mind, spirit, and intellect. When it considers the natures and causes of creatures, it is reason. When it receives the impressions of sensible things through the bodily senses, it is sensation.[30] When it accomplishes its hidden movements in the body, giving it nourishment and growth just as irrational souls do, it is properly called life. But in all these operations it is everywhere whole.

D: Therefore, it is wholly brought forth from the earth in the genus of animals—and wholly made in the image of God.

M: Even so! No right-thinking philosopher is allowed to doubt this lest he seem to split its simple, undivided nature, which is most impious.

## 241. *A fivefold division*

D: How, then, to continue our previous argument, is one and the same human being both an animal and not an animal? Or how does he both have and lack animal nature? How is he flesh, yet not flesh? Spiritual, yet not spiritual? And how can these things, which are mutually opposed and contradictory, be understood to exist in a single, absolutely simple nature?

M: From what we have already said, if someone looks attentively at everything that seems to you contrary to the simplicity of human nature, he will clearly find that not only is it not contrary, but is even entirely fitting. For the wise agree that all creation is contained in the human being. He understands and reasons like an angel, but perceives and controls a body like an animal; and for this reason, all creation is understood to exist in him.[31]

There is a fivefold division of the whole creation: it is either corporeal, or living, or sensitive, or rational, or intellectual.[32] All of these are contained in every way in man. The outermost part of his nature is the body. Then comes the seminal life, which

30. Maximus, *Ambigua* 6.3 (PG 91: 1112d–1113a).
31. Maximus, *Ambigua* 37 (PG 91: 1305a–c).
32. See the diagram, Fig. 1.

sense perception governs, and then reason, which the mind governs. In what human nature shares with animals, then, man is an animal; insofar as he participates in the divine essence, he is not an animal. With animals he shares the body, life, sensation, and the memory of sensible things. But in reason, intellect, and the memory of eternal things, he participates in heavenly being. In this part he was made in the image of God, and "only God himself is better" than this.[33]

### 242. *Animal and spiritual*

It should be noted that even in this life, the whole man can become "animal" or "spiritual."[34] He becomes animal by free will alone, but spiritual by free will together with grace, for without grace the natural power of the will is by no means sufficient to advance a person to the spirit. A person both becomes and is called animal when he is moved by an irrational motion, a spontaneous appetite for bodily desires, like a brute beast. But he becomes spiritual when he is inflamed by the fire of divine love and wholly transformed into the likeness of heavenly beings. For this reason, the animal man is recognized in two ways: one in which he subsists according to nature, and the other when he chooses evil by his free will. Similarly, he is called spiritual by subsisting according to nature, but also according to good will when he is led by divine grace, purified from vices, and redeemed by the ornaments of the virtues.

### 243. *Contradictory things are one in God and in man*

D: Since all species in a genus are one,[35] how can mutually contradictory species subsist as one in the human being? Indeed, the definition of man seems to contradict the definitions of other animals, for man is a rational animal, but other animals are irrational. Rational and irrational are mutually opposed.

M: In many things the preposition "in" has the power to ar-

33. Augustine, *De civitate Dei* 11.2 (CCSL 48, 322).
34. 1 Cor 2.14–15.
35. Dionysius, *De divinis nominibus* 13.2 (PG 3: 977d–980a).

ticulate difference, but not contradiction. For example, "Every creature is either visible or invisible," or, "Every creature is either corporeal or incorporeal." It also distinguishes the relationships of the divine persons: "The Father is unbegotten, the Son begotten," and many similar things. Also, every contradiction is understood to exist in one and the same species or part, but difference is understood in diverse things. If someone were to say of the human being, "Man is a rational animal; man is an irrational animal," one proposition will necessarily be true and the other false. For contradictory predicates about the same subject cannot at the same time be both true and false, whether in general or in particular cases. If someone said, "Man is a rational animal; a horse is an irrational animal," there is no contradiction, but a substantial difference and condition of reason. It is the human condition to possess reason, and the condition of a horse to be without it. Indeed, the horse is not deprived of a condition that it could never possess. Death could not befall an animal if it did not first possess the condition of life. Therefore, we do not properly say that any animal is foolish except for that one who, we see, can possess the condition of reason. Nor do we say that a creature is insensible if it cannot naturally have the condition of feeling.

D: You have said that two mutually opposed predicates cannot be simultaneously false and true of the same subject. Yet you assert that in man both at once are true: "man is an animal" and "man is not an animal." Why is this the case only for man but not at all for other animals, for instance, "This animal is a horse; it is not a horse"?

M: Do you think any animal other than man was made in God's image?

D: By no means.

M: When it is predicated of God that "God is truth, God is not truth," do you deny that both are simultaneously true?

D: I do not deny it. For he himself said, "I am the way and the truth and the life."[36] But Dionysius the Areopagite says, "God is neither truth, nor life, nor virtue, nor light, nor knowledge."[37]

36. Jn 14.6.

37. Dionysius, *De mystica theologia* 5 (PG 3: 1048a).

M: Perhaps Dionysius contradicts Christ?

D: No way!

M: Both statements are true, therefore. "God is truth" because he is the cause of all truths, yet "he is not truth" because he transcends everything that can be said and understood. An affirmation from the creature is transferred to the Creator, but a negation beyond every creature is predicated of the Creator in himself.[38] And because man alone is made in God's image, in him alone contradictory predicates can both be true at once because he transcends the other animals, which were created for his sake.

### 244. *All things exist for the sake of man*

This world with all its parts, from the highest to the lowest, was made for man that he might have dominion over all visible things, as the Lord says: "Let us make man in our image and likeness, and let him have dominion over the fish of the sea, the beasts of the earth, the birds of the sky, and the cattle of the whole earth."[39] This dominion was given to him whether or not he would sin, although if he had not sinned, he would not rule the world in the same way as he rules it after sin.

### 245. *Man is above all things*

D: Is man an animal in the part of him that was made in God's image? Or is the image of God found in the part that was brought forth from the earth among the animals?

M: The whole image subsists in the whole animal, and the whole animal in the whole image, through the whole person. Now the image and likeness of God in human nature is recognized especially in this way: just as God is wholly above all things, within all things, and beyond all things, so human nature exists wholly in itself and in the whole human being, yet wholly transcends itself in order to cleave to its Creator, under whom all

38. Dionysius, *De caelesti hierarchia* 2.3 (PG 3, 140c–141a); 2.5 (PG 3: 144c–145a); *De mystica theologia* 3 (PG 3: 1032d–1033c).

39. Gn 1.26; Gregory of Nyssa, *De hominis opificio* 3 (PG 44: 133cd).

things exist. Augustine testifies that no creature is interposed between God and our mind.[40] But God is above all things; therefore, the man who cleaves to him is above all things and even above himself, insofar as God is in all things: "He who cleaves to the Lord is one spirit with him."[41] Although man cannot yet cleave to God in reality, yet, because this is possible and natural for him, he is not unfittingly said to cleave to him.

### 246. *Man is every creature*

D: I do not clearly see why you assert that the whole, universal creation is found in human nature.

M: Because every creature is established in it, united in it, and will return to it and be saved through it, as the Lord says: "Preach the Gospel to every creature,"[42] which means to man. There you will find intellect, reason, sense perception, seminal life, and the body—not this corruptible body, added as a punishment for sin, but the spiritual and celestial body given before the Fall, which is to be restored in the resurrection. Human nature should not be considered insofar as, to the corporeal senses, it appears similar to irrational animals. Rather, it should be considered in that it was created in God's image before it sinned. In this nature, everything that the Creator primordially created remains whole and inviolate, although it still awaits the hidden "revelation of the children of God."[43]

### 247. *Man is a spiritual animal*

D: Was man an animal before he sinned? If not, why is he said to be created in the genus of animals? But if he was, why does the Psalmist reproach him after the Fall, saying, as if it were a great disgrace: "When man was in honor, he did not understand, but was compared to foolish beasts and became like them"?[44] Here the prophet openly proclaims that before the

40. Augustine, *De vera religione* 55.113 (CCSL 32, 259).
41. 1 Cor 6.17.
42. Mk 16.15.
43. Rom 8.19.
44. Ps 48.13, 21.

Fall, man subsisted in the honor of a spiritual being, beyond the nature of all animals. But when he fell away, failing to understand the dignity of his own nature, he fell into the reproach of being likened to beasts. If he was an animal before the Fall, having been naturally created along with the animals, why is he justly reproached after the Fall for his likeness to them?

M: In his first creation in the image and likeness of God, man was a wise, spiritual animal. But he incurred the likeness of foolish animals and disgraced his natural honor with irrational motions, which is why he is justly reproached. The prophet did not simply say, "He was compared to beasts," but added, "to *foolish* beasts." He is blamed not for being an animal, but because he wished to deform the image of God, although he was unable to lose it. Irrational motions are not shameful in other animals because they inhere in them naturally; without them they could not be animals. But they are reproached in man because they are not natural to him—as if someone willingly imposed a beastly likeness on an honorable form, hastening from a better state to a worse one.

## 248. *All creation is in man*

D: I still ask why God created man, whom he wished to make in his own image and likeness, in the genus of animals. It would have seemed glorious for him to be free of all animality, given that God set him beyond all animals as a participant in supernal nature and chose him as a consort for the celestial beings. Although Plato defines an angel as a rational, immortal animal,[45] and Augustine maintains that angels have spiritual bodies,[46] yet no authority of sacred Scripture compels us to believe that the heavenly beings are animals, for only the joining of an earthly, corruptible body with a sensitive soul produces an animal. And if man is numbered in the genus of animals, but animals are part of this world, which will perish with all its parts, I cannot see where, or how, man as a part of this world will remain after

45. Calcidius, *Commentarius in Timaeum* 135.

46. Augustine, *De diversis quaestionibus* 47 (PL 40: 31); *Epistola* 9.3 (CSEL 34.2, 21).

it ends. For this reason I earnestly beg you to untie the knots of this question.

M: You are requesting a deep philosophical contemplation of the creation of man, which I will offer as far as God grants it. So then, God created man in the genus of animals so that there would be some animal in which he could reveal his image. Indeed, he made the whole visible and invisible creation in the human being, and in him all created nature is understood to exist.[47] There is nothing naturally inherent in the celestial beings that does not essentially subsist in man. For he has intellect and reason and the potential for an angelic body, which will clearly appear in both the good and the wicked after the resurrection. This whole sensible world was created in him, and no part of it is found, either corporeal or incorporeal, that was not created in man. In the human being the whole world subsists, perceives, lives, and is embodied. We must consider in man not his bodily mass, but his natural virtue—remembering especially that the pupil of the eye is the smallest of all members in size, yet has the greatest power. Man, therefore, will not perish with the world, but the whole world will always be in him.

But if anyone asks why God wished to make man specially in his image, beyond the other visible and invisible creatures, he is asking too presumptuous a question. "For who has known the mind of the Lord?"[48] It surpasses all understanding.

### 249. *A great question about the human being*

D: If all things were created in the human being, then all of them also subsist in him.

M: How are you reckoning? According to essence alone, or according to accidents and everything else that is observed in the whole creation? I mean according to essence, species, difference, properties, and everything that is understood to relate to them.

D: According to essence alone.

M: All things, insofar as they exist at all, subsist essentially. But

47. Maximus, *Ambigua* 37 (PG 91: 1305a–c).

48. Rom 11.34; 1 Cor 2.16.

the other phenomena that are understood to relate to essence or substance should not be counted in the universe of created beings, nor do they exist at all. And if that is the case, how then should we understand the phenomena that relate to the essence of things?

D: They were made by God, as I suppose.

M: Why, then, are they not included in the universe that was made in man?

D: Whatever is excluded from man was not made by God.

M: Then such phenomena do not exist. For if they existed, they would come from no other source than the cause of all things, which is God.

D: They are not counted in the number of created beings because they are not from God.

M: How then are they understood? For anything that is not from God cannot be understood at all, for it in no way exists.

D: I think that not only essences, but also everything that is naturally understood in relation to them, come from God and are reckoned among the parts of the universe.

M: Then irrationality was made in man—as well as bestiality, four-footedness, the ability to fly, and all the differences found in diverse animals and other creatures, along with species, properties, accidents, and countless other traits that seem far distant from human nature. If all these traits were innate in man, he would rightly be judged not a human being but a disgusting monster!

D: I beg you, unlock the abstruse difficulty of this question.

M: I will do my best. Do you think that everything that is known by intellect and reason, or imagined by the bodily senses, can somehow be created and produced in the one who understands and perceives?

D: I think it can be. For I believe that the forms of sensible things, which I touch with my bodily senses, are somehow created in me when I imprint their phantasms in memory. When I consider them within myself, I see that a certain knowledge of things outside me is produced within me. Similarly, when I diligently inquire about intelligible things that I contemplate with the mind alone, such as the liberal arts, I understand that certain ideas or intelligible forms are born and take shape within me. But I do not clearly see the difference between knowledge and the things themselves.

### 250. *The idea is better than the thing*

M: Do things and the soul's knowledge of them have the same or different natures?

D: Different. For how can a bodily form, for example, of some animal, plant, or tree, have the same nature as the knowledge of it, which is produced in an incorporeal nature? By the same reasoning, how can the intelligible form of any discipline have the same nature as the knowledge of it?

M: So I ask, if they are of a different genus or nature and not the same, tell me which you think is more excellent? Do things have a higher nature than the ideas of them, or are the ideas higher than the things?

D: Visible forms seem to be of a better nature than the ideas of them. Yet St. Augustine in the ninth book of *On the Trinity* holds otherwise: "When we think of something that the mind knows through the senses of the body, it is not bodies themselves that exist in the mind, but their likenesses. Yet the imagination of a body in the mind is better than the form of that body inasmuch as it exists in a better nature—the vital substance of the mind."[49]

As for intelligible things, they do not seem better than the soul's idea of them because, as reason teaches, that which understands is better than that which is understood. For if the knowledge of all things subsists in divine Wisdom, it is incomparably better than all the things it knows. And if that is the case, I think that by divine providence, such an order pervades the whole creation that every nature, which comprehends in its knowledge the one that follows it, is not only better and superior; but also, knowledge itself by the dignity of its nature far precedes the thing that is known. For this reason, I would easily say that the knowledge of intelligible things is older than the intelligible things themselves.

49. Augustine, *De Trinitate* 9.11 (CCSL 50, 307).

M: Perhaps your opinion would be correct if what is formed were more excellent than that which forms it.

D: Why do you oppose my view?

M: Because knowledge of the arts, which exists in the soul, seems to be formed by the arts themselves. But if you could persuade me by a foolproof argument that knowledge is not formed by the arts, but the arts by the knowledge of them, your reasoning might be off to a good start.

D: Isn't everything that understands more excellent than that which is understood?

M: Yes, it is.

D: Tell me then whether the mind's skill understands a discipline, or the discipline understands the skill?

M: I do not doubt that the discipline is understood by the mind. Similarly, I would say that the skill knows the discipline if I did not seem to assert that these are two things—the mind and its skill—rather than a single essence. True reason teaches that the mind, its skill, and a discipline are one and the same.[50] Or rather, the mind that understands itself to flourish through skill and discipline is both skilled and disciplined. Therefore, it is not older than its idea. To explain this more clearly, tell me this: do you think the nature of a mind that has skill in a discipline is simple or not?

D: I think it is simple. Being incorporeal and intellectual, it is necessarily not composite.

M: That's right. So do you think any accident can befall it that does not naturally inhere in its essence?

D: I do think so, for many things befall the mind that are not itself. It moves through time, yet is not itself time. It acquires skill in disciplines, for it is now skilled and now ignorant, now wise and now foolish—and many things of that kind.

M: Then skill in a discipline, or the discipline itself, are not innate in the mind, but come to it as accidents from without.

D: I do not believe that God created in his own image and likeness a mind in which skill and discipline are not inborn. Otherwise, it would not be a mind, but a brute, irrational life. Man was made in God's image not according to accidents, but

50. A new human trinity: *mens, peritia, disciplina.*

according to his substance, for intellect and reason substantially inhere in him.

M: Therefore, they do not befall him as accidents, but are innate.

D: So I think, although the mind may seem to be born ignorant and foolish. That is an accident that befell it through transgression of the divine command, which made it forget both itself and its Creator.

### 251. *A trinity in the mind*

M: So do skill and discipline inhere in the mind as natural qualities—like wisdom, knowledge, and the other virtues—or as substantial parts of which it consists? In that case there would be a kind of trinity of mind, skill, and discipline, possessing a single essence.

D: It seems to me that there is a substantial, connatural trinity.

M: So the mind understands both its skill and its discipline, and by that skill and discipline we can understand not *what* it is, but *that* it is. Otherwise, it would not be a coessential, coequal trinity.

D: Reason compels us to say so.

M: Are their natures formed by each other or by some other, superior source?

D: I do not doubt that the trinity in the mind is formed by the supreme Trinity.

M: Only the divine mind, then, possesses true knowledge of the skilled, disciplined human mind formed by it.

D: Nothing truer can be thought.

M: Do you think the human mind is one thing, while its idea in the mind of the One who forms and knows it is something else?

D: I understand that the whole human being has no other substance than its idea in the mind of the Maker, who knew all things in himself before they came to be. That very knowledge is their true substance, and the things it knows eternally subsist in it.

### 252. *A wonderful and true definition of man*

M: Then we can define the human being in this way: "Man is a certain intellectual idea formed eternally in the divine mind."

D: This definition of man is most truthful and excellent, but also applies to all things that were made in the divine Wisdom. I marvel at those who define man not according to what he is understood to be, but by traits understood in relation to him. They say, "Man is a rational and mortal animal, capable of sense perception and discipline." What is more marvelous still, they call this definition essential,[51] although it is not substantial but only relative to substance, taken from traits that befall man accidentally from without, through generation. But the idea of man in the divine mind is none of these. There indeed he is simple; he can be called neither this nor that, but transcends every definition and collection of parts. Only being is predicated of the idea, not *what* it is. For the only true definition of a substance is that which merely affirms that it is and does not say what it is.

### 253. *All things are in man through knowledge*

M: There is a certain innate idea in man of all the sensible and intelligible things that the human mind can understand. For this reason especially, he is understood to be man, for it was given to him to have an idea of all creatures, both those created equally with him and those over whom he is given dominion, as Scripture says: "When God had formed from the soil all the animals of the earth and all the birds of the sky, he brought them to Adam to see (that is, to understand) what he would call them." For if he did not understand, how could he rightly name them? "Whatever he called every creature, that is the name (meaning the idea) of a living soul."[52] Thus by likeness to the divine mind, in which the idea of the created universe exists as its unchangeable substance, the idea of things possessed by and created in the human mind is understood to be their substance. And just as the idea of all things understood in the universe or perceived

51. *Usiadem,* from Greek *ousia:* essence, substance, or being.
52. Gn 2.19.

by the senses is called their substance, so too the ideas of differences, properties, and natural accidents are said to be their actual differences, properties, and accidents.

D: Then irrationality was created in man, with all its species and every difference and property of irrationality, and everything that is naturally known in relation to it. The knowledge of all these things was created in man.

M: Yes, that is so. Human nature also possesses a true, innate knowledge of all similar things (other than animals) which the nature of the universe contains—such as the elements of the world and the genera and species of plants and trees, qualities and quantities, and other such things, as they are multiplied through countless differences. This is the case even though such knowledge is still latent in him until he is restored to his former wholeness, in which he will very clearly understand the greatness and beauty of the image created in him. Then nothing will be hidden of all that was created in man, now that his nature is encircled by divine light and turned toward God, in whom he will contemplate all things keenly. This is what the magnificent Boethius meant when he said, "Wisdom is comprehension of the truth of things endowed with immutable substance," such as "qualities, quantities, forms," and similar things.[53] And where do these subsist except in their ideas in the souls of the wise? For wherever they are understood, that is where they exist, or rather, the understanding of them exists.

D: The present question is not unlike the hydra of Hercules, whose heads grow back as fast as they are cut off so that, for a single amputated head, a hundred more bubble up. This implies that human nature, the hydra, is a kind of many-sided well of infinite depth, in which no one can see to the bottom except Hercules—that is, virtue. For no one "knows what is in man except the spirit of the man which is in him."[54] So if the idea of things innate in the human mind constitutes their substance, then we should consequently believe that the idea by which man knows himself is his own substance.

M: Indeed, that follows. The human mind, the knowledge by

53. Boethius, *De institutione arithmetica* 1.1.

54. 1 Cor 2.11.

which it knows itself, and the discipline by which it learns itself subsist as a single essence.

### 254. *The dual substance of human beings*

D: Didn't we define man as a certain intellectual idea formed eternally in the divine mind? If this definition is true, how then is man's substance the idea by which he knows himself?

M: It is a truthful definition that states that man's substance is a certain idea formed eternally in the divine mind. It is also true that the knowledge by which the human mind knows itself is substantially innate in man. For every creature is contemplated one way in the Word of God and a different way in itself, as Augustine proves when he says: "The things that were made through him exist in one way beneath him; in another way, the things that he himself is exist within him."[55] Indeed, the understanding of all things in divine Wisdom is the substance of them all, or rather, it is all things themselves.[56] But the knowledge by which the intellectual, rational creature understands itself in itself is a kind of second substance, by which it knows only that it knows itself and that it exists. That substance fashioned in the Wisdom of God is eternal and changeless, but this substance is temporal and changeable. The former precedes, the latter follows; the former is primordial and causal, the latter proceeding and causative; the former contains man universally, the latter comprehends through particular knowledge; the latter is produced by the former and will return to it. The superessential substance which in itself is God, the sole cause of all things, created the former substance primordially and causally in Wisdom. Its effect is this second substance, or rather, the natural order of all things.

D: Then man has two substances—a universal one in the primordial causes and a special one in their effects.

M: Not two substances, but one understood in two ways. For the human substance is perceived one way through its creation in the intellectual causes, another way through generation in

55. Augustine, *De Genesi ad litteram* 2.6 (CSEL 28.1, 41).

56. Dionysius, *De ecclesiastica hierarchia* 1.3 (PG 3: 376a).

their effects. There it is free of all mutability, here it is subject to mutability. There it is simple, devoid of all accidents, and eludes every created intellect. Here it is composed of quantities, qualities, and forms and open to the mind's gaze. One and the same substance, therefore, is called double because of this double consideration, yet on both sides it is incomprehensible—in the causes and in their effects, whether in its naked simplicity or endowed with accidents. In all of these it yields to no created intellect or sense, nor can it even understand what it is itself.

D: Not long ago you said that the human mind knows itself, but now you assert that it can be known neither by itself nor by any other creature.

M: Reason teaches that both statements are quite true. Indeed, the human mind both knows itself and does not know itself. It knows that it exists, but does not know what it is, and here especially we perceive the image of God in man. For God is comprehensible when we gather from creation that he exists, and incomprehensible because what he is cannot be comprehended by any created intellect—not even by himself. For he is not any particular thing[57] because he is superessential. In the same way, the human mind is only given to know that it exists, but it is in no way permitted to know what it is. For if it were known to be some particular thing, it would be circumscribed in some way and thus could by no means express the image of its Creator, who is utterly uncircumscribed. He cannot be understood because he is infinite and superessential, above all that can be said and understood.[58]

D: How then was every creature made in the knowledge of man, when that knowledge does not even know what it is itself (and this is taken to be great praise!), as it is enclosed by no finite substance?

M: Rather, this is the greatest proof that all creation was substantially created in man. As Gregory the Theologian testifies, no substance of anything that exists can be defined with respect to what it is. It is only understood to exist from the things that relate to it, such as times, places, differences, properties, quanti-

57. *Non est quid.*
58. Gregory of Nyssa, *De hominis opificio* 11 (PG 44: 153c–156b).

ties, and qualities—but what it is, is by no means known.[59] Hence we are not given to understand the subsistence of any creature, except as the reason according to which it was constituted in the primordial causes in the Word of God. Therefore, what it is cannot be defined, for it transcends every substantial definition. But it is defined circumstantially through the accidents that befall it in its proper species as produced through generation, whether intelligible or sensible.

### 255. *Why all things do not exist in the angel as they do in man*

D: Since an angel is an intellectual, rational creature like man, human and angelic natures are either the same or very similar, as divine Scripture and reason prove.[60] Hence it is asked why we read that every creature was created in man but not in the angel.

M: Not without cause, I think. Indeed, a great many things are present in man that do not exist in an angel, such as an animal body, the body's fivefold external senses, and the phantasms of sensible things, as well as the annoying difficulty involved in investigating the natures of things and the laborious skill required to discern virtues and vices. Angelic nature has none of these, yet they are inherent in the nature of things. True reason proves that angels have knowledge of things which neither inhere in them substantially nor befall them by accident.[61] Although the angels govern this world and the whole bodily creation, by no means do they need bodily senses, movement in place and time, or visible appearances for that purpose. All these things come to them as accidents for the needs of our own nature. When they transform their spiritual, invisible bodies into visible forms in order to appear visibly to mortals' senses in space and time, this does not happen for their own sake, but for the sake of human beings, whom they command and to whom they proclaim

59. Maximus, *Ambigua* 13 (PG 91: 1225d–1228a).

60. Mt 22.30.

61. I have not translated what appears to be an erroneous *non* in this sentence, since Honorius's point is that angelic (unlike human) knowledge does not depend on what is intrinsic to their nature.

divine mysteries, as they do to the prophets.[62] They do not see locally by means of sense perception, nor do they learn in time how they must govern things. For they see the causes of their governance eternally, all at once, in contemplation of the truth beyond all time and space.[63]

All this applies only to the highest orders of angels. The lowest order, which is properly called "angelic," is not yet free of all ignorance, as St. Dionysius the Areopagite discusses in his book *On the Celestial Hierarchy*. Therefore, those angels are taught by the higher orders and introduced into knowledge of divine mysteries above themselves.[64] Through this order, the higher orders govern human affairs and aspects of the world by the will of God.[65]

For this reason, the whole visible and invisible creation is believed to have been created in man alone. There is no created substance that may not be understood in man. In the nature of things we can find no species, difference, property, or natural accident that either is not innate in human nature or cannot be known by man. That very knowledge of things is better than the things themselves to the extent that it exists in a better nature. Every rational nature is rightly preferred to every irrational, sensible nature because it is closer to God. So the things that human nature innately knows are understood, as is fitting, to subsist in human ideas of them. They exist more truly where there is better knowledge of them.[66] And if these things subsist more truly in their ideas than they do in themselves, but the knowledge of them naturally inheres in man, then they were universally created in man. Therefore, they will all return to him from whom they also proceeded.

D: Although these things may seem very difficult because they exceed the measure of simple teaching, yet they are rationally suited to the human condition. Therefore, man was duly brought forth in the genus of animals—or rather, every genus of

62. Augustine, *Sermo* 12.9 (CCSL 41, 171).
63. Augustine, *De Genesi ad litteram* 4.24 (CSEL 28.1, 123–24).
64. Dionysius, *De caelesti hierarchia* 5 (PG 3: 196bc); 7.3 (PG 3: 209a–c).
65. Dionysius, *De caelesti hierarchia* 9.2 (PG 3: 260ab).
66. Augustine, *De Genesi ad litteram* 5.15 (CSEL 28.1, 158).

animals was brought forth from the earth (that is, from the solidity of nature) in man. And we can say further that not only every genus of animals, but the whole created universe was made in man. So it is of the human being that we should truly understand what the Truth said: "Preach the Gospel to the whole creation," and the Apostle adds, "The whole creation is groaning in labor until now."[67]

M: So it is. If these things seem too abstruse or thoroughly incredible to anyone, if he is altogether ignorant of the natural disciplines that we call the liberal arts, let him either keep silent or learn, lest he recklessly reject things that he cannot understand. If he is learned he will plainly see, to choose an example from one of them, that geometrical figures do not naturally subsist in themselves, but in the principles of that discipline whose figures they are. A triangle that the bodily senses perceive in some material is indeed a sensory image in the mind of the one who sees it. The triangle that exists in the mind is true because it is immutable; the material triangle is false because it is mutable. And if geometrical bodies rationally subsist in the ideas of them, what wonder is it if natural bodies, which are composed from qualities of the elements of the world, also subsist in that nature which possesses knowledge of them—especially when everything that is perceived in relation to bodies is incorporeal? Even the species in which they are contained are incorporeal. Similarly, no wise person doubts that the quantities and qualities of intelligible nature proceed from the intellectual causes of living substance.

### 256. *Why man was made after all things*

D: Anyone who attentively considers the natures of things will find beyond doubt that these things are true. So it is not unfitting to ask how every creature was created in man, when he himself is said to have been made after the creation of all other things. If the whole visible and invisible creation was created before him, as the divine narrative relates, and we read of no other creation after him, how can we state that every creature was cre-

67. Mk 16.15; Rom 8.22.

ated in man? It is not reasonable to think the creation was fashioned twice: the first time specifically in itself, the second time generally in man. For if that were the case, man would have no substance of his own, but he would be like a composite of many things, or rather of the whole creation made before him—one great, manifold heap of different forms. And what is worse, if the whole creation was made most perfectly in itself, how could it receive a kind of second created perfection in man, who was created last among the divine works? If that were the case, God did not make man in his image[68] out of nothing, but out of the things that were made before him. If anyone were to say that the human body was not created from nothing but from something else, namely clay, what will he say about the better part of man, which doubtless consists in the soul? Do we believe it was created from nothing by the divine breath, or rather *as* the divine breath—but not from anything else?

M: I perceive that this question is wrapped in great darkness, and it will require much skill to resolve. But, lest we skip over it completely untouched, I will try to contemplate it somehow, insofar as an inner ray of divine light smiles on me. But first I ask you to tell me this: are intelligible and sensible things prior to the mind that understands them and the senses that perceive them?

### 257. *The human mind is before all things*

D: When something that understands, such as the mind, is of a better nature than what is understood, I would say it is fitting for it to precede the object that it understands or perceives. But I would not say that beings that understand themselves are prior to themselves. For I know that I exist, but my knowledge of myself does not precede my being. It is not the case that I am one thing, while my knowledge of myself is something else. Everything that either knows it exists, or knows that it does not know it exists, absolutely exists. If anyone is sunk in such ignorance that he neither knows himself to exist nor perceives that he knows himself to exist, I would say he is either not human

68. Gn 1.27.

or utterly dead. Indeed, these two things—knowledge and ignorance—are always innate in the human soul. For it knows itself to be a rational, intellectual nature, but it does not know what intellect and reason are.

M: So then, did you not exist before you knew (or did not know) that you existed?

D: No. At the same time that I received being, I received the knowledge that I am and the understanding that I am ignorant of what I am.

M: Tell me, when does a person receive knowledge of himself? Is it in that creation by which all human beings were universally made in the primordial causes "before the ages,"[69] or in that process of generation by which a person enters this life, in the temporal order known only to God and foreordained by him?

D: In both, I think: in the first according to genus, latent in the causes, and in the second according to species, manifest in the effects. In that primordial, general creation of all human nature, no one specifically knows himself or begins to have a proper idea of himself. There one universal knowledge, known to God alone, is common to all. For there all human beings are one, and that one is made in God's image, in which all humans were created.[70] Just as forms or species subsist as one in the genus and are not distinguished as individuals, so in the communion of human nature, no one can distinguish either himself or others by his own knowledge until he comes into this world in his own time, just as it was decreed in the eternal reasons.

M: Why then doesn't everyone know himself as soon as he is born into this world?

D: This came about through the guilt of the Fall. For if man had not sinned, he would surely not have fallen into such profound ignorance of himself, nor suffered shameful generation from two sexes like irrational animals. This is what the wisest Greeks affirm by the most convincing arguments.[71] He who

69. 2 Tm 1.9; Ti 1.2.

70. Dionysius, *De divinis nominibus* 13.2 (PG 3: 977d–980a).

71. Gregory of Nyssa, *De hominis opificio* 16 (PG 44: 184d–185a); 17 (PG 44: 188c–192a); Maximus, *Ambigua* 27 (PG 91: 1276b); 37 (PG 91: 1305cd, 1309a); 38 (PG 91: 1320d–1321a, 1345d–1348b).

alone was born in the world without sin, the world's Redeemer, never endured such ignorance in any way. Rather, as soon as he was conceived and born, he understood both himself and all things and was able to teach and speak. This is not only because he was the Wisdom of the Father, from whom nothing is hidden, but also because he received his humanity uncontaminated in order to purify contaminated nature. He did not receive a nature different from the one he restored, but in him alone human nature remained uncontaminated, for he was reserved as a medicine for the wound of vitiated nature in its hidden causes. Indeed, all human nature perished in all humans, except for him in whom alone it remained incorruptible. He alone of all humans, with no preceding merits, was joined in unity of substance to the Word of God. In him all the elect, receiving from the fullness of his grace, become children of God and partakers of the divine substance.[72]

M: Human nature, then, had potential for the most perfect self-knowledge if man had not sinned.

D: Nothing is more plausible. For by his Fall, man lost his innate knowledge and wisdom and sank into profound ignorance of himself and his Creator. Yet the desire for this lost beatitude remained in human nature even after the Fall. It would by no means have remained if human nature were entirely ignorant of itself and its God.

M: Then the most perfect knowledge of himself and his Creator was naturally innate in man before sin, insofar as any creature's knowledge can comprehend both itself and its cause.

### 258. *That man is God*

D: I do not think otherwise. For how would he be God's image if he differed in any way from the one whose image he is, except by reason of the subject?[73] From him he received being according to nature and being God according to grace; and everything that is predicated of God essentially can be predicated

72. Jn 1.12, 1.16; Heb 3.14.
73. Gregory of Nyssa, *De hominis opificio* 11 (PG 44: 156a); 16 (PG 44: 184d).

of his image as well by participation. God in himself is goodness; the image is good by participation in the supreme good. God is eternity; his image is eternal. God is omnipotent, and if human nature had not sinned, it would be omnipotent too. For whatever man wished to happen in the nature of things would necessarily happen, since he would wish nothing to happen beyond what he understood to be his Creator's will.

M: Then if perfect knowledge of both himself and his Creator was innate in human nature before sin, it is no wonder if man is reasonably understood to have possessed the fullest knowledge of natures similar to his own, such as the heavenly beings, as well as those beneath himself, such as this world with its principles yielding to the intellect. He still possesses that knowledge, though only potentially—and the highest human beings possess it actually.

D: This will be no wonder, but true and probable, to those who understand clearly.

M: Therefore, just as the understanding of all creatures that the Father made in his only-begotten Word is their being, and the being of all that is naturally understood in relation to it,[74] in the same way the knowledge of all creatures that the Father's Word created in the human soul is their being, and the being of all that is naturally known in relation to it. Just as the divine intellect precedes all things and *is* all things, the knowledge of the intellectual soul precedes all things that it knows, and *is* all things that it foreknows. Just as all creatures subsist causally in the divine intellect, they subsist effectually in human knowledge. The being of all creatures is not one thing in the Word and another in man; rather, the mind beholds one and the same being subsisting one way in the eternal causes and understood another way in their effects.[75] There it transcends all understanding, but here it is understood, from things considered in relation to it, simply to be. No created intellect is allowed to know *what* it is in either aspect.[76] For if this could be known, man would by no means express in himself the image of his Creator, who is

74. Dionysius, *De ecclesiastica hierarchia* 1.3 (PG 3: 376a).
75. Augustine, *De Genesi ad litteram* 2.6 (CSEL 28.1, 41).
76. Maximus, *Ambigua* 13 (PG 91: 1225d–1228a).

known simply to be from the creatures whose principle, cause, and creator he is. But *what* he is eludes all perception and understanding.

### 259. *The angel in the human being*

D: Therefore, no creature, visible or invisible, precedes the creation of man—not in place or time, not in dignity or origin, not in eternity, and in short, by no type of precedence. But in knowledge and dignity (though not in place or time), human nature precedes those things that were created with it, in it, and beneath it. Human nature was created together with the creatures that are its equals in dignity of nature, namely the heavenly beings, for it too is a partaker of the heavenly, intellectual essence. Concerning angelic and human being, it is written, "He who made the heavens in intellect,"[77] that is, who made the intellectual heavens.

But if man was substantially created together with the angelic beings, how could all visible and invisible creatures have been created in him? It makes no sense that he should have had the beginning of his creation with the heavenly powers, yet at the same time, they should have been created in him.

M: Intellectual and rational nature is so reciprocally joined and united that angelic being is constituted within human being, and vice versa. In everything that a pure intellect perfectly knows, the intellect becomes one with the object.[78] The angel understands man, and man the angel; therefore the angel comes to be in man through the intellect, and man in the angel through the intellect—just as I become your intellect when I understand what you understand, and you in turn become my intellect when you understand what I understand. For example, when you understand that I understand that the number six is the sum of its factors, and I understand that you too understand this, then you are created in me, and I in you, and both of our intellects become one. We are not one thing, and our intellect another. But our true and highest being is the intellect ren-

77. Ps 135.5.
78. Maximus, *Ambigua* 11 (PG 91: 1220ab).

dered specific by contemplation of the truth. The intellect can be conformed not only to natures coessential with it, but even to inferior natures by loving them, as the Apostle says: "Do not be conformed to this world."[79]

The angel, therefore, is not rightly believed to precede the human being by any law of creation or any mode of precedence, although the prophetic narrative announces its creation first, as many suppose, and that of man afterwards. For St. Augustine asserts without hesitation that the verse "Let there be light" signifies the creation of the heavenly beings.[80]

### 260. *The angel and man were created together*

D: I would like you to explain why the angelic creation is narrated on the first intellectual day, so to speak—that is, in the first order of prophetic contemplation—while the formation of man is introduced later in the sixth contemplation, interrupted by a fourfold consideration of the sensible world. Why wasn't man introduced at the outset of the whole creation, rather than last of all? Because of this, it seems that the being not just of angels, but even of sensible things precedes the human presence by a certain dignity, not to say temporality.

M: On the contrary! It is especially here that the dignity of the human essence is plainly revealed to be above all that exists. For in everything narrated before the creation of man, he himself was created—or rather, we can clearly understand that all things were established in him. For it was not said, "Let there be an angel," but, "Let there be light."[81] This signifies the creation of man no less than the angel, because man no less than the angel is believed to be a partaker of eternal light. So we can believe that all things related after the creation of light were created in man, not only according to knowledge of them, but also in reality.

79. Rom 12.2.

80. Gn 1.3; Augustine, *De civitate Dei* 11.9 (CCSL 48, 328–30); 11.19 (CCSL 48, 338); 11.32 (CCSL 48, 351).

81. Gn 1.3.

### 261. *The whole world exists for the sake of man and in man*

In fact, this sensible world was made for man's sake, that he might rule it as a king rules his kingdom and a lord his household—or rather, that he might use it for the Creator's praise. He would not have been subject to any of its parts but stood above it, needing it for nothing, brought in solely to rule it. For if man had not sinned, he would not have been governed among the parts of the world, but would himself have governed the whole of it, made entirely subject to him. He would have governed its subsistent beings eternally, without error—needing no bodily senses, but only his rational insight into its natural and internal causes. But if, forsaking the Creator, he fell from the dignity of his nature into the world, he would justly pay the penalty for his transgression by being counted ignobly among its parts.

So after the adornment of the visible world is related, man is introduced as the conclusion of all, to make it clear that everything whose creation is described before him is universally encompassed in him, just as every smaller number is included in a larger one.[82] For if the creation of man had been set first, all other things would have seemed to subsist outside his nature. Therefore, he is introduced at the end of the divine works, revealing that all things subsist in him and are encompassed in him.

### 262. *The first day*

The angelic beings exist in man in two ways. In one way he is coessential with them as a fellow intellectual, rational being. In the second way, the angel is created in man, and man in the angel, through the intellect, in mutual knowledge.

### 263. *The second day*

The firmament in the midst of the waters, that is, the solidity of the elements, was made to separate the primordial causes

82. Maximus, *Ambigua* 37 (PG 91: 1305a–c).

(the upper waters) from changeable bodies (the lower waters). This solidity is present in the essence of man, for he consists of the four elements.

### 264. *The third day*

The dry land (that is, the stability of substance) and the gathering of waters (that is, the instability of accidents) are understood to exist in man. Moreover, the life force of plants and shoots, nourishing and quickening the different species, is reckoned to be in him too.

### 265. *The fourth day*

Because the principal part of man—namely, intellect and reason—is designated by the word "light" on the first day and was formed in the company of angelic nature, external sensation attributed to the four elements is introduced on the fourth day under the name of "sun and moon." This exists in three modes. First is the greater light, which announces the forms of sensible objects to the mind without error, just as the sun reveals all sensible forms and manifests them to the reason. Second is the lesser light, which deceives the mind with ambiguous phantasms, like an oar that appears bent in the water or towers that seem to move, just as the moon overshadows objects in the night with its doubtful light.[83] Third is the light of the different stars. Generated by the tiniest forms of corporeal phantasms, this light impresses certain opinions on the mind, now clearly, now obscurely. None of these exist in the nature of things; they are formed in the senses.

It is no wonder if the lesser things considered in human nature are signified by greater ones, that is, the heavenly bodies. The most truthful reason teaches us beyond a doubt that one single human being is greater than the whole visible world—not in the mass of physical parts, but in the dignity of a rational nature. Augustine proves that the soul of a tiny worm is better than

83. Augustine, *De Genesi ad litteram* 12.25 (CSEL 28.1, 417–18); *Contra Academicos* 3.11.26 (CCSL 29, 50).

the solar body that illumines the whole world.[84] And if the least living thing, whatever it may be, is preferred in the dignity of its being to the first and most precious of bodies, what wonder is it if all the bodies in the entire world are considered secondary to human sensation?

## 266. *The fifth day*

Because this sensation is fivefold, it is inserted in the nature of things on the fifth day, which is allotted to the creeping things of the sea and the birds of the sky, that is, the air.

## 267. *The sixth day*

Man is linked with land animals on the sixth day, for the creatures made on the sixth day seem to have greater kinship with him than those produced from the waters. So all the aforesaid creatures were created in and with man. He was plainly formed last in the whole universe—not in periods of time, but in the order of causes. There is a sixfold repetition to let this number signify not only the perfection of human nature, but also the creation of all things in it,[85] as the Lord says: "Let us make man in our image and likeness, and let him rule over the fish of the sea, the birds of the sky, the beasts of the earth, and the whole creation, and over every creeping thing that moves upon the earth. And God created man in his own image; in the image of God he created him."[86] It should be noted that the Trinity is not mentioned in the other works made in the five intellectual days. But on the sixth, when man is formed, the unity and plurality of the divine nature are openly preached,[87] and rightly so. For when the image is created, the chief exemplar of that image is openly revealed.

84. Augustine, *De libero arbitrio* 3.11.34 (CCSL 29, 295); *De vera religione* 55.109 (CCSL 32, 257).

85. Augustine, *De Genesi ad litteram* 4.7 (CSEL 28.1, 103); *De civitate Dei* 11.30 (CCSL 48, 350).

86. Gn 1.26–27.

87. Augustine, *De Genesi ad litteram* 3.19 (CSEL 28.1, 85–86); *De Trinitate* 7.6 (CCSL 50, 266).

### 268. *The image of God is in the entire soul*

D: Although the human being is one, he is composed of many parts, for he consists of a body formed from sensible matter, vital motion, and a soul—that is, sensation, reason, and intellect.[88] It is asked whether he was made in God's image in all his parts, or only in those of a more excellent nature.

M: Almost all the interpreters of holy Scripture have addressed this question. They unanimously hold that man was not made in God's image *qua* body, for God is incorporeal and no corporeality resides in or befalls him. But whether he was created in God's image in the soul, that is, in all the parts that are understood to belong to the soul, or only its more excellent parts, is a question zealously studied by spiritual men. Some say that he expresses the divine image only in the most excellent part of himself, that is, the intelligible. This part is threefold, consisting of intellect, reason, and interior sensation. But many wise men deny that God's image is present in the life that administers the body (which man shares with plants and trees) and the fivefold external senses (which he shares with animals), even though these parts belong to the soul.[89]

Yet because the whole soul administers its body and is everywhere whole and undivided within itself, as Gregory of Nyssa says,[90] the whole human soul was made in God's image. For the whole soul is intellect understanding; the whole is reason debating; the whole is sensation perceiving; and the whole is the life force quickening. We know that the human soul was made in God's image in two ways. First, just as God is diffused through all creatures that exist but can be comprehended by none, the soul pervades the whole organism of its body but cannot be enclosed by it. Second, just as only being is predicated of God, but what he is can by no means be defined, the human soul is understood only to exist, but what it is, neither the soul itself nor any

88. Gregory of Nyssa, *De hominis opificio* 12 (PG 44: 161cd).

89. Augustine, *De Genesi ad litteram* 3.20 (CSEL 28.1, 86); *De Trinitate* 12.7 (CCSL 50, 366).

90. Gregory of Nyssa, *De hominis opificio* 14 (PG 44: 173d–176b); 15 (PG 44: 177bc).

other creature understands.[91] It should be known that "in the human composite, the mind is governed by God, and the material life by the mind."[92] The body is formed by the life force[93] so that matter may follow the vital motion, vital motion follow the mind, and the mind follow God himself.

## 269. *What the vital motion is*

D: I would like to know whether or not the vital motion belongs to man's substance. If it does not, why is it called "the image of the image,"[94] that is, the image of the mind, and why does the mind give form to matter through it? But if this life force is substantially innate in man, why is he thought to consist only of soul and body? And why, when the matter is dissolved, is this life understood not to exist at all? For it remains neither in the matter, which is now abandoned by all vital motion, nor in the soul, which after ruling the body experiences no further movement toward matter.

M: In my opinion, the vital motion is nothing but a bond joining body and soul, making them cling to each other. Through it the soul quickens and governs the body, waking or sleeping, whether the soul pays attention to what it is doing in the body or recedes from the senses and rests in itself, as if oblivious to its body.[95] Yet it does not cease to govern it in a kind of ineffable silence, distributing the nourishment the body needs to each of its parts. But when body and soul are separated, that vital motion perishes completely. For it is not alive unless it has something to move, that is, unless there is something to be moved by it, for it subsists only as a movement of the mind ruling the body. But when the mover ceases to move or to be moved, the motion in it is utterly destroyed. For the end of all motion is rest

91. Gregory of Nyssa, *De hominis opificio* 11 (PG 44: 153c–156b).

92. Gregory of Nyssa, *De hominis opificio* 12 (PG 44: 164c). I have translated *anima* consistently as "soul" and *animus* as "mind." Normally they are distinct, but in this section, following Gregory of Nyssa, Honorius seems to use the terms synonymously.

93. Gregory of Nyssa, *De hominis opificio* 12 (PG 44: 161d, 164b).

94. Gregory of Nyssa, *De hominis opificio* 12 (PG 44: 164a).

95. This passage may refer to either sleep or mystical ecstasy.

for both the mover and the object moved. Therefore, when the soul rests from moving its body, the whole vital motion, that is, the whole material life, ceases to exist.[96] The mind is not enclosed in any part of the body, but governs the whole body with its presence and is wholly present in all the parts it governs.[97] "The mind commands reason, but nature follows in the footsteps of its commander."[98]

### 270. *Why the mind falls away*

D: Why does the mind fall away from the body?

M: Because the mind's movement falters in any part of the body that is damaged, that is, cannot manifest the power of its governance.[99] This is not a defect of the mind; rather, the damaged part cannot receive the mind's power.

### 271. *All human beings are in the first man*

D: "Some say that man is a little world because he consists of the same elements as the universe."

M: Those who say this have forgotten human nature, comparing themselves to mice and gnats that consist of the same four elements. "What should we think will become of man when heaven passes away, the earth is changed, and everything in it passes away?" The human being in whom the Creator's image is expressed is greater than the world; man does not exist in the world, but the world in man.[100] The image of God is in the human mind, where wisdom, knowledge, reason, and the other virtues dwell.[101] And Gregory the Theologian proves that all human beings were made once and for all in that one man[102] of whom it is written, "Let us make man in our image and

96. Gregory of Nyssa, *De hominis opificio* 13 (PG 44: 165a).

97. Gregory of Nyssa, *De hominis opificio* 14 (PG 44: 173d–176b); 15 (PG 44: 177bc).

98. Gregory of Nyssa, *De hominis opificio* 14 (PG 44: 176a).

99. Gregory of Nyssa, *De hominis opificio* 15 (PG 44: 177c).

100. Gregory of Nyssa, *De hominis opificio* 16 (PG 44: 177d–180a).

101. Gregory of Nyssa, *De hominis opificio* 16 (PG 44: 184b).

102. Gregory of Nyssa, *De hominis opificio* 16 (PG 44: 185a–d).

likeness,"[103] "in whom all have sinned,"[104] for he was all human beings when he was still one,[105] and in him all were expelled from the bliss of paradise.

If man had not sinned, he would not have suffered the division of his simplicity into two sexes. That division has absolutely nothing to do with the image and likeness of the divine nature and would not have existed at all if man had not sinned, just as it will no longer exist after the restoration of nature to its original state, which will be revealed after the universal resurrection of all people. Therefore, if man had not sinned, no one would be born from the coupling of both sexes or from any seed. But just as the angelic essence, being one, was multiplied all at once into infinite myriads with no passage of time, so human nature—if it had wished to keep the commandment and had done so—would have burst all at once into the foreordained number of humans known to the Creator alone. But God, who neither deceives nor is deceived, foresaw that man would forsake the order and dignity of his creation. So he cleverly devised[106] another mode of multiplication for human nature, by which this world would be completed in the course of space and time, so that human beings might pay a universal price for the universal transgression: being born from corruptible seed, just like other animals.[107]

D: Here many questions spring up on all sides, of which the first and greatest makes the most powerful impact. For if all human beings—not only those who have been or now exist, but also those yet to come—were created all at once in that divine word, "Let us make man," and if these corruptible bodies added onto them would by no means have existed if man had not sinned, it is not superfluous to ask how the first creation could have been made in God's image if the second was not in his image, but added later for the aforesaid reason. Was the first

103. Gn 1.26.

104. Rom 5.12.

105. Augustine, *De peccatorum meritis* 3.7.14 (CSEL 60, 141).

106. *Supermachinatus est.*

107. Gregory of Nyssa, *De hominis opificio* 16 (PG 44: 184d–185a); 17 (PG 44: 188c–192a).

creation of the soul alone with no body, or of soul and body together? If it was of the soul alone, how could he have been called man when it is agreed that man is composed of two natures—the invisible soul and the visible body? I could not believe that only part of man was created when it was said, "Let us make man," especially since the fullest, most perfect creation of all natures is recounted in these prophetic words.[108] But if the first creation is rightly understood to involve soul and body, that is, the whole, integral human being, we must ask what the body was like in the first human creation. Indeed, reason cries out that this body, devised as a punishment for sin, was not the one created in the first, natural formation of man.

### 272. *Man was made in a spiritual body*

M: I believe that the body originally made in the creation of man was spiritual and immortal—either the same as or very like the one we will have after the resurrection. For I would not easily concede that it was a corruptible, material body before the cause of corruption and materiality—namely sin—came into being. Moreover, manifest reason teaches that if the same body that was made in the first human creation, before sin, was at once changed and rendered corruptible after sin, then it was not that body devised afterward. Rather, it was transformed from a spiritual, incorruptible body into an earthly, corruptible one. On this point the authority of Gregory the Theologian seems to waver. In fact, he asserts without hesitation that the whole, which was made in the first human creation in the image of God, always remains incorruptible according to the principle of soul and body. He also affirms beyond any doubt that souls were not created before bodies, nor bodies before souls. But the whole was made all at once in the divine counsel when it was said, "Let us make man," and was born into this world simultaneously in the order of time.[109]

Now, even after sin, that spiritual and natural body forever cleaves to the mind and is united to it. It is distinct from what

108. Maximus, *Ambigua* 37 (PG 91: 1305a–c).
109. Gregory of Nyssa, *De hominis opificio* 28–29 (PG 44: 229b–240b).

was added as a punishment for transgression, just as a face deformed by leprosy regains its beauty when the Word removes its deformity, as with Naaman the Syrian or the lepers described in the Gospel. Darkened by disease, their faces shine anew when health is restored in their ideas.[110] So whatever is understood to be immutable in human bodies belongs to the first creation, but whatever appears changeable and various in them was added later, outside of their nature. One and the same shared form is understood to exist universally in all human bodies, and it remains forever changeless in all of them. The innumerable differences that impinge on that form as accidents do not derive from the principle of the first creation; they are contingent on the qualities of corruptible seed.[111]

### 273. *What the spiritual body and the material body are*

That spiritual form, therefore, is the spiritual body made in the first creation of man. But there is no doubt that the one made from matter, that is, from the qualities and quantities of the four elements of the sensible world, along with that qualitative form, pertains to the body that was added on. That material, external body is not unsuitably understood as a kind of garment of the inner, natural body. For it changes over time as it ages, experiencing growth and decay, while the inner body remains forever unchanged in its stability. Yet, because even that external body was made by God and belongs to the lowest order among creatures, it cannot utterly perish and be reduced to nothing. Now everything that is born into this world in space and time through generation must come to an end, whether in the least units (such as days and hours), the greatest (such as centuries), or those in between (such as ages). For everything that begins to exist in the world and is composed from the world, must necessarily be dissolved and perish with the world. Therefore, the external body must be dissolved into the elements from which it

110. 2 Kgs 5.1–27; Lk 17.12–19; Gregory of Nyssa, *De hominis opificio* 27 (PG 44: 225d–228a).

111. Gregory of Nyssa, *De hominis opificio* 27 (PG 44: 225d–228b).

was taken,[112] but it need not perish, because it is from God. The inner body remains forever, abiding without change in the principles by which it was constituted—with the soul, in the soul, through the soul, and on account of the soul.

The rich man's debate with Abraham suggests the notion that bodies cling to souls after death.[113] Because the form of the perishable body remains in the soul, not only while it is alive but even after it dissolves into its elements, the soul cannot forget or be unaware of its parts, wherever they may be in the elements. For even though that body was added to human nature because of sin, it cannot fail to belong to it because it was made by the same Creator of nature. For this reason, it must be received back by the soul at the time of the resurrection.[114] The external body is the seal of the inner body, in which the form of the soul is expressed. On that account it is reasonably called its form.[115]

Do not think I am teaching that there are two natural bodies in a single person. There is just one body, and a human being is produced when it is connaturally and consubstantially united with the soul. But the material, superadded body is rightly taken to be a kind of mutable, corruptible garment of the true natural body, rather than a true body itself. It is not true that it does not abide forever. Therefore, the mortal, corruptible, earthly, or animal body is not posited simply but always with some addition, to distinguish it from the simple body that was originally created in man and is yet to be.

### 274. *On Gregory and Augustine*

D: How then shall we answer the holy, divine theologian Augustine, who seems to oppose these arguments? For in almost all his books he asserts without hesitation that the first man's body before sin was animal, earthly, and mortal, although it would not have died if he had not sinned (for he died by sinning, as the Apostle says: "The body is dead because of sin"),[116] just as now

112. Gregory of Nyssa, *De hominis opificio* 26 (PG 44: 224d).
113. Lk 16.19–31; Gregory of Nyssa, *De hominis opificio* 27 (PG 44: 225c).
114. Gregory of Nyssa, *De hominis opificio* 27 (PG 44: 228b, 225bc).
115. Gregory of Nyssa, *De hominis opificio* 27 (PG 44: 228b).
116. Rom 8.10; Augustine, *De peccatorum meritis* 1.2.2–3.3 (CSEL 60, 4–5); *De*

our flesh "is not invulnerable just because it is not necessarily wounded."[117] He also asserts that Enoch and Elijah, "from the time they were translated, lived and were fed in the same way as Elijah was during those forty days" when he lived after being fed by an angel, or else [Elijah] had such food as Adam had in paradise before sin. He writes that Adam had "refreshment against weakness from the fruit of the trees, and stability against old age from the tree of life."[118] For if his body had not been animal, how would he have been commanded to eat from the fruits of paradise lest he grow weak, and from the tree of life lest he grow old? For as Augustine asserts, the first human beings are said to have eaten corporeally from the fruits of paradise before the Fall.[119]

M: You should know that after the holy apostles, no one has attained greater authority in interpreting the divine Scriptures than Gregory the Theologian among the Greeks and Aurelius Augustine among the Romans. If we wanted to work out some kind of consensus in this controversy between great men, we could say this. The body that, according to Gregory, divine foreknowledge devised on account of sin and added to the external man, is the same body that Augustine calls "animal." Gregory was not silent about the two creations of man—one substantially in God's image, the other far from the image, divided into male and female on account of sin. But Augustine spoke only about that divided creation in two sexes and said nothing about the other, sexless creation in God's image. Still, I never cease to wonder why he calls that body "animal" when he often exalts it with great praise as spiritual and blessed.[120]

D: Didn't we agree that man was made in the genus of animals? How shall we deny that he had an animal body before sin, and if he had not sinned, it could have become blessed?

---

*Genesi ad litteram* 6.19–28 (CSEL 28.1, 192–200); 9.3 (CSEL 28.1, 271–72); 9.10 (CSEL 28.1, 278–79).

117. Augustine, *De peccatorum meritis* 1.3.3 (CSEL 60, 5).

118. 1 Kgs 19.5–8; Gn 2.16; Augustine, *De peccatorum meritis* 1.3.3 (CSEL 60, 5).

119. Augustine, *De Genesi ad litteram* 3.21 (CSEL 28.1, 88); 6.7 (CSEL 28.1, 178); 6.21 (CSEL 28.1, 195); *De civitate Dei* 14.26 (CCSL 48, 449).

120. Augustine, *De civitate Dei* 14.10 (CCSL 48, 430–31); 14.26 (CCSL 48, 449).

### 275. *All things were made at once in man*

M: So do you think that God made everything all at once?

D: Indeed, this is what I believe and understand. All things that are born in the world in the course of time were made all at once, both before the world and with the world, even though they do not sensibly fill the world all at once but in the order of time, as the Lord says: "My Father is working until now, and I work."[121]

M: You perceive rightly. Does it seem to you that God made man in the genus of animals because he foreknew that he would live like an animal and fall into their irrational motions, forsaking the beauty and dignity of the divine image?

D: It seems so. For he who "made all things at once"[122] made future things.

M: So, because he made everything all at once, he also created the animal body added to man on account of sin at the same time, in and with man. We understand that some of the things created all at once in man were made for the sake of divine goodness, like those in which the Creator's image is expressed. These are the mind, reason, and the interior sense—or, so to speak, being, virtue, and operation. But other characteristics were added outside of man, as it were, on account of his foreknown transgression: the animal body, the two sexes, beastly procreation, the need for food and drink, the growth and decay of the body, the unavoidable necessity of alternate sleep and waking, and similar things, from which human nature would have remained entirely free if man had not sinned (as it will be free in the future). Here I follow Gregory of Nyssa and Maximus the philosopher, but I do not refute the sense of the spiritual teaching of other holy fathers who refer these things to the first, substantial creation of man.

121. Jn 5.17.
122. Sir 18.1.

### 276. *To God nothing is past or future*

D: I am troubled to know why God should have made the things that were made on account of sin even before man sinned.

M: Note that for God there is no "before" or "after." For him nothing is past, nothing is future, and nothing is in between, for all things are simultaneous to him. Why then should he not make all at once what he saw and willed should be made? When we say "before and after sin," we demonstrate the mutability of our thoughts while we are still subject to time. But for God, both the foreknowledge of sin and its consequences were simultaneous. To man, not to God, sin was still to come, and the consequences of sin preceded actual sin in man because, in a way, sin preceded itself in man. For evil will, which is hidden sin, preceded the taste of the forbidden fruit, which is actual sin. By the same reasoning we can understand what is written: "I loved Jacob, and I hated Esau."[123] Their good and evil acts had not yet been committed in the order of time,[124] but their consequences already existed in him for whom the whole universe exists simultaneously as one. By "consequences" I mean love and hatred.

Augustine teaches that because man has never been without a mutable will, he has never lacked sin.[125] He also teaches that the first human beings were not in paradise for any period of time, saying: "Man used to live in paradise; he lived in the enjoyment of God; he lived without need."[126] It is as if he plainly said, "Man began to live in paradise, he began to live in the enjoyment of God, he began to live without need." Grammarians call this form of the past tense the "inchoative."[127] He did not

123. Mal 1.2–3; Rom 9.13.

124. Rom 9.11.

125. Augustine, *De civitate Dei* 14.13 (CCSL 48, 434); *De Genesi ad litteram* 9.4 (CSEL 28.1, 272–73).

126. Augustine, *De civitate Dei* 9.26 (CCSL 48, 449). The verb is *vivebat* (imperfect).

127. *Inchoabat homo vivere.* The "inchoative" is the aspect of a verb (not properly a tense) that denotes the beginning of a state. It exists in Latin, Russian, and other "conservative Indo-European languages." In Latin it can be signaled by the infix *-sc-*, as in the case of *amo* (I love) and *amasco* (I'm falling in love).

say man *lived* or *had lived* in paradise,[128] for if he had used such words, man would perhaps be understood, not improperly, to have enjoyed perfect beatitude in paradise without sin for a certain period of time. Often, too, divine authority announces future events as if they had already happened.

### 277. *On the devil*

Who would believe that the devil was in the bliss of paradise? He fell as soon as he was created, for the Lord says in the Gospel, "He was a murderer from the beginning and did not stand in the truth."[129] Augustine asserts, "The devil never stood in the truth, never led a blessed life with the angels, but fell from the very beginning of his creation. Having been made, he at once turned away from the light of truth, swollen with pride and corrupted by delight in his own power. Hence he did not taste the sweetness of the blessed angelic life. It is not that he grew weary of it, for he had never received it—but by not wishing to receive it, he abandoned and lost it. Hence he could not have foreknown his own fall because wisdom is the fruit of piety. He, however, was immediately impious, and consequently blinded in his mind. He did not fall from what he had received, but from what he would have received if he had wished to be subject to God. Because he certainly did not desire this, he fell from what he would have received and, at the same time, did not escape the power of him whose subject he refused to be. In the weight of his punishment, he became such that he could neither take pleasure in the light of justice nor be delivered from his sentence."[130]

### 278. *Neither man nor angel spent any time in paradise*

D: Wasn't the first angel in paradise? For the prophet says, "You are the seal of his likeness and a crown of beauty; you were in the delights of the paradise of God, adorned with every precious stone."[131]

128. The verbs are *vixit* (perfect) and *vixerat* (pluperfect).
129. Jn 8.44.
130. Augustine, *De Genesi ad litteram* 11.23 (CSEL 28.1, 355–56).
131. Ezek 28.12–13; Augustine, *De Genesi ad litteram* 11.25 (CSEL 28.1, 357).

M: In the divine dispensation, the prophet saw these and other things, spoken as if they happened before the devil's fall, as if they had already happened, for they were to be accomplished in him if he had not fallen. In the same way it is also predicated of man that he was in the delights of paradise before sin, for this is what would have happened to him if he had not sinned. No authority, divine or human, reveals how much time man would have lived happily in paradise before he sinned. And if he were understood to have been there, why would Scripture be silent about it? There is no lack of arguments to prove that he lived either very briefly or for no time at all before sin. We nowhere read that he did any of the things he was commanded to do before sin, for example, "Increase and multiply and fill the earth,"[132] namely paradise. Why would he not at once have begotten happy offspring, if he had lived in paradise for any length of time before the Fall? And if he had tasted of the tree of life to prevent corruption, why did the power of its spiritual medicine not prevail in his body, lest by sinning he should fall into corruption? If the food of the tree of life gave his body health and incorruptibility for one or two days, or however many days, but not eternal immortality, then it did not have as much power as we read and believe that it had. Or why should it be called "the tree of life"[133] if it could only delay corruption, but not completely free from corruption those who ate it and grant them a very long life? If the nature of that tree was contrary to all illness, so that it could grant life to all who enjoyed it, why did it not overcome death in those who tasted or ate of it?

D: Sin, I think, overcame its power so that it could not be of such great benefit.

M: In that case, the evil of sin was more powerful than the goodness of life. Rather, we should see what the Lord himself calls the true tree of life. "The devil was a murderer from the beginning."[134] Do you think he killed someone other than the one and only man whom God created in his image?

D: By no means.

132. Gn 1.28.
133. Gn 2.9.
134. Jn 8.44.

### 279. *As soon as they were created, they fell*

M: From what beginning, then, was the devil a murderer? From the beginning of his own creation, the beginning of man's creation, or indeed, from the beginning of the creation of both, if they were created at the same time and one did not precede the other?[135] If the devil's creation preceded that of man, how could the devil have been a murderer from his own beginning? And if man's creation preceded the devil's, how could the devil be called a murderer from the beginning of man's creation? The remaining possibility is that in the beginning, they were both created at the same time. If, then, the devil was a murderer and man was killed, what space is left for man to have lived in paradise before he was killed by the devil?

This is clearly proven in the Gospel parable: "A certain man was going down from Jerusalem to Jericho, and he fell among thieves."[136] It does not say, "There was a certain man in Jerusalem, and he fell among thieves." For if human nature had remained in Jerusalem, that is in paradise, it would not have fallen among thieves—the devil and his followers. So man first went down from paradise, impelled by the irrational movement of his own will, and rushed into Jericho (the weakness and instability of temporal things). In falling, he was wounded and despoiled of all the natural goods with which he was created. Here we are given to understand that man fell within himself even before he was tempted by the devil. Not only this, but we also understand that he was wounded and despoiled by the devil not in paradise, but while descending from it.[137] By his own will he forsook the felicity of paradise, which is called Jerusalem ("vision of peace"), and fell into Jericho, that is, into this world. For it is impossible to believe that the same man both stood in the contemplation of eternal peace and fell through the persuasion of the woman, who was corrupted by the serpent's poison. It is also incredible that the serpent—the devil—who had already fallen from the dignity of paradise (the angelic nature), should have prevailed

135. Augustine, *De Genesi ad litteram* 11.16 (CSEL 28.1, 348–49); 11.19 (CSEL 28.1, 352).

136. Lk 10.30.

137. Augustine, *De Genesi ad litteram* 12.28 (CSEL 28.1, 423).

against man if he had not yet sinned, nor fallen from the loftiness of the divine image.

As Gregory the Theologian testifies, we believe that human nature spent no length of time in paradise where it was naturally created, nor did it experience the effects of any sensible things there. Rather, it immediately strayed from the way of truth and deserved, through the movement of its own perverse will, to be split like beasts into two sexes.[138]

## 280. *Why Adam did not eat from the tree of life*

Following Maximus, the supreme theologian, we say that man did not taste of the tree of life, but first ate the deadly food of the forbidden tree and did not lift the eye of his mind to the divine light. "The first father, Adam," he says, "took the first fruits of the forbidden tree, in which he had already learned that death resided. When sensation offered him the fruit, he borrowed a life befitting that fruit—that is, mortal and fluid because of the corruptible body. If he had believed God rather than his fellow servant (sensation), he would have eaten from the tree of life and perhaps not laid down the immortality given to him, but preserved it forever by participating in life. For every life is preserved through its own appropriate food. But the food of that blessed life is 'the living bread that came down from heaven and gives life to the world.'"[139]

## 281. *That contrary opinions should not be despised*

It is not our purpose to argue against those who say that man lived happily in paradise for some time before sin, though they do not dare to affirm how long that time was. Indeed, we have taken pains only to say what seems probable to us. As for the opinions of others who think differently, it is not our business to refute or despise them, or to pronounce them false. I see that we should now move on to a consideration of paradise itself.

138. Gregory of Nyssa, *De hominis opificio* 17 (PG 44: 189cd).

139. Jn 6.33; Maximus, *Ambigua* 6.28 (PG 91: 1156c–1157a). Underlying this passage is Ambrose's allegorical reading in which Adam represents reason and Eve, sensation. See chap. 283 below.

D: Yes, let us move on. We should follow the correct path of reasoning so that we seem to stray neither to the right nor to the left. That is, we should neither disparage those whom the catholic church has pronounced to be of supreme and holy authority, nor should we despise those whom we know to have a simple understanding, for they possess a sincere catholic faith. "Let everyone abound in his own sense," as the Apostle says.[140] Indeed, we aim to support our own opinion or that of writers who surpass the rest—but to condemn the opinion of others is very dangerous, arrogant in the extreme, or surely contentious. So let us proceed cautiously, humbly, and modestly, following the footsteps of the holy fathers in this affair.

### 282. *On paradise*

M: St. Augustine, then, asserts that there are two paradises: one spiritual, in which man lived happily in the soul, and the other corporeal, in which the same man lived happily in the body.[141] "And in the bodily paradise," as he says, "the animals of the earth lived with the two human beings, subordinate to them and harmless. Among these was the serpent, a slippery animal that moves in a winding, roundabout way. That proud, envious angel, who had already fallen from the spiritual paradise through pride, chose it as a fitting instrument for his work"—that is, deceiving the humans.[142] But the same writer, in his book *On the True Religion*, seems to assert that there was only a single paradise, saying that the soul fell "from the intelligible good to the sensible good."[143]

### 283. *What Ambrose says*

St. Ambrose likewise seems to affirm that there are two paradises. "In this paradise," he says, "God put the man whom he formed—not the one made in God's image, but the embodied

140. Rom 14.5.

141. Augustine, *De Genesi ad litteram* 8.1 (CSEL 28.1, 229); *De civitate Dei* 14.11 (CCSL 48, 432).

142. Augustine, *De civitate Dei* 14.11 (CCSL 48, 432).

143. Augustine, *De vera religione* 20.38 (CCSL 32, 210).

one, for what is incorporeal has no place."[144] He means that spiritually there was only one paradise, that is, human nature planted in eternal delights. He says that Christ was its tree of life and its fountain. The four rivers, he affirms, are the four principal virtues of the soul. The man represents intellect, the woman carnal sensation, and the serpent pleasure.[145]

D: In this it seems to me that he allegorizes the corporeal paradise, rather than denying it. For the same writer says elsewhere, "'God took the man he had made and set him in paradise.' Do you see," he asks, "where he was when he was taken? He was in the land of his formation. The power of God took him and set him in paradise."[146] Again: "Note that the man was made outside of paradise and the woman in paradise, to show that everyone acquires grace for himself not by nobility of place or birth, but by virtue. For the man who was made outside of paradise, that is, in an inferior place, is found to be better, while she who was made in a better place, in paradise, turns out to be inferior. For the woman was deceived before she herself deceived the man."[147] Isn't it clear from these words that he meant to assert that paradise was local, and therefore corporeal and sensual?

## 284. *What Origen says*

M: It is not our purpose to wrestle with those who hold such views. We neither deny nor affirm that there are two paradises, one corporeal and the other spiritual. We shall compare the holy fathers' opinions for ourselves, but it is not ours to judge which ones ought to be followed. "Let everyone abound in his own sense"[148] and choose which ones to follow, laying quarrels aside.

Origen, the supreme interpreter of Holy Scripture, proves that there is no paradise other than the one in the third heaven,

144. Ambrose, *De paradiso* 1.5 (CSEL 32.1, 267).

145. Ambrose, *De paradiso* 2.11 (CSEL 32.1, 271); 3.12–18 (CSEL 32.1, 272–77). This allegory ultimately derives from Philo of Alexandria.

146. Gn 2.15; Ambrose, *De paradiso* 4.24 (CSEL 32.1, 280).

147. Ambrose, *De paradiso* 4.24 (CSEL 32.1, 280).

148. Rom 14.5.

into which Paul was ravished.[149] And if it is in the third heaven, it is certainly spiritual. Indeed, the most important authors in both languages affirm that the third heaven into which Paul was ravished is spiritual.

### 285. *What Epiphanius says*

Epiphanius, bishop of Salamis[150] in Cyprus, maintains that paradise is entirely on earth: a sensible place in the eastern regions of the world, with sensible trees, rivers, and other things that are carnally believed about paradise by those who merely cling to the bodily senses.[151] He has no doubt that the "tunics of skins" that God sewed for the first human beings after the Fall were literally made from the fleece of sheep, which, as he says, were in paradise. Concerning paradise he also rebukes Origen, whom almost all the Greek and Latin authors follow in this theory.[152]

### 286. *What Gregory says*

You should know that Ambrose follows Gregory of Nyssa; let us also follow him.

This Gregory affirms that by the word "paradise," divine Scripture uses figurative speech to signify human nature made in God's image.[153] The true plantation of God is human nature itself, which he created in Eden in his image and likeness—that is, an image totally like himself except by reason of the subject.[154] Eden stands for the delights of eternal felicity and the bliss of the divine likeness; it was greater and better than the whole sensible world, not in mass but in the dignity of its nature. Its fertile earth was the body, potentially immortal, for the first man's body was able not to die—and would not have died if it had not been corrupted by the poison of his transgression.[155]

149. 2 Cor 12.2–4; Epiphanius, *Ancoratus* 54 (PG 43: 112b).

150. Latin *Constantie.*

151. Epiphanius, *Ancoratus* 55 (PG 43: 113b); 58 (PG 43: 117b–120c); 61 (PG 43: 125bc).

152. Gn 3.21; Epiphanius, *Ancoratus* 62 (PG 43: 128b–129a).

153. Gregory of Nyssa, *De hominis opificio* 19 (PG 44: 196cd).

154. Gregory of Nyssa, *De hominis opificio* 16 (PG 44: 184d).

155. Augustine, *De peccatorum meritis* 1.2.2–3.3 (CSEL 60, 4–5); *De Genesi ad*

Rather, it would have remained green with the blossoms of spiritual beauty and never grown old with the passage of time. Its water, capable of receiving forms, was the sense perception of the incorruptible body, formed by the phantasms of sensible things with no deception or falsehood. Its air, illumined by the rays of divine wisdom—that is, the sun of justice—was reason, by which man could have known the natures of all things. Its ether was the mind, which would have circled the divine nature in eternal, unerring motion, changeless in movement and changeable in stability.[156] Because other things that can be predicated of the divine image surpass understanding, they must be honored in silence.

In this paradise, as Scripture testifies, there flowed the fountain of life. It is recounted that four streams of virtues sprang from it, a figure of the four principal rivers of the world: prudence, temperance, fortitude, and justice. Bursting forth from divine wisdom, the wellspring of all life and virtue, these spiritual rivers water the surface of human nature.[157] They first arise as invisible virtues in the secret recesses of human nature, as it were in the most hidden pores of the intelligible earth, then gush up in the manifest effects of good deeds, producing countless forms of virtue and action. For every virtue and action proceeds from these streams and returns to them, while they themselves come forth from divine wisdom and circle back to it.

In the same paradise there were two trees, one called *pan* ("everything") and the other *gnoston* ("mixed").[158] As Scripture says, "The Lord God brought forth from the soil every tree that is beautiful to look at and sweet to the taste, and the tree of life in the middle of paradise."[159] No one who follows Gregory thinks there were many trees in paradise with different shapes and fruits, as in a forest abounding in many trees. There were only two, called *pan* and *gnoston.*

---

*litteram* 6.19–28 (CSEL 28.1, 192–200); 9.3 (CSEL 28.1, 271–72); 9.10 (CSEL 28.1, 278–79).

156. Maximus, *Ambigua* 6.3 (PG 91: 1112d–1113a).

157. Gn 2.10–14; Ambrose, *De paradiso* 3.12–18 (CSEL 32.1, 272–77).

158. Gregory of Nyssa, *De hominis opificio* 19 (PG 44: 196d–197b).

159. Gn 2.9.

### 287. *What* pan *means*

This *pan,* that is, every tree, is the Word and Wisdom of the Father, our Lord Jesus Christ,[160] who is every fruit-bearing tree planted in the middle of paradise (human nature), in two ways. The first is according to his divinity, by which he creates and encompasses our nature. The second is the way that, in order to save our nature, he united it with himself so as to subsist in two natures, divine and human. This is what Scripture says: "God brought forth from the soil," that is, from our material nature, "every tree,"[161] that is, the Word incarnate, in and through which all things were made, and which is itself all things. For the Word alone is the substantial good; other goods are good not in themselves but through it. To eat of this Word is joy and gladness and ineffable delights. The first human beings were commanded to take food from "every tree," that is, from the plenitude of all goods, and all humankind is still commanded to live by this. But since the first parents did not wish to take food from that tree, preferring the deadly fruit of the forbidden tree, not only they but the whole race procreated by them were expelled from the dignity of nature and, by a most just divine judgment, condemned to death.

### 288. *What* gnoston *means*

*Gnoston,* or "mixed," is evil tinged with a fantasy of good, innate in the corporeal senses and utterly contrary to the first tree, or *pan.*[162] Just as all goodness is imagined in the first tree, so is the universality of evil in the second. The first tree, therefore, is all truly subsisting good; this one is every evil, seducing all the wicked through a fantasy of the good.

160. Gregory of Nyssa, *De hominis opificio* 19 (PG 44: 196d–197b); Augustine, *De Genesi ad litteram* 8.5 (CSEL 28.1, 237).

161. Gn 2.9.

162. Gregory of Nyssa, *De hominis opificio* 19–20 (PG 44: 197b–200a).

### 289. *What "in the middle of paradise" means*

D: Why are both trees, that is "every tree" (which is also called "the tree of life") and the other one, the "tree of the knowledge of good and evil," said to be "in the middle of paradise"?[163]

M: According to Gregory, the whole of human nature is divided into six parts, generally in all human beings and specifically in individuals. First it is separated into two principal parts, body and soul. What is ascribed to the body, or exterior man, is divided into three parts: first, the body itself (that is, matter which has received form); second, the vital motion; and third, the fivefold senses. The whole exterior man consists of these three parts. What is ascribed to the soul is likewise divided into three parts: the interior sense, reason, and intellect. The whole interior man consists of these three parts. Human nature is distinguished in these six ways, for it exists, lives, and senses through the body; it also experiences sensation outside of the body, reasons, and understands.[164] The lower triad is corruptible and perishable; the upper, which expresses the image of God, is incorruptible and indissoluble. Beyond the limits of human nature, we understand that no created nature exists. Indeed, only God is above the intellect, and there is nothing below the body.

In the middle of human nature are vital motion in the lower part and reason in the upper part. Between these two are the senses, exterior and interior. We understand that those two intelligible trees were planted in the external and internal senses, as if in the middle of the paradise of human nature: *pan* in the interior sense and *gnoston* in the exterior. "For truth dwells in the inner man," with every good that is the Word of God.[165] Opposed to it are malice and evil, which are possessed by the exterior man.

At the serpent's persuasion, the woman took fruit from the forbidden tree and chose a false good—the transitory goods of this world—suggested by the pleasure of carnal sensation.

163. Gn 2.9.

164. Gregory of Nyssa, *De hominis opificio* 5 (PG 44: 137bc); 8 (PG 44: 144d–148c); 14 (PG 44: 173d–176b).

165. Augustine, *De vera religione* 39.72 (CCSL 32, 234).

By the serpent we should understand pleasure, by the woman carnal sensation, and by the forbidden tree, the false good that deceives all carnal people. Scripture forbids us its fruit: "Do not love the world, nor the things that are in the world."[166] The knowledge of good and evil does not signify any kind of knowledge about nature, but the appetite to experience evil disguised as a form of good.[167]

### 290. *What the tree of the knowledge of good and evil means*

D: I would like to know whether God planted such a tree, whose nature is evil disguised as a form of good and whose fruit was the cause of death, in the paradise of human nature. For if God created it, perhaps he will be judged to be the creator of evil and the cause of death—a thing most impious to say, let alone believe, about the author of all goods! But if it was not planted by God, how did it come to be in human nature?

M: The tree of the knowledge of good and evil, which is understood as false good, is encompassed by God insofar as it is a form of good, for he is the cause of every form and all beauty that is understood or perceived to be in any substance. Or rather, he is himself that form and beauty. But insofar as the tree is evil encircled by a form of good, it is in itself formless, coming neither from God nor from any other fixed and definite cause. Evil is indeed variable and causeless, for it is not substantially found in the nature of things at all.[168] Insofar as it is evil, therefore, that tree cannot be referred to any cause, for it is absolutely nothing. But insofar as it is formed by good in order to deceive the unwary—for the matter from which it was formed was made by God, and is good—it is not entirely evil. So the form by which evil seduced the human beings whom it killed is itself good, since it is a fantasy of some good. But evil itself is absolutely evil and not made by anything good, being contrary to all goodness.[169] Evil, therefore, was not planted in human nature

166. 1 Jn 2.15.
167. Gregory of Nyssa, *De hominis opificio* 20 (PG 44: 197c–200b).
168. Dionysius, *De divinis nominibus* 4.30 (PG 3: 732a).
169. Gregory of Nyssa, *De hominis opificio* 20 (PG 44: 200b–d).

but consists in a perverse movement of free will. That movement is not observed within human nature but taken from outside it, from beastly intemperance. Yet, by the counsel of the ancient enemy, it is mingled with good so as to deceive the affections of carnal sensation, and in this way put them to death.

Now we do not reject the opinion of those who assert that this tree was by nature altogether good and literally planted in a local paradise. They say that its fruit was the experiential knowledge of good and evil. If the first human beings had abstained from tasting it, they would have experienced eternal life and perpetual bliss, uninterrupted by death. But if they illicitly took of its fruit, they would experience eternal death and unhappiness. Just as Sarah and Hagar were really two women who spiritually prefigured the two laws, and as the stone that really poured forth water before the people was a figure of Christ,[170] and many similar things, it is not incredible that a spiritual paradise should be signified by a corporeal one.

### 291. *That no Catholic's opinion should be despised*

Let the reader choose from the aforesaid opinions of the holy fathers whatever seems right to him to follow—but let no one recklessly slander us, thinking what we have said is of no authority. Rather, let him look diligently, and he will find that nothing here is our own except the labor. So let him gratefully accept these views as supported by the highest authorities and proven by reason. But if anyone thinks that he knows something when he knows nothing and blames us because we understand the law spiritually—following the most enlightened doctors of the Church and hearing the Apostle, who teaches, "We know that the law is spiritual"[171]—we refute such a person as possessing carnal wisdom like the Jews and empty of the spiritual sense.

170. Gn 16.1; Gal 4.22–26; Ex 17.6; Nm 20.9–11; 1 Cor 10.4; Augustine, *De Genesi ad litteram* 8.4 (CSEL 28.1, 235).

171. Rom 7.14.

### 292. *What the spiritual paradise is*

D: I approve, but I would like you briefly to recapitulate what is said above. Let everyone choose what he wishes.

M: The paradise planted by God in Eden is human nature, made "in God's image" in the delights of eternal felicity.[172] Its fountain is Christ, "the fountain of life,"[173] who cries out to those who thirst for justice: "If anyone thirsts, let him come to me and drink."[174] Its rivers flowing from the fountain of wisdom are the four principal virtues of the soul, from which every virtue and good action gushes forth. Its every tree is the one of which it is written, "He who conquers, I will give him to eat of the tree of life which is in paradise,"[175] "which is planted beside rushing waters,"[176] that is, the oracles of the prophets. This tree is the Word of God, which is inherent in human nature and became incarnate from it. The tree of the knowledge of good and evil is the carnal senses' undiscerning appetite for false goods, which deceives and destroys souls. The man is the mind, presiding over the whole of human nature. The woman is external sensation, and the serpent is illicit pleasure.

Do you want to hear the view of St. Ambrose on paradise, in which he follows Gregory?

D: Who but a madman will dare to resist the views of such a great, extremely wise man?

M: He says, "This troubles a great many people. If God's great gift to human beings in the beginning was that they should dwell in paradise, and afterwards he seems to reward great merits by ravishing every righteous person into paradise, then why are even beasts, cattle of the field, and birds of the sky said to have been in paradise? For this reason, many have thought that paradise is the soul in which the seeds of the virtues sprout, and man is set there to cultivate and guard paradise. That is, the man is the human mind, whose virtue seems to cultivate and

172. Gn 1.27.
173. Ps 35.10.
174. Jn 7.37.
175. Rv 2.7.
176. Ps 1.3.

guard the soul as it wishes. The beasts that are brought to Adam are our irrational motions because beasts and livestock stand for different bodily passions, some more turbulent, others more languid. The birds are vain thoughts that fly around the soul like birds. Among these creatures, no helper is found similar to the mind except sense perception, which is called in Greek *aisthesis.* This alone could be found similar to *noys,*" the mind.[177] Man's food, "in which eternal life is defined, is the living heavenly bread, the Lord himself, who 'gives life to the world.'"[178]

### 293. *Where the man and the woman were created*

Outside this paradise, that is, outside of God's image, the masculine sex was made from earth, as if in an inferior place, and added onto the nature made in God's image. Because it was added to the divine image as if taken from elsewhere, the male sex was afterwards placed in paradise, that is, alongside the first creation. There the second sex—the woman—was drawn out of the man's side, as if in a superior place, and added to him to help procreate offspring the way foolish animals do. But the creation of the male sex does not precede that of the woman in time, only in dignity. And note that the inner human, made in God's image, is formed in paradise, while the outer, corruptible man is fashioned of mud from the earth[179] outside of paradise, and beneath it. He is then taken up and set in paradise, that is, added to God's image. If he had worked out his salvation there and kept God's commandment,[180] he would have attained the dignity of the superior human being.[181]

See how the Greeks and the Latins agree about paradise![182]

177. Gn 2.20; Ambrose, *De paradiso* 11.51 (CSEL 32.1, 307–8).

178. Jn 6.33; Ambrose, *De paradiso* 9.42 (CSEL 32.1, 299).

179. Gn 2.7.

180. Gn 2.15.

181. Ambrose, *De paradiso* 4.24 (CSEL 32.1, 280). The first half of this paragraph refers to *virilis sexus* and *mulier,* the male sex and the woman, while the second half refers to the *interior* and *exterior homo*—the inner and outer human being. The *interior homo* lacks sex and gender, which belong only to the *exterior homo.*

182. "The Latins" are here represented only by Ambrose, who was of course following the Greeks.

## 294. *That there is only one paradise*

D: I see that Ambrose approves the view of Origen,[183] who asserts that paradise is in the third, intellectual heaven—that is, in the human being insofar as he is intellect. But he refutes the view of Epiphanius, who naively thinks paradise is some place on earth, with earthly trees and sensible rivers.[184]

M: True reasoning laughs at that view. For it is not credible that the Apostle was ravished into any paradise other than the one in which the first human being was made in God's image and from which he was cast out for disobedience. The divine history tells of only one paradise and one human being created in it. In that human being, if we follow the words of the holy fathers, we should understand neither male nor female. In fact, the male aspect of human nature is the intellect,[185] which the Greeks call *noys,* and the woman is sense perception, which they call *aisthesis.* Their marriage prefigures the union of Christ and the Church.[186] Divine law commanded them to eat of the tree of life, which is Christ, the Wisdom and Word of the Father, who was planted "in the middle of the paradise" of human nature.[187] This is the spiritual food on which angels and perfect humans feed. But the law forbade the other tree, that is, the appetite for good and evil, which is planted in imperfect souls through the pleasure of temporal things. To abstain from it earns the reward of eternal life; to abuse it leads to eternal destruction.

## 295. *The double creation of man*

D: I would like to know about the double creation of man.

M: We read about the creation of the inner man: "God created man in his image; in the image of God he created him."[188] The creation of the outer man is expressed here: "So the Lord

183. Ambrose, *De paradiso* 11.53 (CSEL 32.1, 309–10).

184. Epiphanius, *Ancoratus* 54 (PG 43: 112b); 55 (PG 43: 113b); 58 (PG 43: 117b–120c); 61 (PG 43: 125bc).

185. *Humane siquidem nature vir est intellectus.*

186. Eph 5.32.

187. Gn 2.9.

188. Gn 1.27.

God formed man from the mud of the earth, and breathed into his face the breath of life; and man became a living soul."[189] This is said in the same way about the other beasts brought forth from the earth: "Let the earth bring forth a living soul."[190] The division of nature into two sexes follows: "Male and female he created them."[191] The likeness of foolish animals followed that division: "Man became a living soul,"[192] it says, rather than "a life-giving spirit."[193]

### 296. *How Adam saw*

D: What does this verse mean: "Their eyes were opened, and they knew that they were naked"?[194] Didn't Adam have bodily sight when he saw all the animals and gave them names?

M: In the same way that he saw all the animals, he also knew his own nakedness—with the gaze of inner knowledge alone, the simple eye of the mind, with no help from bodily, mortal perception. For he knew that he was naked when he lacked not a garment, but the veil of virtues.[195] Note that before he was despoiled of the covering of virtues, the first human being was able to contemplate all the animals and birds that are said to have been made from the earth and the waters, though they were scattered all over the earth in their natural habitats. He saw them not in any place or with bodily perception, but with the mind's eye alone, beyond all corruptible sensation, beyond all space and time, in the principles according to which they were created.

### 297. *What the sleep of Adam means*

D: What does this mean: "The Lord sent a sleep upon Adam"?[196]

189. Gn 2.7.
190. Gn 1.24.
191. Gn 1.27.
192. Gn 2.7.
193. 1 Cor 15.45.
194. Gn 3.7.
195. Ambrose, *De paradiso* 13.63 (CSEL 32.1, 322–23).
196. Gn 2.21.

M: Ambrose teaches that Adam's sleep was the desire for carnal copulation, which was permitted rather than sent by God.[197] "And while he slept, he took one of his ribs and filled its place with flesh, and the Lord God built the rib that he had taken from Adam into a woman."[198] The rib he took signifies the removal of inner virtue; the flesh set in its place is the weakness of vices and misery; the building of the woman is the splitting of nature into two sexes.

### 298. *What the fig tree and the aprons mean*

D: What do you think about that fig tree from whose leaves the aprons were sewn?[199]

M: The fig tree was the divine commandment given to the first human beings in paradise: "Eat from every tree in paradise, but do not eat from the tree of the knowledge of good and evil."[200] So that they might keep the commandment more carefully, the peril of transgression was not hidden from them: "For in whatever day you eat of it, you will die."[201] St. Ambrose explains that the fig tree is the divine law, whose "fruit is love, peace, joy, patience, kindness," and so forth.[202] Its leaves are the empty words from which people make aprons when they cover their shameful deeds with examples from Scripture. A person "sews leaves together when, wishing to veil his guilt, he either says the devil is the author of his transgression, makes the allure of the flesh his excuse, blames someone else who led him into error," or uses examples from divine Scripture, saying that "Abraham slept with a slave woman, while David had an affair with a foreign woman and killed her husband."[203]

197. Ambrose, *De paradiso* 11.50 (CSEL 32.1, 307).
198. Gn 2.21–22.
199. Gn 3.7.
200. Gn 2.16–17.
201. Gn 2.17.
202. Gal 5.22; Ambrose, *De paradiso* 13.64–65 (CSEL 32.1, 323–24).
203. Gn 16.1–4; 2 Sm 11.1–27; Ambrose, *De paradiso* 13.65 (CSEL 32.1, 324).

### 299. *What the walking of God means*

D: And what was the walking of God in paradise?[204]

M: The Lord walks in paradise when he reminds human nature of the rewards of life or calls future punishments before the mind's eye, rebuking the guilt of transgression with an intelligible voice. "When a sinner reads the divine Scriptures, he hears the voice of the Lord walking in the evening, as it were, when late in the day he recognizes his guilt."[205] He hides in the middle of paradise when he wishes to remain hidden in the secrecy of his conscience.

### 300. *What the speech of God means*[206]

D: "How does God speak? With a corporeal voice?

M: Not at all. But he utters oracles by means of a certain power more excellent than the body's voice. The prophets heard this voice of his, the faithful hear it, and the wicked do not understand."[207] Such speech suggests that paradise is not local—some forested place—but spiritual, sown with the seeds of virtues and planted in human nature. In this paradise the Word of the Father speaks, condemning faults and promising pardon. So the man (the mind) is interrogated first as the guardian set over the whole paradise of human nature, lest it violate the divine commandment. "Adam, where are you?[208] Before you sinned, you had been set beyond all places and times; you were in heaven, blessed like the angelic creation. Now you are on earth like the brute animals, a proud transgressor."

Adam said, "The woman you gave me as a companion gave me fruit from the tree, and I ate."[209] Such a distancing of the crime offered no defense but only increased the weight of condemnation. "The Lord God said to the woman, 'Why did you

204. Gn 3.8.

205. Ambrose, *De paradiso* 14.68 (CSEL 32.1, 326).

206. This exegesis of the Fall is by far the longest chapter of the *Clavis physicae.* It continues from Book IV into Book V of the *Periphyseon.*

207. Ambrose, *De paradiso* 14.69 (CSEL 32.1, 327).

208. Gn 3.9.

209. Gn 3.12.

do this?'"[210] The inquiring judge's sentence against the man and the woman is not pronounced immediately, so as to grant a space to correct the wicked excuse and prepare a place for indulgence. "She answered, 'The serpent deceived me, and I ate.'"[211] The author of the fault is the woman (carnal sensation), not the serpent (pleasure). So the pride of the mind, united with the illicit pleasure of carnal sensation, betrayed human nature to the condemnation of death, from which only the humility of Christ and the pleasure of spiritual things in faithful souls can recall and liberate it.

But the serpent, the primordial cause of all evil, at once experienced the just judge's sentence. "The Lord said to the serpent, 'Because you have done this, you are cursed among all the animals and beasts of the earth.'"[212] Note that neither the man nor the woman, but only the serpent is cursed. For God does not curse the things he makes, but blesses them, and the mind and senses are God's creation. Carnal pleasure, however, arose outside the divine creation in the irrational passions of the human soul. Therefore, it succumbs to the severity of the divine sentence, for it is found to be outside the nature made by God. The divine curse is the most just, irrevocable damnation of those who are outside of nature and contaminate it. The beasts and animals of the earth are the irrational passions of our rational nature, called by the name of earth.[213] "Upon your breast you shall walk, and earth shall you eat all the days of your life."[214] The serpent is carnal pleasure or diabolical cunning. Its breast is "the prudence of the flesh,"[215] governed by the cleverness of diabolical fraud, as well as vain philosophy that does not build up the mind but puffs up the breast.[216]

D: What is the difference between the prudence of the flesh and vain philosophy?

M: The prudence of the flesh is false virtue simulating good-

210. Gn 3.13.
211. Ibid.
212. Gn 3.14.
213. Ambrose, *De paradiso* 11.51 (CSEL 32.1, 308).
214. Gn 3.14.
215. Rom 8.6.
216. Col 2.8; 1 Cor 8.1.

ness, which deceives the senses. It deludes souls, overwhelms them with the fallacious fantasies of false virtues, and oppresses them with the darkness of eternal death. But vain philosophy thrives especially among the perfidious Jews. It follows only the literal sense of the divine narrative but hates, spurns, neglects, and ignores the spirit, which is the mystical understanding. It devises false and empty fables about the nature of things with no resemblance to truth, to delude the souls of carnal people.[217] Despising the truth of the natural causes by which the whole creation was made, it speaks pretentiously with the grandiloquent charm of unusual words, or else it simulates the form of truth with the intricate curls of fallacious propositions and syllogisms, by which it can deceive the unwary. On this breast the serpent walks (or is lifted up) and he boasts of it, tripping up the whole person.

"And you shall eat earth" means you shall feed on carnal desires and the actions of carnal people "all the days of your life."[218] That is, your reign will last as long as a certain false light smiles and prevails in human nature. "I will set enmity between you and the woman."[219] The woman is bodily sensation; the serpent is lustful pleasure in temporal things. God has established enmity between them because the sense perception of the perfect hates the carnal appetite for material things, but pleasure hates spiritual and divine virtues. "And between your seed and her seed": the seed of the woman is the perfect, natural, and manifold knowledge of visible things, with all error purged away, but the serpent's seed is the deadly increase of countless offenses. "She will crush your head": the head of this serpent is the beginning of sin, which is crushed in the senses of the perfect faithful. When one head is cut off, it splits into an infinite number, for universal evil is so manifold that there is no part of it from which the poisonous shoots of vices do not spring. Yet the woman crushes them all when sense perception overcomes evil with good.

217. The association of Jews with literalism and carnality goes back ultimately to Paul. See 2 Cor 3.4–6; Gal 4.21–31.

218. Gn 3.14.

219. Gn 3.15.

"And you will lie in wait for her heel": the woman's heel is the image of bodily things impressed on the five senses—sight, hearing, smell, taste, and touch—among which sight extends far beyond the body of the perceiver. For I perceive that the sun, moon, and other stars are far from the place where the bulk of my little body walks. Wherever they are, I perceive them with the rays from my eyes, which rise up to them without delay, and in those rays the phantasms of the aforesaid stars are formed.[220] It is similar with objects that we understand to be nearby or in the middle distance. Hearing also reaches beyond the limits of the body to receive the forms of sounds or voices impressed on it, produced by striking the air, whether they are distant or near. Smell too leaps out to perceive pleasant or unpleasant scents, far or near. Taste distinguishes sweet and bitter flavors within the body. Touch fulfills its office both within and outside its body. The cunning serpent lies in wait for these five senses, informed by phantasms of sensible things, when he perniciously persuades unwary souls to desire outward things perceived by the bodily senses. Therefore, Scripture says, "The woman saw that the tree was good to eat, beautiful to the eyes, and delightful in appearance, and she took of its fruit and ate, and gave it to her husband."[221] That is, bodily sensation, delighted by the forms of sensible things, corrupts the mind through consent and turns it away from contemplation of the truth within.

D: What does this saying to the woman mean: "I will multiply your hardships and your offspring; in pain shall you bring forth children"?[222]

M: If the human being had not sinned, he would not only have contemplated truth most purely with the intellect within. He would also have observed the natures and causes of things with the outer senses with the greatest ease, having no need for laborious reasoning.[223] But after sin, the mind perceives only

220. This is the optical theory of extramission: vision takes place when rays emitted by the eyes pass through space to strike the object of perception.

221. Gn 3.6.

222. Gn 3.16.

223. The subject is *homo*. I use "he" to indicate that this punishment allegorically refers not to gender relations, but to the functioning of the fallen mind and senses in all human beings.

the surfaces of sensible things, with their quantities and qualities, positions and conditions, through the organs of the exterior senses. It attains knowledge of all these not as they are in themselves, but through their phantasms; and it is not without multiple hardships (that is, laborious study) that it can arrive at multiple offspring (the first stages of understanding intelligible things) and procreate children (correct reasoning about the nature of things), with the aid of the same senses. This verse follows: "And you will be under your husband's power, and he will rule over you."[224] This will happen when nature is restored and recalled to its natural order and converted to the peace of the spiritual, natural marriage, when the body is submissive and obedient to the senses, the senses to the mind, and the mind to God.

D: What is the meaning of what is said to the man: "Cursed is the earth in your work," and so forth?[225]

M: The earth cursed in the works of Adam is the flesh made by Adam's works, that is, by the passions of the mind, flesh that is unfruitful in the works of virtue, from which he eats "in sadness." That is, he enjoys pleasure only briefly. The earth brings forth "thorns and thistles" for him—that is, it stings him with cares, temptations, and dangers. "In the sweat of his face" he eats bread, for he feeds on the contemplation of intelligible things through the laborious work of considering sensible things. Adam's earth is also the heart cursed by the loss of celestial goods. Earth well eaten is the purification of the heart through action. The grass of the earth is the knowledge of created things; the bread, the teaching of mysteries.[226] The days of the life of the mind, in which it labors to purify the earth of its heart, constitute the whole span of life, including life after death, until bodies rise again. For we believe that souls can be purified in both this life and the life after bodily death, up until the day of judgment. These are the days in which the mind eats the earth of its heart, that is, performs acts of purification. For

224. Gn 3.16.

225. Gn 3.17. *Terra* (earth) can also mean land, ground, or dust, as in most English Bibles. Honorius uses the same term with multiple senses.

226. Gn 3.17–19; Maximus, *Quaestiones ad Thalassium* 5 (PG 90: 277c–280b).

we read that after the end of sensible things, there will be no act of purification when nature has returned to its original purity. Therefore, this verse follows: "Until you return to the earth from which you were taken."[227] This is as if to say: "Your face"—that is, the rational inquiry into truth—"will sweat" in the labors of your purification, through action and knowledge, "until you return to the earth from which you were taken." For you will no longer sweat when you have arrived at the changeless stability of the primordial causes, from which you take your beginning.

D: How do you prove that the word "earth" signifies the happiness of eternal life and the stability of the primordial causes, from which all that exists has its origin?

M: This is clearly suggested by many passages of divine Scripture. For example, Abraham was told, "Go forth from your land and your kindred and your father's house, and come into the land that I will show you."[228] And "Abraham proceeded from there to a southern land and dwelt between Kadesh and Shur,"[229] that is, between sanctification and equanimity. All the happiness of the saints in eternal rest stands between these two, for they are sanctified—that is, purified from every taint of body and soul—to live with equanimity according to the laws of nature. Again, Isaac said to Jacob, "Go forth to the land of Mesopotamia, to Syria,"[230] and Jacob went "to an eastern land."[231] Syria means "contemplation of heavenly things," while Jacob means "wrestler." Wrestling against vices, they dwell in an eastern land, for after the resurrection they shall be deified and contemplate the glory of divinity in the heavens. Mesopotamia both is and means "between the rivers."[232] The dwelling place of holy souls and of the whole of restored human nature will be nowhere else but between the rivers of spiritual virtues that flow from the fount of all goodness. This is also signified by the "promised land"[233] to which God led his people after they were freed from

227. Gn 3.19.
228. Gn 12.1. "Land" is once again *terra,* or earth.
229. Gn 20.1.
230. Gn 28.2.
231. Gn 29.1.
232. Ambrose, *De paradiso* 3.14 (CSEL 32.1, 273).
233. Heb 11.9.

bondage in Egypt.[234] This is "the land of the living," in which the saints "will possess double portions," that is, happiness of body and soul.[235] Of this earth the Lord himself says, "Blessed are the meek, for they shall possess the earth."[236]

D: What is the following verse: "You are earth, and into the earth you shall go"?[237]

M: This means that you took your beginning from the fertile earth of the primeval causes, and you will necessarily return to it.

D: Doesn't another translation read, "You are dust, and unto dust you shall return"?[238]

M: This is because, just as everything that is born from the dust of this sensible earth takes the cause of its birth from it, the great abundance of all visible and invisible things is generated from the fertility of the primordial causes, and will return to them when the world ends.

When you asked about and (in part) explained these things, I have expounded them from the opinions of the holy fathers Ambrose and Augustine, as well as Gregory of Nazianzus and the monk Maximus.

234. Ps 26.13, 141.6; Is 38.11.
235. Is 61.7.
236. Mt 5.4.
237. Gn 3.19 (LXX); Augustine, *De Trinitate* 13.12 (CCSL 50a, 403).
238. Gn 3.19 (Vulgate).

# BOOK V

D: So far I have not read or heard of anything written about the return of human nature (with the other creatures that exist in and for it) to the eternal reasons from which it was produced, or its restoration to its original dignity. Yet often the glimpse of such a teaching smiles out here and there in the divine books and writings of the holy fathers. So I would like to hear about these things because they are very necessary and, as I believe, few have discussed them.

M: The great prophet Moses foresaw in his spirit that human nature would return to the happiness that it had lost by sinning. He concealed that return in these words: "And the Lord God made tunics of skins for Adam and his wife, and clothed them."[1] That is, after sin he added mortal bodies to the human being formed in God's image, and clothed them in the likeness of beasts to procreate children.[2] "And he said, 'See, Adam has become like one of us.'"[3] This is spoken ironically, as if to say that Adam, who wished to be like God, has become so far unlike God that he is similar to "foolish beasts."[4] "And the Lord God cast him out of paradise"—out of the delights of eternal happiness—"that he might work the earth from which he was taken,"[5] or do things by which he could return to the former glory of his nature. "Now then, lest perhaps he put forth his hand and take

1. Gn 3.21.

2. "The human being" here is singular (*homo*), but Genesis refers to "Adam and his wife" as separate individuals. Honorius imagines the *homo* who sinned as a single person composed of mind and sense perception, who as a result of the Fall has become two persons, divided into male and female.

3. Gn 3.22.

4. Ps 48.13, 21.

5. Gn 3.23.

also of the tree of life, and eat, and live forever."[6] This is as if he said: let him put forth his zeal for good action in the virtues, by which he can take the fruits of the tree of life, which are the spiritual gifts of the Word of God; and let him eat the food of pure contemplation, by the strength of which he can live forever. He will never return to the poverty of temporal things, which will perish utterly with this world, but will pass wholly into God and become one with him. In this passage, "lest perhaps" is the voice of God not forbidding but doubting, as it were.

As for those who think man was expelled from paradise to keep him from eating of the tree of life and living forever, they are in error. For how could man eat of the tree of life and live forever when he was not yet delivered from sin and death, which is the penalty of sin? Indeed, even before sin he neither took nor ate from that tree, as a diligent inquiry into divine Scripture suggests. For if he had eaten, he would surely not have sinned or fallen, but would have lived happily forever. If the paradise from which man was expelled was local and earthly, and if the tree of life planted in paradise was an earthly, sensible tree producing fruit suitable for the use of the body,[7] why didn't God remove the man from the tree of life alone and enclose him in some other part of paradise, where he could not reach that tree? For if the only way to live happily in paradise forever was to eat of the tree of life—which was granted to the rational creature alone—why could wretched, mortal man not have lived out the time of his life in some part of paradise after he sinned? If we believe that the other animals, especially the serpent, through which the ancient enemy exercised his malice, were in paradise, yet could not live in eternal happiness because they were not created to eat of the tree of life, then why was the offending man not allowed to live among them? True reason teaches that a rational creature, even a sinful one, by the dignity of his nature excels every irrational creature, even if it is sinless. So if the irrational animals remained in paradise after man was cast out, although he is more excellent than the rest, why was he not al-

6. Gn 3.22.

7. Epiphanius, *Ancoratus* 55 (PG 43: 113b); 58 (PG 43; 117b–120c); 61 (PG 43: 125bc).

lowed to remain with them in paradise even as a sinner? Or perhaps the other animals were expelled from paradise with him?

If anyone says such a thing, let him seek a text in divine Scripture, the authority of the holy fathers, or both, to prove that the animals that man had named in paradise before he sinned were expelled from paradise along with sinful man. If he cannot find one, let him cease to hold carnal views about paradise and its animals and hasten to the spiritual interpretations taught by Truth. This is the one and only way to pass through the gates of the mystic writings.

D: I am ready and prepared to learn what this means: "And he cast Adam out, and set before the paradise of pleasure a cherubim and a flaming, revolving sword to guard the way to the tree of life."[8]

M: The paradise from which man was expelled was the human nature created in God's image. By despising the divine commandment, he fell from that dignity. His ejection or banishment is the loss of the natural happiness he was made to possess. But man did not lose his nature, which, being made in God's image, necessarily remains incorruptible. Rather, he lost the happiness that he would have attained if he had not scorned to obey God. If we understand the cherubim in this place as a heavenly being, we are compelled to say that paradise has a spiritual nature because reason does not let us believe that a spiritual nature—the nearest to God—could be set before a local, earthly paradise. And if we say that the cherubim set another angel from the lowest order before paradise, the same difficulty will remain because an angelic substance, even from the lowest order of heavenly beings, could not be set in any earthly place.

From the interpretation of its name alone, we must realize that there is no heavenly substance here on earth. For "cherubim" means "abundance of knowledge" or "outpouring of wisdom"[9] and signifies the Word of God, "in whom all the treasures of wisdom and knowledge are hidden."[10] It is set before

8. Gn 3.24. Although *cherubim,* which appears in the text, is plural in Hebrew, a single being is understood here.

9. Dionysius, *De caelesti hierarchia* 7.1 (PG 3: 205b).

10. Col 2.3.

paradise—that is, before the sight of human nature—that our nature might examine itself in wisdom and purify itself through knowledge and action to enable it to return to its original happiness. So we are given to understand that there was more divine mercy than punishment in man's expulsion from paradise. For the Creator did not want to condemn his image altogether, but to renew it so that it would not perish, but live forever.

The flaming sword is the Word of God, burning and dividing.[11] It burns away our offenses and divides human nature from the filth that comes upon it through transgression. This sword is revolving because the Word of the Father is moved by ineffable kindness and mercy toward the salvation of human nature, to guard the way to the tree of life. In other words, it will not let us forget the way to the tree of life, namely Christ, who is the way to life.[12]

### 301. *On the return of sensible things*

D: Since we are discussing the return of our nature, I think we should take up certain well-established arguments from sensible things, by which we can prove what is to come without hesitation.

M: I suppose it is very clear to all who consider the nature of things, by speculative thought and sensory observation, that the ever-revolving celestial sphere of the fixed stars returns to the same position in space in the course of 24 hours. Similarly, the sun arrives at the same point on the equinoctial diameter after four years, returning at the same moment of time (I mean at sunrise). The moon also returns to the same place in the zodiac where it first began to shine in a little more than 27 days and 8 hours. All experts in astronomy are familiar with the cyclical return of the other planets, so let us speak of the two great lights of the world. The moon is recalled to the beginning of its course after 19 years have passed, the sun after 28. If these two numbers are multiplied, they yield a figure of 532 years. When that time has passed and the two luminaries have completed the

11. Heb 4.12.
12. Jn 14.6.

whole paschal cycle, they are said to return to the same numbers and positions in the zodiac and times of the Great Year, fulfilling the entire harmony of their course.

The air too returns to the same qualities of cold, heat, or temperate weather in definite seasons. Likewise, the ocean follows the course of the moon in all things and observes the regular intervals of its return. In its daily ebb and flow and in the seasonal high and low tides,[13] it never interrupts the fixed, cyclical returns of nature. In the same way all animals, shoots, and plants observe their seasons when they bear young and produce flowers, leaves, and fruit. There is no corporeal creature quickened by vital motion that does not return to the beginning of its motion. For the end of a motion is its beginning; it terminates nowhere but in its principle,[14] from which it begins to move and to which it always desires to return, so that there it may cease and come to rest. The same thing must be predicated not only of the parts of the sensible world, but also of the whole—for its end is its beginning, which it desires. Having arrived there, it will cease to move, not that its substance may perish, but that it may return to its reasons, from which it set out. "For the form of this world," says the Apostle, "is passing away."[15]

Augustine explains that "form" (*figura*) here does not mean "nature" (*natura*),[16] though the Greeks often use the words *physis* (nature) and *ousia* (being or essence) interchangeably. *Ousia* is the essence in every creature, whether visible or intelligible; it can neither be corrupted nor increased nor diminished.[17] But *physis* or nature refers to the generation of a being or essence in space and time, in some matter that can be corrupted, increased, diminished, and affected by a variety of accidents. *Ousia* is derived from the verb *eimi,*[18] which means *sum,* or "I am." Its masculine participle is *ôn,* and the feminine is *ousa,* whence *ousia.* But *physis* comes from the verb *phyomai:* to be born, planted,

13. *Sive malinas sive ledones.*

14. *Principium* means both "beginning" and "principle." Both senses are operative throughout this passage.

15. 1 Cor 7.31.

16. Augustine, *De civitate Dei* 20.14 (CCSL 48, 724).

17. Dionysius, *De divinis nominibus* 4.23 (PG 3: 724d).

18. The Latin text reads *oni.*

or generated.[19] Every creature, therefore, is *ousia* insofar as it subsists in its reasons, but *physis* insofar as it is procreated in matter.[20] The Greeks refer to the beginning and end as *telos* because when the motion of the universe begins from it, it is the beginning; when it ceases in it, it is called the end. All these things suggest the return of our nature to its beginning: the principle by which it was made, in and through which it moves, and toward which it always tends to return.

There is a universal desire in all human beings, be they perfect or imperfect, pure or defiled, renewed in Christ through knowledge of the truth or detained in the old man in the darkness of ignorance.[21] All have one and the same natural appetite for being, well-being, and perpetual being[22]—or, as St. Augustine briefly sums it up, living happily and fleeing misery.[23] This movement toward living and subsisting happily is innate in all people, deriving from Him Who Is, who exists blessedly forever. And if, by necessity, natural motion never ceases or rests until it arrives at the end that it seeks, what can prevent, check, or stop the necessary motion of human nature before it arrives at that which it naturally desires? For there is no creature that wishes or desires to be nothing. Rather, every creature flees from the threat of non-being, especially because it is difficult for anything made by him who truly is, and is above being, to return to nothing.

But if a nature similar to God is by any chance estranged from its principle through unlikeness, it always strives to return to its principle to regain the likeness it had corrupted. If visible fire burning in any material always tends upward, how much more does that intelligible fire always raise itself from the abyss of death and misery by a natural appetite for the sublime heights of life and beatitude? We say this not because nature will

19. The Latin text reads *fismai.* Latin *natura* similarly derives from the verb *nasci,* to be born.

20. This linguistic explanation clarifies some ambiguities earlier in the *Clavis physicae,* where terms with distinct meanings are indeed used interchangeably.

21. Eph 4.22–24.

22. Maximus, *Ambigua* 3 (PG 91: 1084bc); 6.3 (PG 91: 1116b); 38 (PG 91: 1329b); 61 (PG 91: 1392a).

23. Augustine, *De beata vita* 4.23 (CCSL 29, 78).

be equally blessed in all people, but because it will be free from death and misery in all. For being, living, and immortality will be common to all, both good and bad; but well-being and beatitude will be special and proper only to those who are perfected in action and knowledge. Indeed, the Creator of the rational nature does not prevent its rational motion from attaining him.

### 302. *On the return of intelligible things*

D: As we have cited examples of the return of nature from sensible things, it seems necessary that we should also bring in examples from intelligible things—that is, the disciplines that philosophers call the liberal arts. Arguments derived from the unshakable rules of the true arts have greater ability to inspire belief in a doubtful matter than those drawn from conjectures of the bodily senses, although even those cannot be discovered or proven without the guidance of reason and intelligence. For it is impossible to attain true knowledge of sensible things with the bodily senses alone.

M: The art that the Greeks call dialectic, which is defined as the knowledge of arguing well, revolves first of all around *ousia*, or being, as its proper principle. From this begins every division and multiplication of the realities about which this art disputes. The art descends from the most universal genera through the intermediate ones down to the most specific forms and species. By the rules of its unfolding, it then proceeds back through the same stages by which it departs until it arrives again at the *ousia* from which it issued forth. It does not cease to return to that, always desiring to rest in it and revolve around it with solely or primarily intelligible motion.

Arithmetic too, beginning from the monad and passing through the different species of numbers, returns again after their resolution to the same monad, beyond which it cannot ascend. For all numbers and species of numbers begin from it, come to rest in it, and subsist in it both potentially and actually, just as all genera and species are contained and resolved in being.

We should think no differently about geometry. Beginning in

the same way from its principle, the point (which the Greeks call *semeion* and the Latins *signum,* or sign), it constructs plane and solid figures, surfaces, sides, and angles, and completes spaces with length, breadth, and depth. When all these have been resolved, it returns to its proper principle, the sign, in which the whole virtue of the art resides.[24]

Music likewise begins from its principle, called the tone, and moves around simple or compound harmonies. Resolving these, it once again seeks out the tone, its beginning, for there resides all its act and its potency.

So too astronomy, whose greatest power is to consider the movement of the stars through space and time, begins its course from the atom, and once the intervals of time have been resolved, ends its return in the same. Don't you see how the aforesaid concepts of the rational mind seek to return to their beginnings, in which they find the end of their movement? In all these things, as we have said before, the beginning and end are the same.

D: This seems credible; but I don't see why you omitted grammar and rhetoric.

M: For three reasons. First, because these two arts seem to many philosophers, not without reason, to be branches of dialectic. Second, for the sake of brevity. Finally, because they do not seem to treat the nature of things. Instead, they concern either the rules of human speech, which do not exist according to nature but according to the custom of speakers (as Aristotle and his followers claim),[25] or else special cases and persons, which are far removed from the nature of things. When rhetoric strives to treat commonplaces that pertain to the nature of things, it uses not its own resources, but those of dialectic. But even grammar and rhetoric do not lack their own principles, for the first begins from the letter, the second from the hypothesis or finite question. They are resolved into the same principles: the knowledge of writing well resolves into the letter, the skill of speaking well into the hypothesis. But arguments drawn from the nature of things have more power than those derived from human in-

24. The *signum* or sign denotes a geometrical point.

25. Aristotle, *De interpretatione* 2, 16a, 19–29.

ventions, and the arts of writing and speaking well emerge from human reasoning.

D: Then why are they counted among the liberal disciplines, if they are not according to nature but according to human ingenuity?

M: Only because they always cling to the mother of arts, which is dialectic. They are like her arms, or streams flowing from her, or indeed, instruments by which she manifests her intelligible discoveries for human use.

D: I would like you to prove by authority that the beginning and end of natural motions are the same and in no way different.

M: Maximus proves that "a single cause is the beginning and end of all that exists in any way and is moved according to nature. Everything that exists and moves both exists and moves through that cause."[26]

D: This concerns God, who is the beginning and end of all things. Yet you do not seem to be discussing God, but rather the temporal origins of sensible things or the first principles of intelligible things.

M: Just as each thing is naturally compelled to return to its principle,[27] whether sensible or intelligible, we also believe without hesitation that human nature will return to its principle, which is none other than the Word of God in which it was made and changelessly exists and lives. This is corroborated by the most certain arguments from nature. For if God is the beginning of all things that are and that are not (I mean those that can and cannot be perceived by sensation or intellect), and if all things desire him, and there is no reason that prevents the desire of all from attaining him, then what wonder is it if human nature, which was specially made in the image and likeness of the Beginning of all, should return to the source from whence it set forth? It did not depart from thence in order to forsake its principle entirely, but is said to have withdrawn by a certain unlikeness, defaced by sin. For likeness made it near, and unlikeness distant.

...*gua* 19 (PG 91: 1257d).

...slate *principium* as both "principle" and "begin-

### 303. *What it means to be distant from God*

It is not by physical steps, but by the mind's affections that a person is distanced from God or draws near to him. We do not withdraw from sunlight by spatial distance, but by the loss or closing of our eyes, or by the sun's setting. Health is not lost in space but in pain. Similarly, life, blessedness, wisdom, and all the virtues are not lost except by deprivation, that is by death, misery, folly, and vices. Just as the skin of a human body is smitten by the infection and deformity of leprosy, human nature is infected and corrupted by proud disobedience and made deformed and unlike its Creator. But it has been delivered from this leprosy by the medicine of divine grace and will be recalled to its former beauty. For the nature made in God's image has never lost and cannot lose the vigor of its beauty and the integrity of its being. Rather, the divine form remains forever changeless, though it has become capable of corruption as a penalty for sin.[28]

### 304. *The meaning of Naaman the Syrian*

This is suggested under the figure of Naaman the Syrian and the ten lepers cleansed by the Lord in the Gospel.[29] They did not lose their human likeness, but were only smitten and completely covered by the swelling and deformity of leprosy. In the same way our nature is not lost or altered, but tainted by the deformity of vices. That Syrian was obviously a figure of human nature, for Naaman means "beautiful," and Syria, "contemplation of heavenly things." This is what human nature would have been if it had not sinned, for it was beautiful and created for the contemplation of heavenly things, but it was smitten by leprosy because of the transgression. Naaman, descending to Judea and returning again to Syria, laid down his leprosy in the Jordan River at the command of the prophet Elisha, and his bodily skin was renewed. When our nature has recognized its sickness and the deformity of its vices, it will descend into the confession of

28. Gregory of Nyssa, *De hominis opificio* 27 (PG 44: 225c–228b).
29. 2 Kgs 5.1–27; Lk 17.12–19.

its misery, and on returning to itself, it will be purified by Elisha (which means "God's Savior" or "God's salvation")—that is, by the Lord Jesus Christ, the divine Savior. On our return, he will save our nature when he commands us to return to our original state in the contemplation of intelligible virtues.

Where will our nature be purified? In the Jordan, a name that means "descent of the Lord," "descent of judgment," "power," "distant land," or "their ascension." For the salvation and return of our nature to the Syria of heavenly contemplation will take place when the Lord descends in glory to judge the living and the dead, and to manifest his power in a distant land—that is, at the end of the world—when "heaven and earth will pass away"[30] in their ascension, that is, the exaltation of the saints to eternal beatitude, or the common resurrection of all. Indeed, the common resurrection of all is an ascent from death to life, from an animal, corruptible body to a spiritual, incorruptible one.[31] All the leprosy and corruption of human nature will be heaped up and converted in Jezi, which means "seeing the valley" or "departure from vision."[32] This signifies the devil, the wicked servant of our Savior, who always looks into the depth of perdition and eternal death through malice, and departs from the vision of truth through pride. So our leprosy, which had contaminated the image of God through his malicious envy, will be driven back and poured out upon him. His penalty will be increased by his pain at our salvation and restoration.

## 305. *The meaning of the ten lepers*

The ten lepers also bear a distinctive mark of our nature, which has been redeemed by its Redeemer. It is daily redeemed in individuals, and at the consummation of the world it will be universally redeemed and liberated in all. Human nature is often signified by the number ten, which encompasses soul and body. The body flourishes in the number five: the four bodily

30. Mk 13.31.

31. 1 Cor 15.44–53.

32. No such place is mentioned in the Bible, but Jezi may be an error for Jezreel, a valley where several ancient battles were fought. Some thought it would be the site of the apocalyptic battle of Armageddon (Rv 16.16).

elements plus the form that composes and configures the elements. The soul too conforms to the number five, consisting of intellect, reason, the twofold senses (inner and outer), and the vital motion that governs the body. By the grace of its Redeemer, this tenfold character of man will be liberated from every misery added to it, like a kind of leprosy, and restored to oneness. Then it will no longer be tenfold, but the unified intellect alone will remain in pure contemplation of the simple truth. This is signified by the sole leper who returned to the Lord and gave glory to God for his cleansing.[33] Like a foreigner returning from the distant land of unlikeness, he clung to the one who had liberated and purified him. But the other nine were no longer found, for the whole of human nature will be poured into the intellect alone, so that nothing will remain in it but the intellect alone, by which it will contemplate its Creator.

### 306. *Whence man fell and where he returns*

D: Whence and where did human nature fall? Where or how will it return? By what stages does it ascend, what does it desire, and in what will it rest?

M: The Psalmist tells whence it fell and where it arrived: "When man was in honor, he did not understand; he was compared to foolish animals and became like them."[34] So he abandoned the honor of the divine image and equality with the heavenly powers, but fell into the likeness of irrational animals. A nature that was naturally created to desire and love heavenly things is oppressed by earthly greed and carnal desires; a nature that was prepared to enjoy God by reason is whirled around by irrational motion. For there is no beastly motion that cannot be detected in man after he sinned—and as assured reason teaches, what is praised in a beast is reproached in man. For irrational motion exists naturally in a beast, but in man it is against nature. Fear, ferocity, desire, hatred, and other passions are natural in beasts, which are far from the character of divine beauty. Thus no wise person doubts that man fell into these irrational mo-

33. Lk 17.11–19.
34. Ps 48.13, 21.

tions, which belong naturally to beastly life, but to human life as a form of suffering.[35] From these he fell once again into the death and dissolution of the body. He could go no lower, for indeed, there is nothing lower in the nature of things than a life that lacks reason and sense. The lowest of all things is the corruptible body, for no nature is allowed to return to nothing. Where man set an end to his ruin, at that point he began his return. The end of ruin is the dissolution of the body.

## 307. *What death is*

The return of nature, therefore, proceeds from the dissolution of the body, and that is why the death of the flesh confers more utility than vengeance on human nature, even though it has been considered a punishment for sin. In fact, the dissolution of the flesh, customarily called death, might more reasonably be called the death of death than the death of the flesh. For if human life in this corruptible flesh is rightly termed death by the wise, why should the end of that life be called by the name of death, since it liberates the dying rather than inflicting death on them? Maximus asserts that "the end of the present life should not be called death but alienation from death, separation from corruption, liberation from bondage, peace after struggle, the termination of wars, a way out of confusion, a return from darkness, a rest from sufferings, the abolition of sin, and the end of all evils."[36] Thus the end of the present life is the beginning of the future life, and the death of the flesh is an omen of the restoration of nature and its return to its ancient wholeness.

## 308. *The stages of ascent: on the return of human nature*

The first return of human nature is when the body is dissolved and recalled to the four elements of the sensible world, from which it is composed. The second will be fulfilled in the

35. *Passibiliter insunt.* The term implies passivity: human beings suffer the passions ("irrational motions") against nature and, in some cases, against their will.

36. Maximus, *Ambigua* 6.29 (PG 91: 1157cd).

resurrection, when all persons will receive their own bodies from the communion of the four elements. The third is when the body will be changed into spirit. The fourth is when the spirit and, to speak more plainly, the whole of human nature will return to the primordial causes, which exist forever immutably in God. The fifth is when that nature with its causes will move into God just as air moves into light.[37] For "God will be all in all"[38] when nothing exists but God alone.

D: Then will the substance of the universe perish?

M: Rather, it will return to a better state through the aforesaid stages. For how can something perish when it is proven to return to a better state? So the transformation of human nature into God should not be judged a destruction of its substance, but rather a marvelous, ineffable return to its original state, which it had lost by sinning. If everything that understands purely becomes one with what is understood,[39] what wonder is it if our nature can become one with God and in God, when it is to contemplate him face to face[40] in those who are worthy (insofar as he can be contemplated) and to ascend in the clouds[41] of contemplative vision?

## 309. *On the various opinions of the fathers*

D: Doesn't St. Augustine say that no body can be changed into a soul, nor any soul into a body?[42]

M: Concerning the return of nature, we ourselves follow Gregory the Theologian and Maximus the monk (later bishop), as well as St. Ambrose. The tradition of the theologians fully agrees on certain stages of the return of nature, but on others there is sharp disagreement. As for the body's return to the elements from which it came and its return to itself at the time of resurrection, no one disagrees. But as for the passage or trans-

37. Maximus, *Ambigua* 3 (PG 91: 1073d–1076a and 1088d); 6.19 (PG 91: 1137bc); 6.20 (PG 91: 1140c).

38. 1 Cor 15.28.

39. Maximus, *Ambigua* 11 (PG 91: 1220ab).

40. 1 Cor 13.12.

41. 1 Thes 4.16.

42. Augustine, *De Genesi ad litteram* 10.4 (CSEL 28.1, 300).

mutation of the body into the soul, of the soul into the causes, and of all things into God, they almost all have very different opinions and various doctrines. Many argue only for the dissolution of the body into the elements and its return to its own state at the moment of resurrection. But they seem to ascend no further, for they end their argument with the quality of bodies after the resurrection. Some utterly deny the transformation of bodies into souls, of souls into the causes, and of the causes into God. Some hesitate so cautiously that they dare not even say that the humanity of Christ is converted into divinity.

### 310. *What Augustine says*

Aurelius Augustine says, "Let us hold most firmly that the nature of the soul is converted neither into the nature of the body, so that what was once a soul should become a body; nor into the nature of an irrational soul, so that what was a human soul should become that of a beast; nor into the nature of God, so that what was a soul should become God."[43]

### 311. *What Boethius says*

Boethius also says, "If neither the body nor the soul could be converted into divinity, by no means could humanity be converted into God. Much less can it be believed that both should be converted into each other, for incorporeality cannot turn into body, nor conversely can body turn into incorporeality."[44]

### 312. *What Gregory says*

D: From the words of these authors, we gather that no corporeal nature can be changed into an incorporeal one.

M: Not only do we not blame their opinion; we even willingly accept it. Nevertheless, we are not unaware that Greek theologians have thought otherwise. Among them, Gregory of Nazianzus argues concerning the resurrection that the soul "will draw the whole body into itself to be assumed, when, to-

43. Ibid.
44. Boethius, *Contra Eutychen et Nestorium* 6.

gether with the body, it will become one spirit, one mind, and one God, and what is mortal and ephemeral will be swallowed up by life."[45] Maximus explains this sentence: "Just as the flesh has been swallowed up by corruption through sin, so too the soul, rendered earthly by its activities, has been swallowed up by the flesh; and the knowledge of God has been swallowed up by the soul through consummate ignorance, so that it cannot even know if God exists. Thus at the time of the resurrection, according to the happy conversion that will take place in the Holy Spirit by the grace of God incarnate, the flesh will be swallowed up by the soul in the Spirit, and the soul by God, who is truly life. The whole soul will manifestly possess him as a most singular whole through all things."[46]

## 313. *What Ambrose says*

Following these writers, Ambrose expounds that passage in Luke about the woman who hid [leaven in] three measures of flour until they were fermented into one.[47] "If the three measures in this life," he says—namely body, soul, and spirit—"remain in the same leaven" (the unity of the Church) "until they are fermented and become one, there will be no inequality, nor will we seem to be composed of three different parts. So in the future those who love Christ will enjoy an incorrupt communion, and we will no longer be composite. For we who are now composite will be one, and we will be transformed into one substance. Nothing will be inferior to anything else in the resurrection, the way the weakness of our flesh now is frail and the condition of our bodily nature lies open to wounds and injuries. Oppressed by the weight of its burden, it cannot rise higher and lift its steps above the earth. But we will be conformed to the grace of a simple creation when the prophecy of John has been fulfilled: 'Beloved, we are now children of God, and it has not yet been revealed what we shall be. But we know that when it is

45. 2 Cor 5.4; Gregory of Nazianzus, *Epitaphios in Caesarion,* cited in Maximus, *Ambigua* 17 (PG 91: 1249d–1252a).
46. Maximus, *Ambigua* 17 (PG 91: 1252a).
47. Lk 13.21.

revealed, we shall be like him.'[48] Because the nature of God is simple, for 'God is spirit,'[49] we too 'shall be conformed to the same image'[50] so that 'as the heavenly man is, so shall the heavenly ones be.'"[51]

This should not be understood as a confusion or transmutation of substances, but as a kind of ineffable, intelligible union. Indeed, nothing subsists in human nature that is not spiritual and intelligible, for surely even the substance of the body is intelligible. So it is not incredible or contrary to reason if intelligible substances should be united with each other. They may become one while each retains its own property and subsistence, yet in such a way that the inferior is contained in the superior. For true reason does not allow what is superior to be contained in, attracted to, or consumed by what is inferior. Rather, the inferior is naturally attracted to and swallowed up by the superior—not that it might cease to be, but that it might be saved in it, as their subsistence becomes one. Air does not lose its substance when it is wholly changed into sunlight until nothing but light appears in it, even though light is one thing and air another. Yet the light prevails in the air so that it seems to be light alone. Iron or any other metal melted in fire seems to be changed into fire so that it looks like pure fire—yet the substance of the metal remains. In the same way I think bodily substance will pass into the soul, not that its being should perish, but that it should be saved in a better essence. Likewise, we should understand that the soul itself will pass into intellect, in order to be preserved in it as more beautiful and more like God. I should not speak otherwise about the passage—I do not yet say of all—but of rational substances into God, in whom all will be one and come to their end.[52]

48. 1 Jn 3.2.

49. Jn 4.24.

50. 2 Cor 3.18.

51. 1 Cor 15.48; Ambrose, *Expositio evangelii secundum Lucam* 7.194 (CCSL 14, 282); 7.191 (CCSL 14, 281); 7.190 (CCSL 14, 280–81).

52. Maximus, *Ambigua* 3 (PG 91: 1073d–1076a and1088d); 6.19 (PG 91: 1137bc); 6.20 (PG 91: 1140c).

### 314. *What Maximus says*

Maximus proves this. Eternal life, he says, "is not constituted by the air we breathe or by the streams of blood that flow from the liver. But God in his wholeness is wholly participated in by the soul and, by means of the soul, the body as well—as he himself knows—so that the soul might receive immutability and the body immortality, and the whole man be deified through the grace of the humanized, deifying God. The whole person remains human in soul and body by nature, yet is made wholly God in soul and body by grace and by the divine radiance of blessed glory, tempered to human capacity. Nothing more luminous or lofty than that light can be conceived. For what is more worthy of love than *theosis,*" or deification, "by which God is united to those he has made into gods, and makes the whole universe divine through his goodness?"[53] What is proper to nature will remain, therefore, and there will be a unity of natures. The distinct property of each will not obstruct the union of natures, nor the union the property of each.

D: Although these things seem to resemble what is true and rational, yet to those who are less capable of contemplating the nature of the universe, I believe they will seem like self-contradictory nonsense. First you introduced Gregory of Nazianzus, asserting that the soul "will assume its whole body into itself and, along with it, the spirit, the mind, and God will become one."[54] Afterwards you introduced Maximus, proving that "the whole person will remain human in soul and body by nature, yet be made wholly God in soul and body by grace."[55] What do these words mean except that the bodily nature will always remain in itself and will by no means pass into the soul, the mind, or God himself—even though the blessed, incorruptible glory of the future resurrection will unite the soul, the mind, and God? As for the nature of the soul and the mind, I think

53. Maximus, *Ambigua* 3 (PG 91: 1088bc). The quotation is grammatically difficult and probably corrupt.

54. Gregory of Nazianzus, *Epitaphios in Caesarion,* cited in Maximus, *Ambigua* 17 (PG 91: 1249d). This is quoted in a different form in chap. 312 above.

55. Maximus, *Ambigua* 3 (PG 91: 1088c).

he understood in the same way that they will not pass away, but each will remain in its own substance. For there is no small difference between the soul and the mind: the latter is concerned only with the divine, but the former is concerned with creatures.

### 315. *Three things to be noted: being, virtue, and operation*

M: The union of intelligible natures can take place without addition or composition, while the properties of each are preserved and remain unchanged. For there are three aspects of every substance, corporeal or incorporeal, that remain changeless and immutable: being, virtue, and operation.[56] These three are one, not as a composite but quite simply one, an inseparable unity. None of them can exist without the other, for they are of one and the same substance. Yet, considered rationally, some differences can be discerned. It is one thing to be, another to be able to do something, and another to do it. It is one thing to be a tree, another to be capable of growth, and another to grow. It is one thing to be human, another to be capable of understanding, and another to understand what one can. There is no doubt that these three properties are innate in every creature, visible and invisible.[57]

56. *Essentia, virtus, et operatio.* In this context *virtus* refers to the potential, and *operatio* to the act. Dionysius, *De caelesti hierarchia* 11.2 (PG 3: 284d); *De divinis nominibus* 4.23 (PG 3: 724c–725a).

57. Here the *Clavis physicae* as an abridgment of Eriugena breaks off. Honorius adapted only the first 12.5% of *Periphyseon,* Book V, ending at paragraph 881b. The manuscripts continue by transcribing the rest of Eriugena's work verbatim.

# INDICES

# GENERAL INDEX

# INDEX OF HOLY SCRIPTURE

*Old Testament*

*New Testament*

## RECENT VOLUMES IN THE FATHERS OF THE CHURCH, MEDIAEVAL CONTINUATION

ST. ALBERT THE GREAT, *On Job, Volume 2*, translated by Franklin T. Harkins, Volume 23 (2024)

RUPERT OF DEUTZ, *Commentary on the Songs of Songs*, translated by Jieon Kim and Vittorio Hösle, Volume 22 (2024)

BL. HRABANUS MAURUS, *On the Formation of Clergy*, translated by Owen M. Phelan, Volume 21 (2023)

ST. ALBERT THE GREAT, *On Resurrection*, translated by Irven M. Resnick and Franklin T. Harkins, Volume 20 (2020)

ST. ALBERT THE GREAT, *On Job, Volume 1*, translated by Franklin T. Harkins, Volume 19 (2019)

ST. HILDEGARD OF BINGEN, *The Book of Divine Works*, translated by Nathaniel M. Campbell, Volume 18 (2018)

ALBERT THE GREAT, *On the Body of the Lord*, translated by Sr. Albert Marie Surmanski, OP, Volume 17 (2017)